HOW *to* USE

Windows® Me

Millennium Edition

SAMS

A Division of Macmillan USA
201 W. 103rd Street
Indianapolis, Indiana 46290

Douglas A. Hergert

Visually in **Full Color**

How to Use Windows® Me

International Standard Book Number: 0-672-31937-3

Library of Congress Catalog Card Number: 00-102116

Printed in the United States of America

First Printing: August 2000

03   02   01   00   4   3   2   1

Trademarks

Warning and Disclaimer

Acquisitions Editor
Elizabeth Brown

Development Editor
Alice Martina Smith

Managing Editor
Charlotte Clapp

Project Editor
Carol Bowers

Copy Editor
Rhonda Tinch-Mize

Indexer
Sheila Schroeder

Proofreaders
Kimberly Campanello
Maryann Steinhart
Mary Ellen Stephenson

Technical Editor
Dallas Releford

Interior Designers
Nathan Clement
Ruth Lewis

Cover Designers
Aren Howell
Nathan Clement

Layout Technicians
Jeannette McKay
Michael J. Poor

Contents at a Glance

Contents

About the Author

A former teacher, **Douglas Hergert** began his current career in 1980 as an editor for a major West Coast computer book publisher. After helping to develop works by other authors, he began producing his own books, initially as a staff writer. His earliest books were tutorials on the popular programming languages of the time. He eventually left his editorial job to continue writing computer books on his own. In the years since, he's developed more than 50 titles with eight of the industry's major publishers. He's written extensively about spreadsheets, database management, programming languages, and Windows. His work is known internationally and has been translated into more than a dozen languages.

Dedication

To Regina Piper,
Claudia Carter,
Robert Murray,
Sallou Cole,
Jim Cartwright,
Mary Lou Johnson,
and everyone in Room C-203,
with admiration, gratitude, and friendship.

Acknowledgments

My sincere thanks to **Alice Martina Smith**, who gracefully and professionally guided this book through the development process; to **Betsy Brown**, who efficiently managed the project from the very beginning and was always ready to answer questions; to **Dallas G. Releford**, who checked the manuscript for technical accuracy; and to the team at Macmillan USA, including **Carol Bowers, Rhonda Tinch-Mize, Kimberly Campanello,** and **Maryann Steinhart**. Thanks also to **Cynthia Hudson, Lysa Lewallen, Carol Burbo, Barbara Dahl, Kim Haglund,** and **Stephanie Raney** for their contributions to previous versions of this work; and to **Claudette Moore** of Moore Literary Agency for her guidance, advice, and support.

Tell Us What You Think!

As the reader of this book, *you* are our most important critic and commentator. We value your opinion and want to know what we're doing right, what we could do better, what areas you'd like to see us publish in, and any other words of wisdom you're willing to pass our way.

You can fax, email, or write directly to let me know what you did or didn't like about this book—as well as what we can do to make our books stronger.

Please note that I cannot help you with technical problems related to the topic of this book, and that because of the high volume of mail I receive, I might not be able to reply to every message.

When you write, please be sure to include this book's title and author as well as your name and phone or fax number. I will carefully review your comments and share them with the author and editors who worked on the book.

Fax: 317-581-4770

Email: office_sams@mcp.com

Mail: Mark Taber
              Associate Publisher
              Sams Publishing
              201 West 103rd Street
              Indianapolis, IN 46290 USA

How to Use This Book

The Complete Visual Reference

Each part of this book is made up of a series of short, instructional tasks, designed to help you understand all the information you need to get the most out of Windows Millennium Edition.

 Click: Click the left mouse button once.

 Double-click: Click the left mouse button twice in rapid succession.

 Right-click: Click the right mouse button once.

 **Drag and drop:** Position the mouse pointer over the object, click and hold the left mouse button, drag the object to its new location, and release the mouse button.

 Selection: This circle highlights the area that is discussed in the step.

 Keyboard: Type information or data into the indicated location.

Each task includes a series of easy-to-understand steps designed to guide you through the procedure.

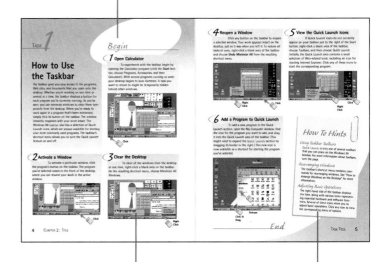

Each step is fully illustrated to show you how it looks onscreen.

Extra hints that tell you how to accomplish a goal are provided in most tasks.

Menus and items you click are shown in **bold**. Words in *italic* are defined in more detail in the glossary. Information you type is in a **special font**.

Continues

If you see this symbol, it means the task you're in continues on the next page.

Introduction

*I*n all kinds of work places—offices, homes, schools, labs, and even spots as unlikely as lakeside resorts, airports, and coffee shops—Microsoft Windows defines the way people use their personal computers. Thanks to Windows, users can work confidently and consistently on all important computer tasks. People everywhere have come to recognize Windows as the basis for a practical and reliable approach to personal computing.

How to Use Windows Me is an illustrated, task-oriented tutorial, introducing the latest version of the system. If you're a newcomer to the desktop computing environment, the step-by-step instructions in this book will help you explore the software resources that Windows Me provides. In the first several parts of the book, you'll master the basics—the desktop, the **Start** button, the taskbar, and a variety of tools designed to help you adjust the Windows environment to your own work patterns. Then you'll learn how to use Windows programs to accomplish specific tasks on your computer—produce documents; work with files and folders; go online and search for information on the Web; send email; effectively manage your printer and other devices attached to your computer, such as digital cameras, scanners, and game controllers; and take advantage of the many software tools included in Windows. Along the way, you'll actually *see* what Windows does and how it works. And because this book provides a *hands-on* approach to new topics, you'll learn by performing each step on your own computer.

In addition to covering familiar features that have been part of Windows from the beginning, this book also introduces you to the important new components of Windows Me and its accompanying Web browser, **Internet Explorer 5.5**. The browser software is designed to help you find, view, and use information online. The vast network of resources known as the Internet continues to generate dramatic interest and enthusiasm among computer users worldwide. This book will help you join all the activity, even in innovative areas such as Internet games and multimedia content.

If you work with two or more computers in your home or small office, Windows Me provides the easiest techniques ever to create a *home network*. After you've connected your machines and set up your network, all your computers will be able to share essential resources, including printers, documents and programs stored on hard disks, and your Internet connection. When you're ready to experience the distinct advantages of a home network, look to Parts 17 and 18 of this book for complete instructions.

In short, whether you're just starting out in the Windows environment or upgrading to the new features of Windows Me, this book guides you step by step through all the practical tasks you'll want to master. You'll learn to complete your work with confidence, expertise, and style.

Task

1

Getting Started with Windows Me

*T*he *desktop* is your own workspace in Windows Millennium Edition—the place where you run programs, open documents, view Web sites, manage your home network, and organize your work in just the way you want to see it. Whatever your current task—writing a memo, reviewing an inventory database, working up a quarterly budget, searching for information on the Internet, designing a logo, or even playing a surreptitious card game on the side—you can view a combination of programs, documents, and Web content on the desktop at once.

Windows Me allows you to coordinate all your computer work in a single software environment. The Windows desktop recognizes a consistent set of mouse and keyboard operations and gives you simple ways to interact with programs and Web sites. *Consistent* is the key word here. By providing intuitive mouse actions, keyboard techniques, and visual tools, Windows ultimately shortens the learning curve for each new program you run. Whether you regularly use 2 applications or 20, you can count on predictable operations for every task you perform. ●

How to Start Your Work

When you start your computer, your screen becomes a visual desktop with graphics that represent your activities and options. Your work appears in individual *windows*, framed areas that display your activity in particular programs. You can place many tasks on the Windows Me desktop at once, and you can arrange your work in many convenient ways. An important center of operations in Windows is the *taskbar*, which initially appears at the bottom of the screen. The taskbar's **Start** button is the key to many of the tools that Windows has to offer.

Begin

1 Explore the Desktop

Turn on your computer and take a first look at the desktop. Arranged down the left side of the screen are *icons* representing essential Windows services and applications. This selection of icons varies according to the way your computer has been set up. At the bottom of the screen, the taskbar displays its **Start** button along with other Windows shortcuts.

2 Find the Start Button

The *mouse pointer*, initially displayed as a bold arrow, flows around the desktop as you move the mouse itself. Without clicking a mouse button just yet, move the pointer to the **Start** button at the left side of the taskbar. The message **Click here to begin** appears near **Start**.

3 Click to View the Start Menu

With the mouse pointer positioned over **Start**, click the left mouse button to view the Start menu. Move the mouse pointer up and down the menu to highlight individual items in the list. The Start menu gives you access to programs, documents, Web sites, and tools for changing the Windows Millennium Edition settings.

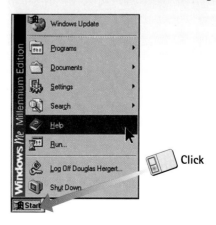

4 Click Help

Experiment with the Start menu by clicking **Help**. Windows closes the Start menu and opens the **Help and Support** window, an important resource for guiding your activities in Windows Me.

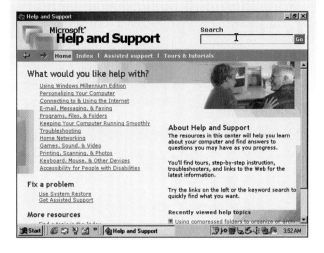

5 Select a Help Topic

Move the mouse pointer inside the **Help and Support** window and stop at any of the help topics listed on the left side of the window. As you do so, notice that the mouse pointer changes to an upward-pointing hand, and the current topic is highlighted in a new color. When you click a topic, you might be presented with yet another list of options to choose from.

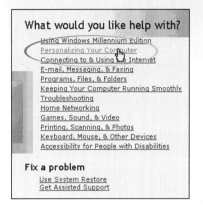

6 Find the Information You Need

Continue using the **Help and Support** window by clicking specific topics that interest you. At the right of the topic list, you can read specific information about the selected topic. When you finish reading and experimenting, click the **X** button at the far upper-right corner of the window to close **Help and Support**.

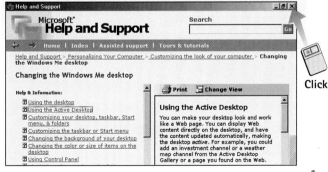

Click

End

How-To Hints

Getting More Help

Read more about the features of the **Help and Support** window at the end of Part 2, "Working on the Desktop."

Using the Mouse

The mouse is essential for making selections and starting programs in Windows Millennium Edition. To learn more about basic mouse operations, turn to Task 3, "How to Use the Mouse," later in this part.

How to Use the Desktop

On the Windows Me desktop, your daily work with applications and documents can merge with the constantly changing content of the World Wide Web. In a set of options known as the *active desktop*, Windows can perform regular updates of any Web content you choose to display. Furthermore, the visual tools of the active desktop are consistent with the interface of Internet Explorer, Microsoft's Web browser. You'll learn about the active desktop throughout this book, but for now you'll focus on techniques for turning specific features of the active desktop on or off.

Begin

1 Experience the Active Desktop

On the active desktop, icons are single-click tools, similar to links and objects you might select on a Web page. Move the mouse pointer to an icon; the pointer takes the shape of an upward-pointing hand. Windows underlines the icon's caption to show that you've selected the item. (If this doesn't happen on your desktop, see Steps 3 and 4.)

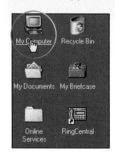

2 Try a Single Click

To experiment, open the **My Computer** folder, which contains icons representing the various storage components of your computer: Position the mouse pointer over the **My Computer** icon on the desktop and click the mouse button. Windows opens the **My Computer** folder onto the desktop. If you are already familiar with the Internet Explorer browser window, notice that this Windows folder has similar features—including **Back**, **Forward**, and **Search** buttons and an **Address** bar.

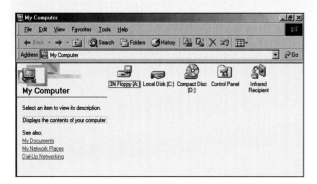

3 View the Folder Options

You can use the **Folder Options** dialog box to specify how you want the desktop and its icons to behave. One way to view these options is to click the **Tools** menu at the top of the **My Computer** window, and then click **Folder Options**. The **Folder Options** dialog box appears on the desktop. (See the How-To Hints for another way to open the **Folder Options** dialog box.) You can opt for an *active* desktop (with regularly updated Web content) or a *classic* desktop (without Web content). Notice that you can also choose between single-clicking or double-clicking icons to open windows or start applications.

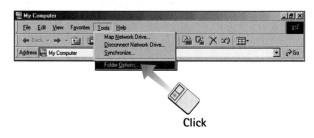

Click

4 Select the Options You Prefer

If you change an option and click **OK**, the new setting applies to the entire desktop. (To close **Folder Options** without making any changes, click **Cancel**.)

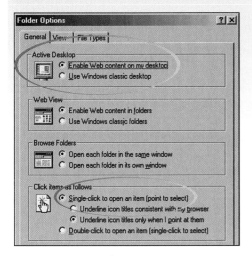

5 Customize the Active Desktop

Another way to change the characteristics of the active desktop is to open the **Display Properties** box. Position the mouse pointer over an empty area on the desktop and click the right mouse button. On the resulting pop-up menu, choose **Active Desktop** and then **Customize my Desktop**. The **Display Properties** box appears on the screen. (The **Web** tab is selected by default.)

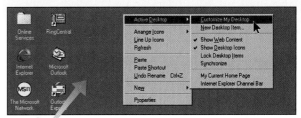

Right-click

6 Display the Channel Bar

If you want to display the Internet Explorer **Channel** bar on your active desktop, click that option in the **Display Properties** box. Click **OK** to confirm. See the How-To Hints for more information about the **Channel** bar.

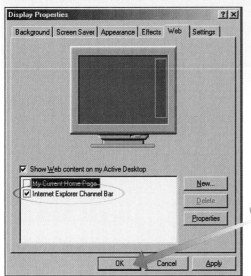

Click

End

How-To Hints

Using the Channel Bar

The **Channel** bar provides one-click links to selected entertainment and news sites on the Internet. This desktop item is actually a left-over feature from Windows 98 and Internet Explorer 4. If you have a new computer on which Windows Me is the *original* operating system, the **Channel** bar is not available.

Opening Folder Options from the Control Panel

The **Control Panel** is a centralized collection of tools designed to help you change and customize the way Windows Me works on your computer. (An icon for the **Control Panel** appears in the initial content of the **My Computer** window.) For example, the **Control Panel** contains a **Folder Options** icon, representing the same options you worked with in Step 4. Windows Me often gives you more than one way to view a particular set of options. You'll learn more about the **Control Panel** throughout this book.

How to Use the Mouse

Using your mouse, you can get things done quickly, efficiently, and intuitively on the Windows desktop. The mouse pointer first appears as an arrow pointing up and to the left, but changes shape as you move to different parts of the desktop or as you perform tasks in particular applications. If you prefer to use the mouse with your left hand, Windows Me allows you to reverse the roles of the left and right mouse buttons. (See Task 4, "How to Change the Mouse Settings," in Part 4.)

Begin

1 Point to an Icon

To move the mouse pointer to a new position on the desktop, slide the mouse over a flat surface. To *point* to an icon on the desktop (in this example, the **Outlook Express** icon), position the mouse pointer directly over the item. If you're using the single-click icon option, this pointing action selects the icon for a subsequent action; Windows underlines the icon's caption. (If you're using the double-click option, you can click the item once to highlight it for a subsequent action.)

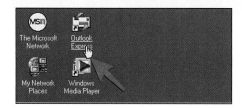

2 Click an Object

To *click* an item, position the mouse pointer directly over the object and click the left mouse button. If you're using the single-click option, this action opens a document or starts a program. For example, a single click on the **Outlook Express** icon opens the window and starts the program. (Quit the program by clicking the **X** button at the far upper-right corner of the window.)

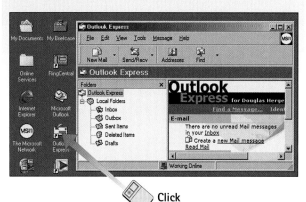

Click

3 Double-Click an Object

To *double-click* an item, position the mouse pointer over the object and click the left mouse button twice in quick succession. If you're using the double-click option, this action starts a program or opens a document. But if you choose the single-click option on the active desktop (as is assumed in the remainder of this book), you'll quickly break yourself of the double-click habit. Double-clicking is still a useful action in other contexts; for example, in a word-processing application, you might double-click a word to select it, as shown here.

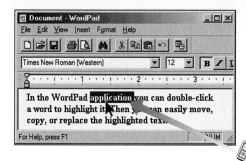

Double-click

4 Drag an Object

To *drag* an object, point to the item and hold down the left mouse button. Move the mouse to reposition the object on the desktop. Finally, release the mouse button to settle the object in its new location. For example, you can move a window by dragging its title bar. As you perform this action, an outline shows you the window's new position.

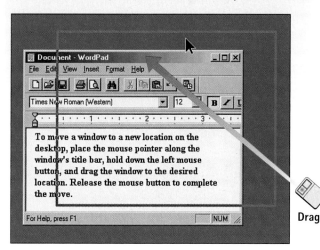

Drag

5 Pull Down a Menu

To pull down a menu in an open window, place the mouse pointer over a selected item on the menu bar and click the left mouse button. You can then choose a command by clicking an entry in the menu list. In response, Windows carries out the command you've chosen.

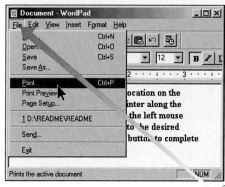

 Click

6 Click a Button in the Title Bar

To change the appearance of a window, click one of three buttons located at the upper-right corner of most open windows. Click the **Minimize** button to clear a window temporarily from the desktop. (A button representing the window remains on the taskbar at the bottom of the desktop; click this button to redisplay the window.) Click the **Maximize** button to expand a window to its largest possible size on the desktop. When you maximize a window, **Maximize** is replaced by the **Restore** button. Click **Restore** to return the window to its previous size. Click the Close button when you're finished working with the window.

7 Right-Click an Object

Using the right mouse button, click any object on the desktop (including the taskbar or the background area of the desktop itself) to view a *shortcut* menu. This menu contains useful commands that apply specifically to the object you've selected. In many shortcut menus, the **Properties** command allows you to change the appearance or behavior of that particular object.

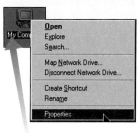

 Right-click

End

How to Start a Program

After you learn your way around the desktop, you're ready to begin working with programs. The **Start** menu lists a variety of everyday programs that come with Windows Me, along with any other applications installed on your computer. To start a program, select its name from the **Start** menu. By the way, with the new **Personalized Menus** option, Windows Millennium hides menu items you haven't used recently—but keeps them conveniently available nonetheless. As a result, your own menus might not be identical to those shown on these pages. (See the How-To Hints for details.)

Begin

1 Click the Start Button

Click the **Start** button to view the **Start** menu, and then move the mouse pointer to **Programs**. A secondary menu of program names appears to the right of the main **Start** menu.

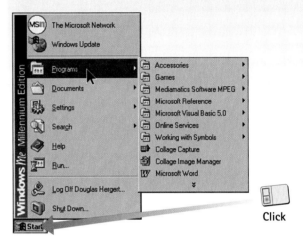

Click

2 Start the Calculator Program

Move the mouse pointer to **Accessories** at the top of the **Programs** menu. The list of accessories appears to the right. *Accessories* are simple but useful applications that come with Windows; they include a word processor, a paint program, a calculator, and others. Click **Calculator**. Windows starts the Calculator program.

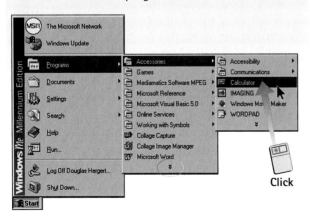

Click

3 Minimize the Application Window

The application's window opens on the desktop so that you can begin working with it. The Calculator contains buttons that look like those of an ordinary handheld calculator. By clicking these buttons with the mouse, you can perform any kind of arithmetic calculation. If you want to put your work temporarily aside so that you can focus on another activity, click the **Minimize** button at the upper-right corner of the application window.

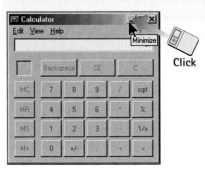

Click

4 Reopen the Window

Note that the minimized Calculator program is represented by a button on the taskbar. Click **Calculator** on the taskbar to return to your work. The **Calculator** window reopens, displaying any work in progress just as you left it. For example, if you were in the middle of a calculation, you can now complete the task.

Click

5 Close the Application

Close the application when you complete your work. Typical Windows programs contain a **File** menu with an **Exit** command, but the Calculator does not. To quit the program, simply click the **Close** button (represented by an **X** icon) at the upper-right corner of the window. Alternatively, click the **Control** menu icon at the left side of the title bar and then choose **Close**.

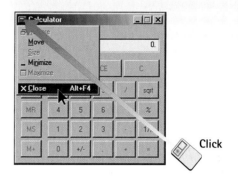

Click

End

How-To Hints

Deactivating Personalized Menus

With the **Personalized Menus** option activated, you may have to click the down-arrow at the bottom of the menu list to view all the options in the menu. You can turn off the **Personalized Menus** option if you prefer to see all the programs available in the **Start** menu, with no hidden items. Right-click the taskbar and choose **Properties** from the resulting shortcut menu. In the **Properties** box, click **Use Personalized Menus** to remove the check from the corresponding check box. Then click **OK**.

Running Multiple Programs

Windows Me allows you to run many programs at once. Each running program is represented by a button on the taskbar. In Part 2, "Working on the Desktop," you'll learn more about working with multiple programs on the desktop.

Using the Keyboard

You can use the keyboard to navigate the **Start** menu. Press **Ctrl+Esc** to open the **Start** menu. Press the up- or down-arrow key to select and highlight a menu item. Press the right-arrow key to view a secondary menu. When you've highlighted the program you want to start, press **Enter**.

How to Use the My Computer Window

The **My Computer** window gives you easy access to tools and resources available on your computer, including programs, documents, and Web sites. Files are organized in folders. With a few mouse actions, you can quickly open any folder on a selected disk and examine the files it contains. After you've opened a target folder, you can run a program or open a document by clicking the appropriate icon. You can also use the **My Computer** window to start your browser and jump to a specific Web site.

Begin

1 Open the My Computer Window

Click the **My Computer** icon on the desktop. The **My Computer** window appears.

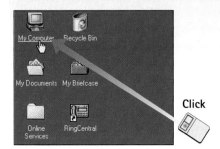

Click

2 Select a Drive

The **My Computer** window contains icons representing your hard disk, floppy disk drive, CD-ROM drive, as well as some other important folders. Click the icon for the drive you want to investigate—for example, your hard disk drive, typically named **C:**. After this action, the **My Computer** window displays information about the selected disk. To view all the files and folders stored on the disk, click **View the entire contents of this drive** at the left side of the window.

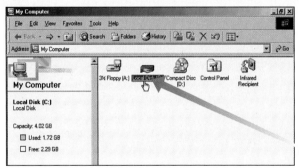

Click

3 Select a Folder

Click any folder icon to view the files stored in the folder. Keep in mind that a folder can contain files alone or a combination of files and additional folders. (Icons can appear in a variety of ways, depending on the current **View** setting. See the How-To Hints for details.)

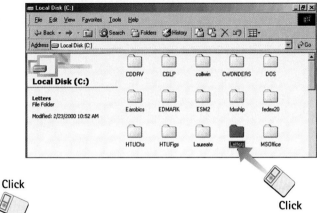

Click

4 Open a File

After you open a folder, position the mouse pointer over the icon representing a file you want to identify. A description of the file appears on the left side of the **My Computer** window. If you want, click the icon to open the file. If the file is a document, Windows starts the appropriate application and opens the document.

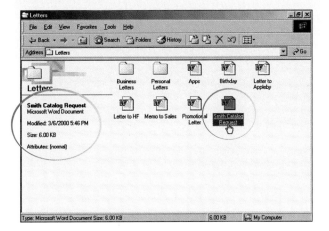

5 Visit a Web Site

To visit a Web site, pull down the **Favorites** menu and choose the name of a site. (The **Favorites** menu contains any number of sites that you choose to add to your own list as you explore the Internet over time.) Alternatively, enter the address for a target site in the **Address** bar. The **My Computer** window becomes a browser view of the site you've selected.

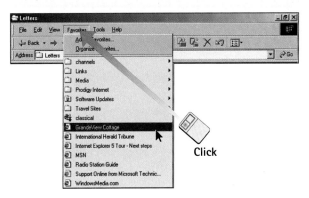

Click

6 Navigate Between Folders

To navigate among the files or sites opened during your current session in the **My Computer** window, click the **Back** and **Forward** buttons. To close the window, pull down the **File** menu and choose **Close**.

Back   Forward   Address bar

End

How-To Hints

Recognizing Shared Disks

If your system is part of a home network, Windows Me displays a blue-sleeved hand beneath the icons for any *shared* disks or folders in the **My Computer** window. This means that the content of the disk or folder is available to other computers attached to the network. Turn to Parts 17 and 18 for detailed information about setting up a home network.

Managing the My Computer Window

Before automatically showing you the entire contents of a selected disk or folder, **My Computer** presents you with a convenient list of specific items that may interest you. These options appear at the left side of the **My Computer** window. Click **View the entire contents of this drive** (as directed in Step 2) to see all the files and folders of a drive; to switch back to the original view, click **Hide the contents of this drive**.

How to Shut Down Your Computer

As long as your computer is on, Windows Millennium Edition remains in charge of operations. When you're ready to turn off your computer, you must follow a few simple steps to end your Windows session in an orderly way. The **Shut Down** command is on the **Start** menu, just a mouse click away. When you choose this command, Windows checks all open documents to make sure that you've saved any changes you've made. If any unsaved files are found, Windows gives you the opportunity to save them before you quit.

Begin

1 Choose the Shut Down Command

Click the **Start** button and choose the **Shut Down** command. The **Shut Down Windows** dialog box appears on the desktop and the desktop behind the dialog box dims.

Click

2 View the Shut Down Options

Click the down arrow to the right of the list box to display the three available options.

Click

3 Choose an Option

Choose the **Shut Down** option and click **OK** if you're ready to turn off your computer. (Choose **Restart** if you want to begin a new Windows Me session; choose **Stand by** to keep your current activities in memory while your computer rests in a low-power mode.)

Click

4 Save Your Documents

If Windows detects any unsaved documents on the desktop, a dialog box gives you the option of saving the modified document to disk or abandoning the changes. Click either **Yes** or **No**. (If you click the **Cancel** button, you will cancel the **Shut Down** command.) Windows notifies you when it's safe to switch off your computer. (If you're using a laptop, the computer shuts down automatically at this point.)

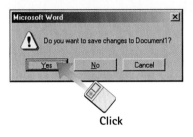

Click

End

How-To Hints

Suspending Operations

If you choose the **Stand by** option, Windows retains all your current work on the desktop and "rests" your computer. When you next turn on the computer, your desktop activity reappears just the way you left it.

Retaining Desktop Settings

Any desktop settings changed during the current Windows session are retained for future sessions. You learn to change a variety of settings in Part 4, "Changing the Windows Me Settings."

Logging Off

The **Start** menu also has a **Log Off** command. If your computer is used by more than one person, the **Log Off** command allows you to end your own work and prepare for someone else to take over the computer.

Task

Working on the Desktop

*I*n the flurry of activity that sometimes takes place on your desktop, Windows Millennium Edition helps you maintain a tidy and usable workspace. Using commands available from the taskbar, you can organize all open windows in *cascade* or *tile* arrangements. To avoid clutter, you can *minimize* any or all of the windows you're currently working on, temporarily clearing them from the desktop. You can also attach a variety of navigational toolbars to the taskbar, giving you convenient ways to jump directly to folders on your computer or to sites on the Web.

When any icon, document, or program becomes extraneous to your work, you can quickly delete it. But just in case you later change your mind, Windows keeps deleted files in the **Recycle Bin**, which gives you the option of restoring them to their original locations.

Windows Me provides an extensively cross-referenced **Help and Support** center to guide you in your work on the desktop. When you have a question about the steps of a procedure—or when you want to investigate a tool in greater depth—you can quickly look up the relevant help topic. Online support is also available on the Web, just a mouse click away whenever the **Help and Support** window is open.

In the following tasks, you'll practice effective techniques for organizing your work in Windows Me and for switching among the programs you run on the desktop. You'll also learn how to find relevant and useful help when you need it. ●

How to Use the Taskbar

The **taskbar** gives you easy access to the programs, Web sites, and documents you open on the desktop. Whether you're working on one open item or several at a time, the taskbar displays a button for each. The taskbar also has a selection of **Quick Launch** icons, initially displayed to the right of the **Start** button. These icons are available for starting several commonly used programs. The taskbar's shortcut menu—which appears when you right-click the taskbar itself—allows you to turn the **Quick Launch** feature on and off.

Begin

1 Start Some Applications

Open any group of programs from the **Start** menu. In this example, you see windows for the FreeCell, WordPad, Paint, and Calculator programs.

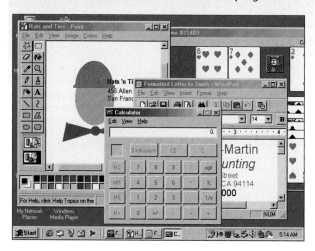

2 Activate a Window

To activate a particular window, click the program's button on the taskbar. That program comes to the front of the desktop, where you can resume your work in the active window.

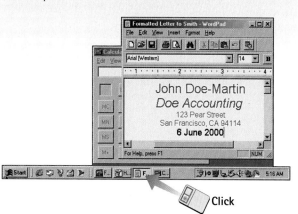

Click

3 Clear the Desktop

To clear all the windows from the desktop at one time, right-click a blank area on the taskbar. From the resulting shortcut menu, choose **Minimize All Windows**. (Alternatively, click the **Show Desktop** icon in the **Quick Launch** section of the taskbar.) Your windows disappear from the desktop, but are still represented by buttons on the taskbar.

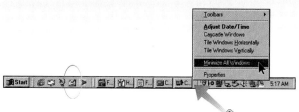

Right-click

4 Reopen a Window

Click any button on the taskbar to redisplay a selected window. Your work reappears intact on the desktop, just as it was when you left it. To restore all tasks at once, right-click a blank area of the taskbar and choose **Undo Minimize All** from the resulting shortcut menu (or click the **Show Desktop** icon on the **Quick Launch** toolbar).

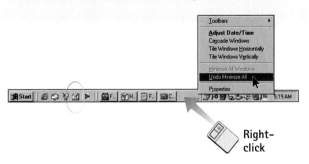

Right-click

5 View the Quick Launch Icons

If the **Quick Launch** icons do not currently appear on your taskbar to the right of the **Start** button, right-click a blank area on the taskbar, choose **Toolbars**, and then choose **Quick Launch**. Initially, the **Quick Launch** area contains a preset selection of tools, including icons for launching Internet Explorer and Outlook Express.

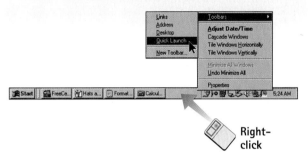

Right-click

6 Add an Icon to Quick Launch

To add a new program to the **Quick Launch** toolbar, point to the icon for the program you want to add (from the **My Computer** window, for example, or even directly from the desktop), hold down the right mouse button, and drag the icon into the **Quick Launch** area of the taskbar. Choose **Create Shortcut Here** from the resulting shortcut menu. (You might have to expand the length of the **Quick Launch** toolbar by dragging its border to the right.) This new icon is now available as a shortcut for starting the program you've selected.

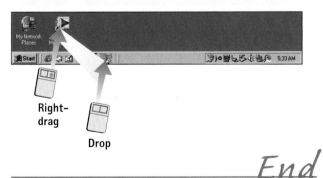

Right-drag

Drop

End

How-To Hints

Using Toolbars on the Taskbar

Quick Launch is only one of several toolbars you can place on the Windows Me taskbar. The taskbar is one of most important and commonly used tools on the desktop. Its effectiveness depends partly on simplicity and clarity. You may find that the taskbar becomes cluttered and difficult to use if you add too many **Quick Launch** icons and other toolbars. Experiment with the taskbar format that best suits your own work habits on the desktop. For more information about toolbars on the taskbar, turn the page.

Rearranging Windows

The taskbar's shortcut menu contains commands for rearranging windows. See Task 4, "How to Arrange Windows," for more information.

How to Use Toolbars on the Taskbar

You've already worked with **Quick Launch**, one of the standard toolbars that can appear on or with the taskbar. There are three others: The **Address** toolbar provides an easy way to open folders or Web sites; the **Links** toolbar displays a list of one-click connections to selected Web sites; and the **Desktop** toolbar places your entire set of desktop icons onto the taskbar. In addition to these toolbars, you can create your own toolbars from the contents of any folders on your hard disk. To accommodate the toolbars, you can increase the height of the taskbar by one or more lines.

Begin

1 Add a Toolbar

Right-click a blank area of the taskbar and choose **Toolbars** from the resulting shortcut menu. From the **Toolbars** list, select the item you want to add to your taskbar. Repeat this step for any additional toolbars you want to include.

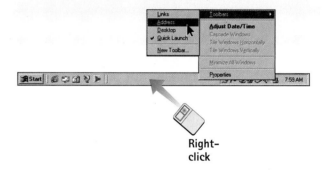

Right-click

2 Increase the Taskbar's Height

To make room for a newly displayed toolbar, position the mouse pointer over the top border of the taskbar and drag the border up. As you drag, the mouse pointer appears as a bold two-headed arrow.

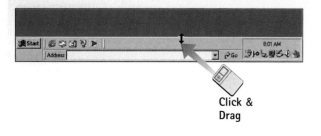

Click & Drag

3 Add a Custom Toolbar

To add a nonstandard toolbar, right-click a blank area of the taskbar, choose **Toolbars**, and then choose the **New Toolbar** command. Windows opens the **New Toolbar** dialog box, which displays the hierarchy of folders stored on your computer.

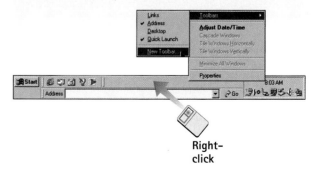

Right-click

4 Select a Folder

Select the folder from which you want to create the new toolbar. Click the small + symbol to the left of any folder icon to open it; keep opening contained folders until you find the one you want. Click **OK** to create the new toolbar. Optionally, you can increase the height of the taskbar to create room for the new toolbar.

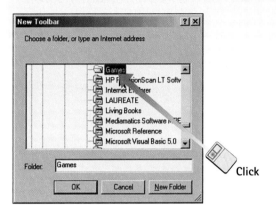

Click

5 Click an Icon in the Toolbar

Click any of the icons on the new toolbar to start the corresponding program.

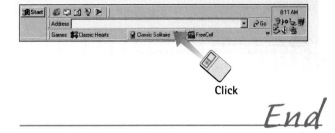

Click

End

How-To Hints

Changing the Appearance of a Toolbar

You can change the display properties of a toolbar, including the size of icons and the appearance of captions. Right-click the title of the target toolbar (for example, Desktop). On the resulting shortcut menu, the **View** command provides **Large** and **Small** options for the size of icons, and the **Show Text** and **Show Title** commands are toggles that determine whether captions appear on the toolbar.

Removing a Toolbar

To remove a toolbar, right-click a blank area on the taskbar and choose **Toolbars**. In the **Toolbars** list that appears, a checked item means that the toolbar is currently displayed. Click the name of the checked toolbar you want to remove from the taskbar.

Restoring the Taskbar's Height

To restore the taskbar to its original height, position the mouse pointer along the upper border of the expanded taskbar and drag down.

How to Switch Between Applications

Even in a mouse-oriented environment such as Windows, you might occasionally prefer to use keyboard techniques for some common operations. Lifting your fingers off the keyboard to click a button with the mouse sometimes seems inconvenient and inefficient. In particular, when you are running several programs at once, you might want to use the keyboard to switch between applications on the desktop. Windows provides a simple two-key shortcut for activating the program of your choice.

Begin

1 Start Some Programs

Start the applications you plan to use during your current session with Windows. Optionally, maximize any of the applications you want to work with, or minimize them all as shown here.

2 Press Alt+Tab

To switch to an application and display its window, hold down the **Alt** key and press **Tab** once. (Don't release **Alt** yet.) A box appears, displaying the icons of all the programs currently running on the desktop. Holding down **Alt**, press **Tab** one or more times to step through the icons in the box. A frame marks your current selection.

3 Activate a Program

When you've selected the program you want to activate, release the **Alt** key. The program you've selected comes to the front of the desktop in the active window. Optionally, press **Alt+Tab** to switch to and display another running application.

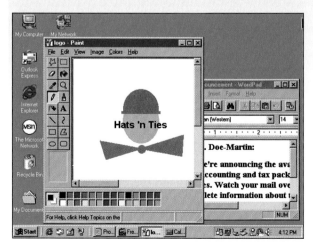

4 Open the Start Menu

Keep in mind that you can also use a keyboard shortcut to open the **Start** menu: Hold down the **Ctrl** key and press **Esc**. Press the up- or down-arrow key to select and highlight a menu item. Press the right-arrow key to view a secondary menu. When you've highlighted the program you want to start, press **Enter**.

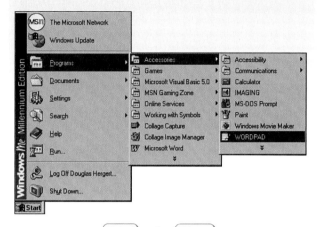

Ctrl + Esc
↑ → ↓

End

How-To Hints

Restoring a Window

When you use **Alt+Tab** to activate a window, the program you select is restored to its previous size and position on the desktop. If the application was maximized the last time it appeared, it will be maximized again.

Canceling the Switch

If you are in the middle of using the **Alt+Tab** technique and decide not to switch programs after all, press the **Esc** key once and release the **Alt** key. The current application remains active.

Changing the Size of a Window

You can use yet another keyboard shortcut to minimize, maximize, or restore the previous size of the active window. Press **Alt+Spacebar** to view the **Control** menu for the active window. Then press **N** for **Minimize**, **X** for **Maximize**, or **R** for **Restore**.

How to Arrange Windows

When you right-click the taskbar, you see a shortcut menu containing a variety of convenient commands. Among these are three options for rearranging open windows on the desktop: **Cascade Windows**, **Tile Windows Horizontally**, and **Tile Windows Vertically**. In the cascade arrangement, windows are stacked, overlapping, one on top of another. Because the windows overlap, only the front window is fully visible; others are identified by their title bars. In the tile arrangements, windows are automatically resized so that they can appear side by side or one above another on the desktop. The more windows included in the tiling, the smaller each appears.

Begin

1 Start Some Programs

Start the applications you want to work with. Minimize any windows you do not want to include in the cascade arrangement. Only those programs displayed as windows on the desktop are affected by the arrangement commands.

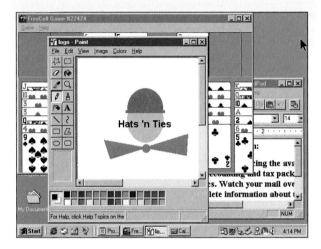

2 Arrange Windows in a Cascade

Right-click a blank portion of the taskbar and choose **Cascade Windows** from the shortcut menu. Windows rearranges the current tasks in a cascade of windows.

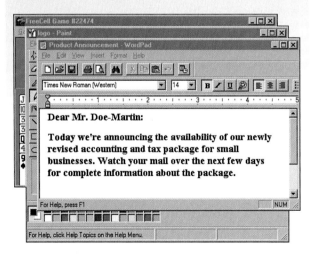

3 Tile Windows Horizontally

Right-click the taskbar again and choose **Tile Windows Horizontally**. Windows arranges the current tasks one above another on the desktop.

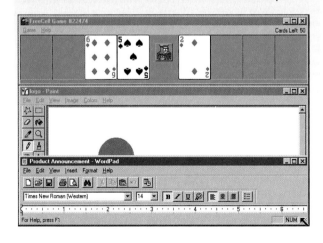

4 Tile Windows Vertically

Right-click the taskbar and choose **Tile Windows Vertically**. Windows displays tasks in a side-by-side arrangement.

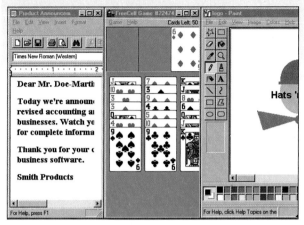

End

How-To Hints

Returning to a Previous Arrangement

To return to the previous window arrangement, choose **Undo** from the taskbar's shortcut menu.

Using the Show Desktop Button

Keep in mind that the **Quick Launch** toolbar on the taskbar contains a **Show Desktop** button. Click this button to minimize all open windows.

Resizing Windows

The cascade and tiling options are not the only ways to change the size and shape of a window. You can use the mouse to resize a window by dragging any of its borders or corners. When you position the mouse pointer over a side or corner of a resizable window, the pointer takes the shape of a two-headed arrow pointing vertically, horizontally, or diagonally. Hold down the left mouse button and drag toward the window's center to reduce the size; drag away from the center to increase the size. Note that some application windows, such as the calculator, cannot be resized.

How to Use the Recycle Bin

You can delete files, folders, and shortcut icons from the desktop or from a folder whenever you want. To safeguard against inadvertent deletions, Windows Me maintains an intermediate location called the **Recycle Bin**. When you delete an item, it goes temporarily into this bin. If you later decide that you want to restore the item to its original location, you can choose the **Restore** command from the **Recycle Bin**. Alternatively, you can empty the bin when you're sure that you want to confirm the deletion process.

Begin

1 Delete an Item

To delete a shortcut icon from the desktop or from a folder, drag the icon to the **Recycle Bin**. Alternatively, right-click the item and choose **Delete** from the shortcut menu.

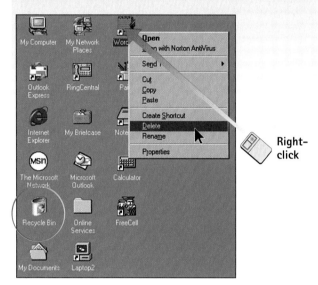

Right-click

2 Confirm the Deletion

If a dialog box asks you to confirm sending the item to the **Recycle Bin**, click **Yes**. (Be sure to read the cautionary note in the How-To Hints.) When the Recycle Bin contains one or more objects, its icon appears as an overflowing trash can.

Click

3 Delete Several Items

To delete several items at once, begin by dragging the mouse around the group of items. This action selects all the items in the group.

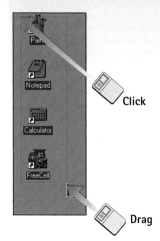

Click

Drag

4 Drag the Items to the Bin

Drag the selected items to the **Recycle Bin** and release the mouse button when the trash can icon is highlighted.

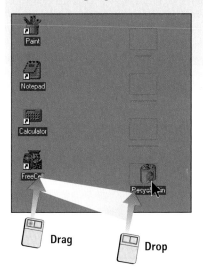

Drag

Drop

5 Open the Recycle Bin

Click the **Recycle Bin** icon to open its window and view the current contents.

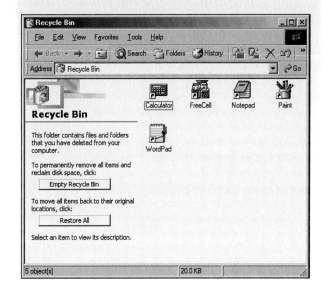

6 Delete or Restore a File

To delete a single item permanently, or to restore it to its original location, begin by selecting its name in the **Recycle Bin** window. Then pull down the **File** menu and choose **Delete** or **Restore**. Alternatively, click one of two available buttons to delete or restore all files: **Empty Recycle Bin** or **Restore All**.

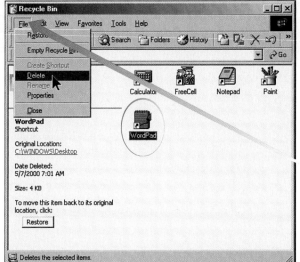

Click

How-To Hints

Avoiding Permanent Deletions

Some desktop items cannot be stored in the Recycle Bin and will be removed permanently if you choose to delete them. In this case, Windows displays an appropriate cautionary note in the **Confirm Delete** dialog box.

Deleting Shortcut Icons

Deleting a shortcut icon does not delete the application that the icon represents. (See Task 3, "How to Create a Shortcut Icon" in Part 3 for more information.)

Changing the Recycle Bin Properties

To change the behavior of the **Recycle Bin**, right-click its icon and choose **Properties**. You can change the amount of disk space reserved for maintaining the bin. You can also de-activate the bin, although this is not advis-able, by selecting the option labeled **Do not move files to the Recycle Bin**.

End

How to Get Help

Windows Me provides a cross-referenced **Help and Support** center you can turn to whenever you have questions about features or procedures on the desktop. The answers to your questions appear in an easy-to-use help window. Information is organized by major topics and is also indexed intuitively by keywords. This feature is always available directly from the **Start** menu.

Begin

1 Open Help and Support

Click the **Start** button on the taskbar and choose **Help**. The **Help and Support** window appears on the desktop.

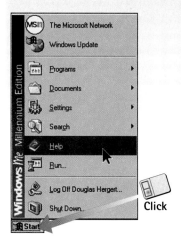

Click

2 Choose a Topic

Begin by examining the major topics listed at the left side of the window under the heading **What would you like help with?**. Click a topic that interests you; a new list of more specific subtopics appears. Continue making selections until you find the particular item you want to read about.

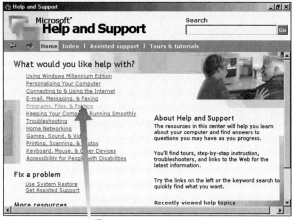

Click

3 Read the Help Text

Scroll through the information displayed in the box at the right side of the **Help and Support** window. You'll find steps for performing a particular task along with notes about completing the task. Click **Related Topics** at the bottom of the box for a convenient list of references to additional help information. Click any item in the **Related Topics** list to jump to another topic.

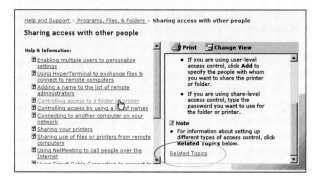

4 Look up an Index Topic

Click the **Index** link at the top of the **Help and Support** window. In the **Type in the keyword to find** text box, type a keyword for the topic you want to look for. In response, the index list scrolls to the corresponding topic. Select an item from the index list and click the **Display** button to view the information you want.

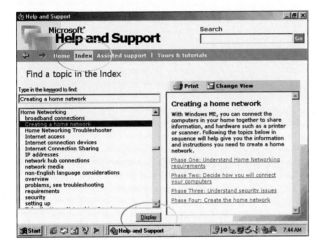

5 Start a Program

Some help topics contain special shortcut links to relevant programs. Click a link if you want to start a program discussed in the help topic.

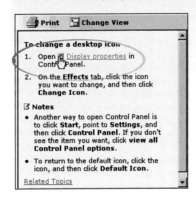

End

How-To Hints

Printing a Help Topic

When you've located a help topic you want to keep on paper, click the **Print** icon displayed at the top of the topic box (shown in Step 3) to print the topic.

Navigating through Help Topics

The help window has **Back** and **Forward** icons that allow you to review previous topics. Above the topic list you'll also find the sequence of topic selections that led to the current topic (as shown in Step 3). You can click any entry in this horizontally arranged list to jump back to an intermediate topic location.

Pressing F1

The F1 function key is the shortcut for finding context-sensitive help in your current activity in Windows. Each major Windows application provides its own help system, which is designed to assist you with the operations of that specific program.

Task

Working with Programs and Documents

From word processing to Web browsing, from spreadsheets to Solitaire, applications are Windows' true *raison d'être*. Your own library of favorite programs might include applications that come with Windows, along with a variety of software packages that you buy separately to install and run on the desktop. The essential purpose of Windows Me is to guarantee a consistent and manageable environment for all the programs you use on your computer.

Before you begin learning about applications, take a moment to review a few of the essential terms you'll encounter in the tasks ahead. A *file* is the basic unit for storing information on disk. A file can contain a *document* you've created in a particular application—for example, a word-processed report, a spreadsheet, a database, or a drawing—or a file might store part of a program that you run on the desktop. A *filename* is the unique identifier for a file. Windows Me allows you to write free-form multiword filenames that are long enough to describe the contents and purpose of each file. A *folder* provides a practical way to organize files related to a specific purpose. Given the large amounts of space available on hard disks, folders provide an important multilayered structure for organizing your files. You can create folders on a disk or directly on the desktop. You can also create folders inside other folders. The many programs and documents on a hard disk are typically stored in a hierarchy of folders within folders. ●

How to Save a File

In an application designed for creating specific kinds of documents—such as a word processor, a spreadsheet application, or a graphics program—you'll typically find two save commands in the **File** menu: The **Save As** command is for storing the initial file version of each new document you develop, and the **Save** command is for updating the file with any changes you make in the document. The **Save As** dialog box allows you to designate a location for the new document file and to assign the file a name. You can choose any folder on your hard disk—or elsewhere—to save a new file that you create.

1 Use the Save As Command

Start an application and begin developing a new document. When you are ready to perform the first save operation, pull down the **File** menu and choose **Save As**. The **Save As** dialog box appears on the desktop. (This example shows the **Save As** dialog box from the WordPad program.)

2 Choose a Disk Location

If you want to save your new file somewhere other than the default folder (often **My Documents**), pull down the **Save in** list by clicking the down-arrow button on the right side of the list. Then choose the disk destination for the save operation; for example, your hard disk.

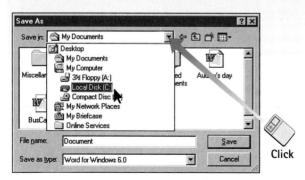

Click

3 Choose a Folder

If the selected disk location contains a structure of folders, the icons for these folders appear in the **Save As** dialog box. Click any folder icon to open the folder and choose it as the destination of the save operation.

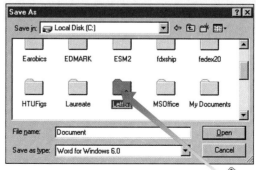

Click

4 Create a New Folder

Alternatively, click the **Create New Folder** button at the top of the dialog box. A new folder appears at the current disk location. Enter a name for the new folder. Then click the folder icon to select it as the destination of the save.

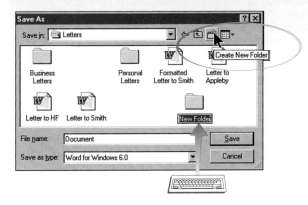

5 Name the File

Type a name for the new file and then click the **Save** button to complete the save operation. (See the How-To Hints for information about filenames in Windows Millennium Edition.)

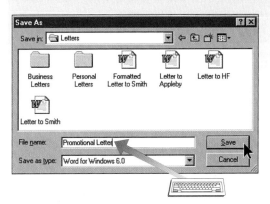

6 Update the File as You Work

As you continue developing your document, you should periodically update the file on disk with the latest version of your work. To do so, pull down the **File** menu and choose **Save**. Alternatively, press **Ctrl+S** or click the **Save** icon on the application's toolbar.

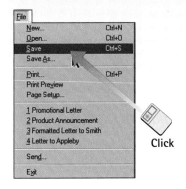

Click

End

How-To Hints

Naming a File

Windows Millennium Edition supports long, multi-word names for the files you create. A name can contain as many as 215 characters and can include spaces. Note that reasonably short names are generally more convenient than very long ones. Several characters are restricted from the names you assign to files, including /, \, :, *, ?, ", <, >, and |

Assigning a File Extension

Each application typically appends its own three-character *extension* to the name of a file, in the form **name.ext**. For example, the WordPad program identifies word-processed documents with the extension **.doc**.

Using Toolbar Buttons

The toolbar in the **Save As** dialog box includes a variety of useful buttons. You've seen how to use the **Create New Folder** button. In addition, the **Up One Level** button allows you to navigate to the next-higher folder level in the current structure of folders. The **View Menu** button allows you to change the way files and folders are displayed in the content area of the dialog box itself.

How to Open a Document

As you've seen, a *document* is a file you create in a particular application. For example, you can create a text document in WordPad, a graphic file in Paint, or a numeric worksheet in a spreadsheet program such as Microsoft Excel. Windows Me gives you a variety of convenient ways to open and manage documents. Most Windows programs have an **Open** command you can use to open a file from disk and display its contents in the work area of the application. Alternatively, the **Documents** list in the **Start** menu gives you a quick way to open recently used documents, and the **My Documents** folder is a convenient default location for frequently used files.

Begin

1 Start an Application

To open a document, begin by running the application in which the document was created. Click the **Start** button, choose **Programs**, choose **Accessories**, and then click the name of the application you want to start.

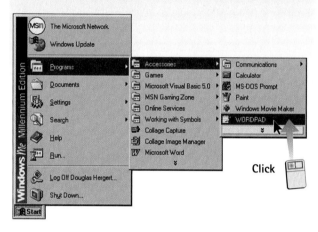

Click

2 Choose the Open Command

When the application window appears (WordPad in this example), pull down the **File** menu and choose **Open**, or simply click the **Open** button on the application's toolbar. The **Open** dialog box appears on the desktop.

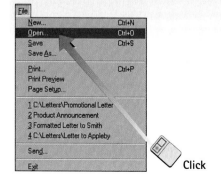

Click

3 Locate the Document

In the **Open** dialog box, pull down the **Look in** list and select the drive where the target file is stored. If necessary, open the folder where you expect to find the document.

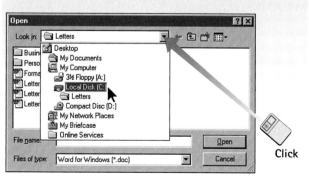

Click

4 Open the Document

When a list of documents appears, select the one you want to open. Click **Open** to open the document and view its contents.

Click

5 Use the Documents List

To view a list of documents you've worked on recently, click **Start** and choose **Documents**. When you click the name of a file from the resulting list, Windows starts the appropriate application and opens the document.

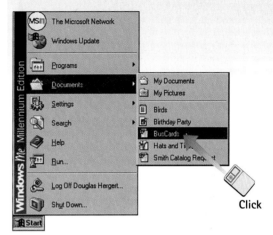

Click

6 Open from My Documents

The **My Documents** folder is another convenient location for organizing and opening your everyday files. Applications often suggest this folder as a default storage destination for new files. Open the **My Documents** folder by clicking its icon on the desktop. Then open any document in the folder simply by clicking an icon.

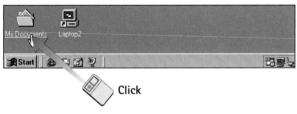

Click

End

How-To Hints

Creating Shortcut Icons

You can place shortcut icons for frequently used documents directly on the desktop. See Task 3 to explore this technique.

Selecting Documents from the File Menu

Many applications maintain a list of recently opened documents at the bottom of the **File** menu. To reopen a recently used file, pull down the **File** menu and chose an entry from the list. But note that this action does not add the file's name to the **Documents** list in the **Start** menu.

Clearing the Documents List

Occasionally, you might want to remove files from the **Start** menu's **Documents** list. To do so, right-click the taskbar and choose **Properties**. Click the **Advanced** tab and then click the **Clear** button to clear the **Documents** list. (This action does not delete the actual documents from disk, only their names from the list.)

How to Create a Shortcut Icon

Are there a few Windows programs that you use every time you turn on your computer? Or is there a set of documents—budgets, schedules, forms, templates—that you open on a daily basis? If so, you can easily place shortcut icons for these items directly on the Windows Me desktop. A *shortcut* gives you instant access to a program, document, folder, printer, disk drive, Web site, or any other object you use regularly in Windows. After you create a shortcut, you simply click it to open the application it represents.

Begin

1 Open My Computer

Open the **My Computer** window by clicking its icon on the desktop.

Click

2 Select the File

In the **My Computer** window, open the appropriate disk and folders to locate the program or document for which you want to create a shortcut. Position the mouse pointer over the target item to select it.

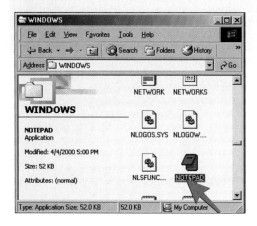

3 Drag the Icon to the Desktop

Hold down the right mouse button and drag a copy of the selected item onto a blank area of the desktop.

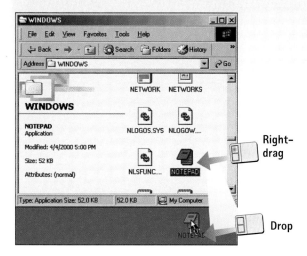

Right-drag

Drop

4 Create the Shortcut

When you release the mouse button, a menu pops up. Choose **Create Shortcut(s) Here**. In response, Windows creates a shortcut icon for the program or document you've selected.

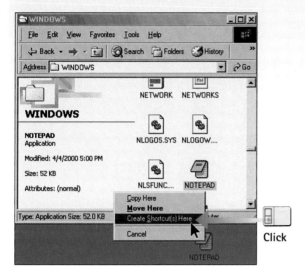

Click

5 Rename the Icon

If you want to rename the shortcut icon, right-click it and choose **Rename**. Then type a new name and press **Enter**.

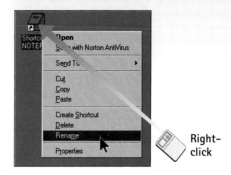

Right-click

6 Use the New Shortcut

To run the program or open the document, simply click the shortcut icon

Click

End

How-To Hints

Using Auto Arrange

By default, Windows arranges icons in neat columns on the desktop. If you prefer a free-form arrangement, turn off the **Auto Arrange** option: Right-click the desktop, choose **Arrange Icons**, and click **Auto Arrange** to deselect the option. You can now drag icons to any position on the desktop.

Using the Send To Option

Another quick way to create a desktop shortcut for a selected program or document is to right-click the target icon, choose **Send To** from the shortcut menu, and then click **Desktop (create shortcut)** in the **Send To** menu.

Using the Create Shortcut Tool

Here's yet another technique: Right-click the desktop, choose **New**, and click **Shortcut**. In the resulting sequence of dialog boxes, identify the location of the program, document, or Web site for which you want to create a shortcut and type a name for the icon.

How to Find Files or Programs

Windows Me supplies a simple but powerful **Search** tool that helps you find files, wherever they are stored in your system. By using the **Search** application, you can find files by name, size, category, date, or content. You can also search through all the folders on a given disk, or through a specific set of folders. When **Search** displays a list of files that match your criteria, you can open any file simply by clicking its icon.

Begin

1 Start the Search

Click the **Start** button and choose **Search**. Then choose **For Files or Folders** from the **Search** menu. When the **Search** window appears, select the text box labeled **Search for files or folders**. Type the name (or part of a name) of the file or files you want to search for.

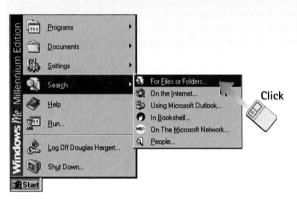

Click

2 Select a Location for the Search

Pull down the **Look in** list and select the drive or folder where you want to perform the search. (Click **Browse** if you want to specify a particular folder.)

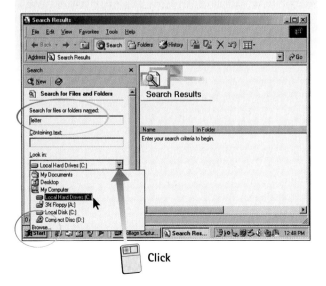

Click

3 Click the Search Button

Click the **Search Now** button. Windows searches in the specified location for files whose names match your entry.

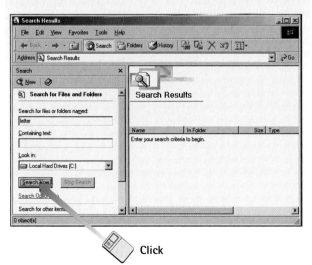

Click

4 Examine the Results

The **Search** window displays a list of the files and folders that match the target name. You can scroll through the search results by dragging the scrollbars located below and to the right of the file list.

Click

5 Change the View Setting

To view the files as icons, click the **View** button on the **Search** window toolbar and choose the **Large Icons** option. To open any file in the **Search Results** pane, click its icon.

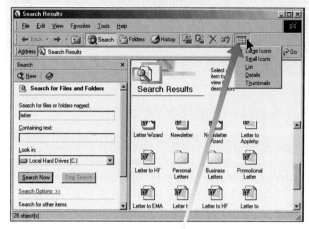

Click

End

How-To Hints

Searching by Content

To search for files that contain a specified text content, type an entry in the **Containing text** box in the **Search** window before you click the **Search Now** button.

Searching by Date

You can also search by other criteria, including date of last revision, file type, and file size. Click **Search Options** at the lower-left corner of the **Search** window, and then scroll down the left pane to view the options box. For a date search, check the **Date** option and type date entries in the **between** and **and** boxes.

Previewing the File Contents

To get an idea of the content of each file in the **Search Results** pane, try switching to the **Thumbnails** view. (Click the **View** button in the **Search** window toolbar and choose **Thumbnails**.) To the extent possible, Windows provides a small picture of each file's contents.

How to Use Windows Explorer

Windows Explorer is another tool you can use to locate and manage files on your computer. When you start Explorer, it displays two panes of information. On the left, you see the hierarchy of folders on your current disk. You can quickly open any folder by clicking its icon in the list. On the right, you see the file contents of the selected folder. Files in the content list can be displayed as icons, descriptive lines of text, or thumbnail pictures—arranged by name, size, type, or date. Explorer gives you simple techniques for copying, moving, opening, renaming, and deleting files in a selected folder.

Begin

1 Start Windows Explorer

Click the **Start** button and choose **Programs, Accessories**; then click **Windows Explorer**. (If the **Personalized Menus** option is active on your computer, you may have to click the down-arrow icon at the bottom of the **Accessories** menu list to find Windows Explorer.) The **Explorer** window opens on the desktop.

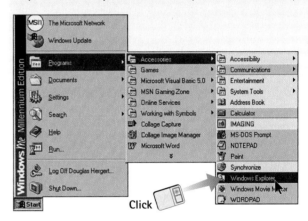

2 Open a Folder

To open a folder and view its contents, click the folder's name in the list on the left. The pane on the right displays all the files and folders contained in the selected folder. A folder containing an additional structure of folders is marked by a plus sign in the left pane. Click the plus sign to view the folder structure.

3 Change the View Mode

In the toolbar, click the **Views** button. Choose **Large Icons, Small Icons, List, Details,** or **Thumbnails** to change the display format of the files in the right pane.

4 Change the Order of Files

To change the order in which files are displayed, pull down the **View** menu and choose **Arrange Icons**. Then choose an option to arrange the files by name, type, size, or date. (Alternatively, click the heading at the top of any column in **Details** view to change the order of the list.)

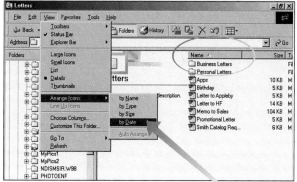

Click

5 Copy or Move a File

To copy a file to another disk, use the mouse to drag the file from the pane on the right to the appropriate disk icon in the pane on the left. Explorer copies the file to the destination disk. To move a file to a new folder on the same disk, drag the file from one folder to another; in this case, the file disappears from the source folder and is moved to the destination folder. (See the How-To Hints for more information.)

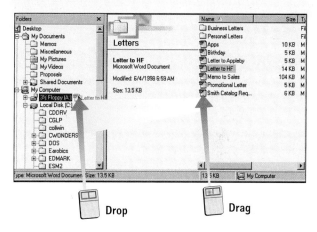

Drop   Drag

6 Start a Program

To start a program or open a document, click its icon in the pane on the right.

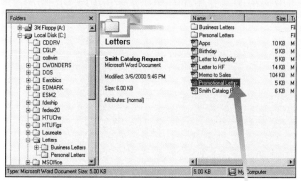

Click

End

How-To Hints

Copying a File

Another way to copy a file is to select the file and then choose **Copy** from the **Edit** menu. Then select the destination folder and choose **Paste** from the **Edit** menu. Alternatively, hold down the **Ctrl** key while you drag a file from one folder to another. The mouse pointer displays a plus sign to show that you are performing a copy operation.

Exploring a Home Network

If you have set up a home network with two or more computers, the **Explorer** window can display contents from each computer in the network. See Parts 17 and 18 for information about home networks.

How to Create a Folder

You can use the **My Computer** or **Windows Explorer** window to create a new folder at any location on your hard disk or on a floppy disk. For convenient access to everyday files, you can even place folders directly on the desktop. You also can add new program folders to the **Start Menu** folder to expand the options presented in the **Start** menu itself.

Begin

1 Choose a Location

Click the **My Computer** icon on the desktop to open the **My Computer** window. Then click the icon for the disk on which you want to create a new folder. Optionally, you can open existing folders until you reach the location where you want to create a new folder.

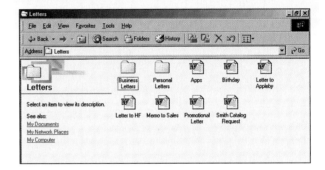

2 Create a New Folder

Pull down the **File** menu, choose **New**, and then choose **Folder**. A **New Folder** icon appears in the folder that you opened in the **My Computer** window in step 1. The folder's initial name is highlighted so that you can immediately enter a new name. Type the name you want to assign to this folder and press **Enter**. You can now click this icon to open the new folder. (You can use this same technique in **Windows Explorer**.)

Click

3 Create a Folder on the Desktop

To create a new folder on the desktop, right-click any empty portion of the desktop, choose **New**, and then click **Folder**. Type a name for the new folder and press **Enter**.

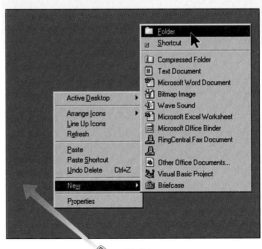

Right-click

4 Explore the Start Menu

The **Start Menu** folder contains a hierarchy of folders that define the contents of the **Start** menu itself. By inserting a new folder into this group, you can create a personalized entry in your **Start** menu. To view the **Start Menu** folder, right-click the **Start** button and choose **Explore**. Open the **Programs** folder inside the **Start Menu** folder.

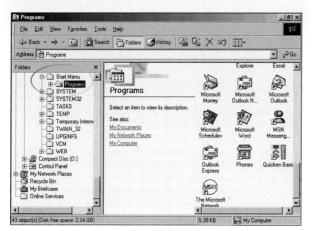

5 Add a Folder to the Programs Menu

The **Programs** folder represents the contents of the **Programs** menu. To add a new folder to the **Programs** menu, pull down the **File** menu, choose **New**, and then choose **Folder**. Inside this new folder, you can place any number of program shortcuts to reorganize and personalize your **Start** menu.

End

How-To Hints

Adding Items to a New Folder

Use the **Save As** command in any application to save documents in a new folder location you create. (See Task 1 in this part for details.) Alternatively, use the copy or move techniques described in Task 5 of this part to place existing files in a new folder.

Creating New Folders

There are two techniques for creating a new folder in **My Computer**: Choose **New** from the **File** menu; or right-click inside a folder window, choose **New**, and then click **Folder**.

Deleting a Folder

To delete a folder, right-click the folder icon and choose **Delete** from the shortcut menu. In the **Confirm Folder Delete** dialog box, click **Yes**. The folder and all its contents are moved to the **Recycle Bin**.

Task

4

Changing the Windows Me Settings

When you're ready to add some flair to your desktop—or to adjust it to the way you like to work—you'll find that Windows Millennium Edition provides many important options for customizing the interface. These options are generally easy to use and often fun to explore. In the tasks ahead, you'll learn to make important changes in the **Start** menu, the taskbar, the mouse pointer, the date and time settings, and the desktop itself.

The final two tasks in this part show ways to make the computer more accessible for users with disabilities. Always adaptable, Windows Me provides an important set of options to respond to special needs. A choice of high-contrast colors and large fonts makes the desktop easier to read. Keyboard adjustments allow a user to type information without having to press multiple keys at once. Other keyboard techniques are available as substitutes for mouse actions.

Although designed to address specific disability issues, options like these will appeal to a broad range of users. Like the urban curb cut—meant to facilitate wheelchair access, but also ideal for baby strollers and shopping carts—the opportunity to accommodate personal preferences on the computer is a boon to everyone. Whatever your needs or inclinations, you'll be glad that Windows can adjust to your style of work. ●

How to Designate StartUp Applications

StartUp is a special folder that allows you to define *automatic applications*—programs that start at the beginning of every Windows session. You can place shortcut icons in the **StartUp** folder for the applications you use every day. By doing so, you save yourself the trouble of having to start these applications yourself when you begin your work.

Begin

1 Open the StartUp Folder

Right-click the **Start** button and choose **Explore** from the resulting shortcut menu. **Windows Explorer** opens, displaying the contents of the **Start** menu folder. Click the **Programs** folder and then click the **StartUp** folder. If you haven't yet designated any startup programs, the **StartUp** folder may be empty.

Right-click

2 Add a New Shortcut to the Folder

Pull down the **File** menu and choose **New**. Then click **Shortcut** to begin the process of adding a new application to the **StartUp** menu. The **Create Shortcut** window appears on the desktop.

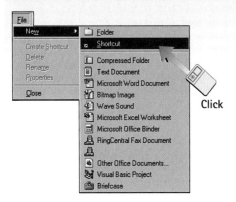

Click

3 Identify the Target Program

If you know the full path of the program you want to add to the **StartUp** folder, type it in the **Command line** box. If you don't know the path, click **Browse** to search for the program.

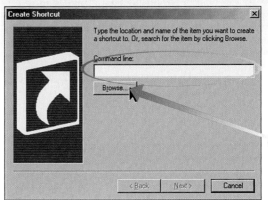

Click

4 Use the Browse Window

In the **Browse** dialog box, navigate to the folder that contains the target program and select the program file. Then click **Open**. This action returns you to the **Create Shortcut** window, where the program's full path now appears in the **Command line** box. Click **Next** to continue.

Click

5 Enter a Name for the Program

In the **Select a Title** window, type a name to identify the new program you're adding to the **StartUp** menu and then click **Finish**. The program you've selected appears inside the **StartUp** folder.

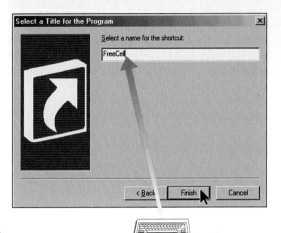

6 Add More Programs

Repeat Steps 2 through 5 for any other programs you want to place in the **StartUp** folder, and then close the **Explorer** window. The next time you start Windows, all the programs in your **StartUp** folder will automatically open onto the desktop. You can view the contents of the **StartUp** folder by clicking **Start**, **Programs**, and then **StartUp**.

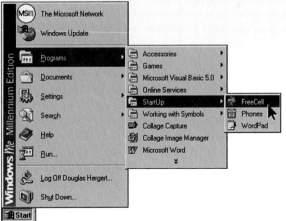

End

How-To Hints

Dragging Icons to StartUp

You can drag icons from other folders directly into the **StartUp** folder, as described in Task 5, "How to Use Windows Explorer," in Part 3.

Deleting Icons from StartUp

If you no longer want an application to start automatically, you can delete the program's icon from the **StartUp** folder. Open the folder, select the icon you want to delete, and press the **Delete** key. Windows asks you to confirm the deletion; click **Yes** if you're sure. The icon moves to the **Recycle Bin**. Alternatively, you can delete **StartUp** items directly from the menu itself. Click **Start** and choose **Programs** and **StartUp** to view the current list of **StartUp** programs. Right-click the name of the program you want to remove from the list and choose **Delete** from the shortcut menu.

How to Select Screen Options

You might have several reasons for wanting to change the colors and patterns that appear on your desktop. Different visual effects can prove more soothing to the eye, or your display hardware might produce better images with particular colors. Whatever your reasons, you can choose from pre-defined lists of patterns and color schemes that Windows supplies. In addition, you can install a *screen saver*, designed to prevent damage to your screen resulting from the long-term display of a single image.

Begin

1 Open the Display Properties Window

Right-click a blank area of the desktop and choose **Properties** from the resulting shortcut menu. The **Display Properties** window appears on the desktop.

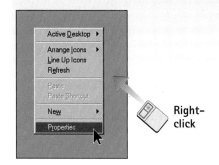

Right-click

2 Choose a Wallpaper

In the **Background** tab, select a graphic from the **Wallpaper** list, and then choose **Center**, **Tile**, or **Stretch** from the **Picture Display** options. The sample screen in the **Properties** window shows what the desktop will look like with the selected wallpaper.

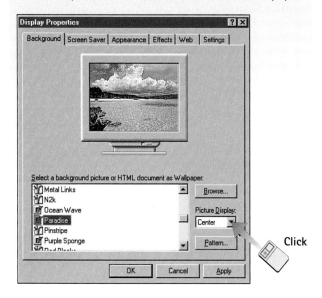

Click

3 Select a Pattern

Alternatively, select **(None)** from the **Wallpaper** list and click the **Pattern** button. In the resulting **Pattern** dialog box, select the name of a pattern and examine the preview to see whether you like it. Select **(None)** if you decide not to place a pattern on your desktop. Click **OK** to confirm.

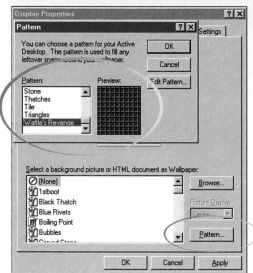

4 Select a Color Scheme

Click the **Appearance** tab and then click the down-arrow button at the right of the **Scheme** box to view the list of color combinations available for the desktop. Select the name of a color scheme.

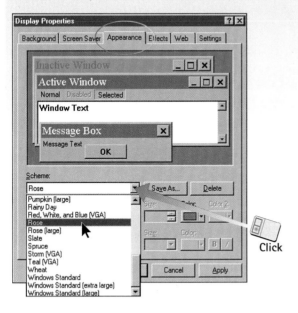

Click

5 Select a Screen Saver

Click the **Screen Saver** tab and select an option from the **Screen Saver** list. The sample screen shows the appearance of the screen saver you've selected. Optionally, change the numeric value in the **Wait** box. Windows will activate the screen saver whenever your computer has been idle for the specified number of **Wait** minutes.

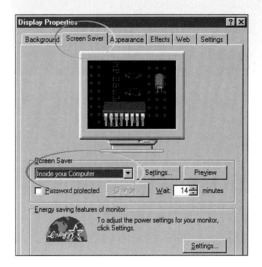

6 Try Other Options

The **Settings** tab provides options for color and resolution. Change any of these options to experiment with the result. Then click **OK** to confirm all your **Display Property** options and to close the window.

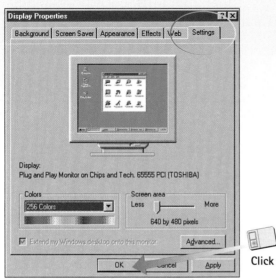

Click

How-To Hints

Choosing a Desktop Theme

Desktop Themes provide another way to customize your desktop environment. See Part 19 for details.

Defining a Password

You can define a password to secure your computer from other users while you're away from your desk. In the **Screen Saver** tab, click the **Password protected** check box, and then click **Change** to define a password. The password you specify will subsequently be required to return to the desktop from the screen saver you've selected.

End

How to Add Items to the Active Desktop

The *Active Desktop* gives you ways to combine Web content with your other work in Windows Millennium Edition. For example, you can place active content from your favorite sites directly on the desktop, where online information can be updated regularly. To begin, make sure that you know the Web address of the target site. Then follow these simple steps. (You'll learn more about the Internet in Parts 5 and 6.)

Begin

1 Open the Display Properties Window

Right-click a blank area of the desktop, and then choose **Active Desktop** and **Customize My Desktop** from the resulting shortcut menu. The **Display Properties** window appears on the desktop; the **Web** tab is selected. (Note that you can also add an item to the Active Desktop by clicking **New Desktop Item** directly from this shortcut menu; but the **Display Properties** window supplies a convenient visual preview of the changes you make.)

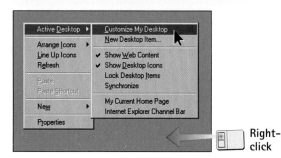

Right-click

2 Click the New Button

Click the **New** button to add a new Web item to your desktop. The **New Active Desktop Item** dialog box appears.

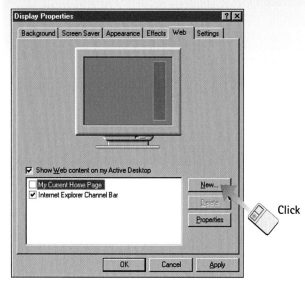

Click

3 Enter a Web Address

In the **Location** box, type the address of the Web site you want to add to your desktop. Click **OK** to confirm your entry. Then wait for your computer to connect you to the Web. (You might have to supply a password and click a **Connect** button to go online.)

4 Confirm the Item

The **Add Item to Active Desktop** window appears next. Click **OK** to confirm.

Click

5 Wait for the Content to Download

Wait while the site's content is downloaded to your computer. As soon as the download is complete, you can disconnect from the Web whenever you want.

6 View the Web Page on the Desktop

In the **Display Properties** dialog box, make sure that a check appears in the box next to the name of the new active item. (If not, click the corresponding check box to confirm that you want the item to appear on your desktop.) Then click **OK**. Optionally, use your mouse to move the active item to a convenient position on the desktop and to change its size and dimensions appropriately.

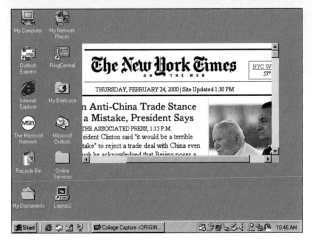

End

How-To Hints

Scheduling Updates

You can schedule regular updates for a Web item, or you can request a new update at any time. Move the mouse pointer to the upper-left corner of the item and click the down-arrow button on the resulting bar; then select **Properties**. Click the **Schedule** tab, select **Using the following schedule(s)**, and click the **Add** button to add a new schedule.

Updating Now

To update the site at any time, click the down-arrow button at the upper-left corner of the item and choose **Synchronize**.

Removing an Active Site

To remove an active item from the desktop, click the item's **Close** button (the × in the upper-right corner). You can always restore the item using the **Display Properties** dialog box, as described in Step 2.

How to Change the Mouse Settings

Windows Me allows you to change several mouse characteristics, including the clicking rate required for a successful double-click; the speed at which the pointer moves across the screen in relation to the movement of the mouse itself; and the roles of the left and right mouse buttons. By default, the left button is for standard click-and-select operations, and the right button is for displaying shortcut menus (also known as *context menus*), but you can reverse these roles whenever you want. If you are left-handed, this can be one of the most important changes you make.

Begin

1 Open the Control Panel

Click the **Start** button, choose **Settings**, and then click **Control Panel** to open the **Control Panel** folder. The Windows Me **Control Panel** can display *all* available options or a short list of the half-dozen most commonly used options. If the short list is initially displayed in your own folder, click **view all Control Panel options** at the left side of the folder.

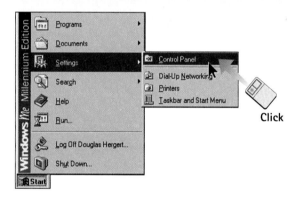

Click

2 Click the Mouse Icon

Click the **Mouse** icon in the **Control Panel**. The shape of this icon and the content of the resulting **Properties** box might vary, depending on the type of pointing device you have on your system.

Click

3 Change the Button Assignments

If you want to reverse the roles of the mouse buttons, select the **Left-handed** or **Right-handed** option in the **Buttons** tab. To activate this setting immediately, click the **Apply** button.

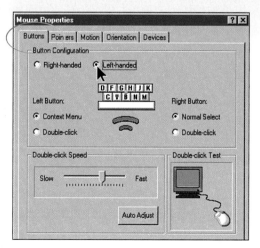

4 Change the Double-Click Speed

To increase or decrease the double-click speed, drag the slider toward **Slow** or **Fast** in the **Double-click Speed** box. To test the effect of this change, try double-clicking inside the **Double-click Test** box. An animated graphic indicates a successful double-click.

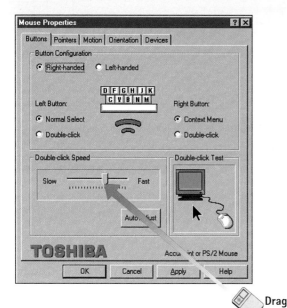

Drag

5 Adjust the Pointer Speed

Click the **Motion** tab, and drag the **Speed** slider toward **Slow** or **Fast** to decrease or increase the pointer speed. Click the **Apply** button, and then test the effect by moving the mouse pointer around the desktop. Optionally, experiment with other property settings available for the mouse, and then click **OK** to confirm the changes you've made.

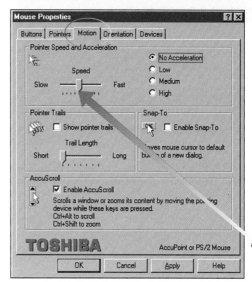

Drag

End

How-To Hints

Viewing Pointer Trails

The **Motion** tab also offers a setting known as "pointer trails." Activate this option by clicking the **Show pointer trails** check box and then clicking **Apply**. Subsequent mouse movement produces a trail of pointers. On some monitors, this effect can help you keep track of the mouse's position on the desktop.

Using the Default Button Actions

Throughout this book, the left mouse button is assumed to be the button you use to perform click-and-select operations; the right button is assumed to be the button you use to view shortcut menus. If you reverse these roles, you'll have to adjust the instructions given in this book accordingly.

How to Change the Date and Time

Your computer's internal clock and calendar provide the time and date for many important operations. Individual applications use these settings for their own purposes. In addition, every file you save to a disk is automatically stamped with the current date and time. You might occasionally have to adjust the time and date to keep them accurate. The **Date/Time Properties** window allows you to change these settings quickly and efficiently.

Begin

1 Double-Click the Time Display

Position the mouse pointer over the time display at the far right side of the taskbar, and double-click the left mouse button. In response, the **Date/Time Properties** window appears on the desktop.

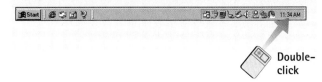

Double-click

2 Adjust the Date

Check the current date setting to see whether it is correct. If necessary, select a new month setting, adjust the year, or click the correct date in the calendar display.

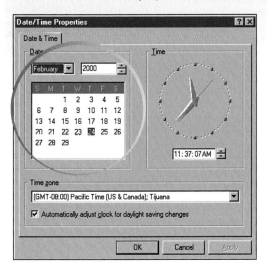

3 Adjust the Time

Check the current time to see whether it is accurate. If necessary, double-click any portion of the digital time display (hours, minutes, seconds) and enter a new value from the keyboard to change the time setting.

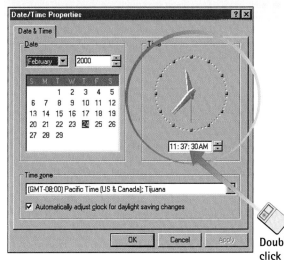

Double-click

4 Change the Time Zone

To change the time zone, click the down-arrow at the right end of the **Time zone** box and select a new setting. Optionally, you can also instruct Windows to adjust the clock automatically for Daylight Savings Time.

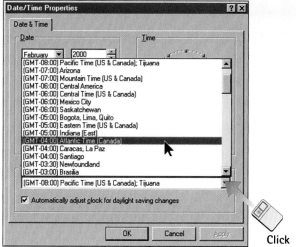

Click

End

How-To Hints

Viewing the Date/Time Properties

Another way to open the **Date/Time Properties** box is to click the **Date/Time** icon in the **Control Panel**. Open this folder by clicking the **Start** button, and then choosing **Settings** and **Control Panel**.

Changing Regional Settings

The date and time formats used on your computer are determined by options you can select in the **Regional Settings Properties** window. Click the **Regional Settings** icon in the **Control Panel** to open this window.

Viewing the Current Date

To view the current date at any time, hold the mouse pointer over the time display at the right side of the taskbar. A box pops up to show the date.

How to Change the Taskbar

The taskbar and the **Start** button are at the heart of operations in Windows Me. Together, these tools provide access to documents, Web sites, programs on disk, and applications currently running on the desktop. Because the taskbar is so important, Windows allows you to customize its use and appearance in ways that suit your own work habits. For example, you can add toolbars to the taskbar, as you learned back in Part 2. In addition, you can add new entries to the **Start** menu for your own most frequently used applications. You can also control where and when the taskbar appears on the desktop.

Begin

1 Open the Taskbar Properties Window

Click the **Start** button, choose **Settings**, and then choose **Taskbar and Start Menu**. The corresponding properties box appears on the desktop.

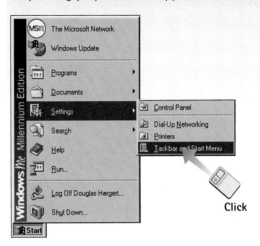

Click

2 Add an Item to the Start Menu

Click the **Advanced** tab. Then click the **Add** button in the **Start menu** section. The **Create Shortcut** window appears.

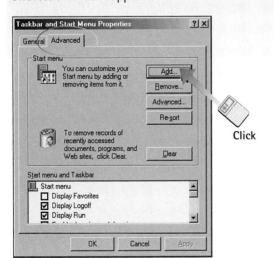

Click

3 Identify the Program

In the **Command line** box, type the path to the program you want to add to the **Start** menu. (Alternatively, click the **Browse** button to search for the program on disk.) Click **Next** to continue.

Click

4 Select a Menu Location

In the **Select Program Folder** window, highlight the name of the folder in which you want to display the new menu entry. For example, click **Accessories** if you want your program entry to be included in the **Accessories** list. Then click **Next**.

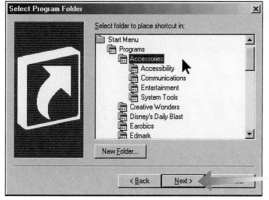

Click

5 Enter a Display Name

In the **Select a Title for the Program** window, type the program name just as you want it to appear in the menu. Click **Finish**, and then click **OK** in the properties box. You can now run the target program by selecting it directly from the **Start** menu.

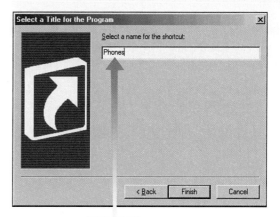

6 Move the Taskbar

Optionally, you can move the taskbar to a different location on the desktop. Use your mouse to drag it to the top, left, or right edge of the desktop.

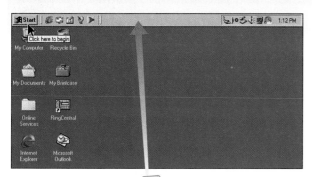

 Drag

End

How-To Hints

Opening Taskbar Properties

Another way to open the taskbar properties box is to right-click the taskbar itself and choose **Properties** from the shortcut menu.

Removing Menu Entries

To remove an entry from the **Start** menu, click the **Remove** button in the **Advanced** tab of the **Taskbar and Start Menu Properties** box (see Step 2), and select the item you want to remove.

Hiding the Taskbar

You can increase the amount of space available on the desktop by hiding the taskbar temporarily from view. To do so, click the **General** tab of the **Taskbar and Start Menu Properties** box, select the **Auto Hide** option, and click **Apply**. The taskbar disappears. To view it again, move the mouse pointer to the bottom of the desktop.

How to Change the Display for Accessibility

If you have trouble reading text on the screen or seeing activities on the desktop, the accessibility options offer several solutions. You can choose a high-contrast display (black-on-white or white-on-black), or a screen design from the list of preset color schemes. Several of these schemes use large text fonts for the elements of the desktop, including the **Start** menu, title bars, captions, and so on.

Begin

1 Open Accessibility Properties

To open the **Accessibility Properties** window, click the **Start** button, choose **Settings**, and then click **Control Panel**. Then click the **Accessibility Options** icon.

Click

2 Activate the High Contrast Option

Select the **Display** tab and then check the **Use High Contrast** option to select a new appearance for the display screen. Click the **Settings** button to set the details.

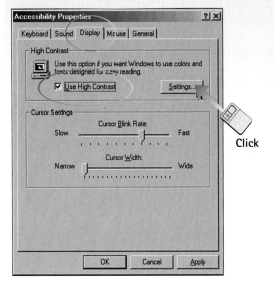

Click

3 Adjust the Settings

The **High Contrast color scheme** section shows three options for improving the visibility of the display. If you choose the third option, **Custom**, you can also select a specific color and font scheme. Click **OK** to confirm the new settings.

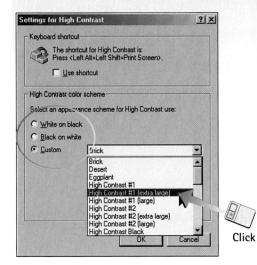

Click

4 Examine the General Options

Click the **General** tab to view some important options that apply to all the changes you make in the **Accessibility Properties** window.

5 Choose Automatic Reset

The **Automatic reset** options arrange to restore your original settings after a period of inactivity on your computer. Check the **Turn off accessibility** option and then specify the number of minutes Windows should wait before a reset.

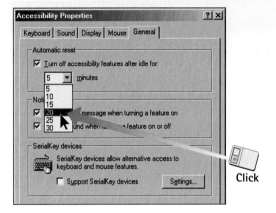

Click

6 Choose Notification Options

Check any combination of **Notification** options to activate visual and audible signals when changes occur in the Accessibility options. These signals are designed to help you keep track of options that are active or inactive as you work on the desktop. Click **OK** to confirm the changes you've made in the **Accessibility Properties** window and to close the window.

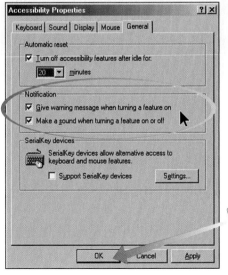

Click

How-To Hints

Using the Accessibility Wizard

Windows Me provides a convenient tool that will help you set a variety of accessibility options in a single process. To start the **Accessibility Wizard**, click the **Start** button and choose **Programs, Accessories, Accessibility,** and **Accessibility Wizard.** The wizard takes you step by step through the available options and gives you the opportunity to customize settings according to your own requirements.

Using the Magnifier

Another important tool available in Windows Me is the **Magnifier.** It is designed to provide visual magnifications (up to 9 times larger) of portions of the desktop. Using this tool takes some practice, but it can significantly improve the visibility of desktop details. To experiment with this tool, click **Start, Programs, Accessories, Accessibility,** and **Magnifier.**

End

How to Change the Keyboard for Accessibility

Many Windows applications have keyboard short-cuts that require you to press two keys at once, often with one hand. Some people find these key combinations difficult to carry out. The **StickyKeys** option changes these shortcuts to sequential keystrokes rather than simultaneous ones. Along with **StickyKeys**, the **Accessibility Properties** window offers two other keyboard options: **FilterKeys** and **ToggleKeys**.

Begin

1 Open Accessibility Properties

Open the **Accessibility Properties** window by clicking its icon in the **Control Panel** folder.

 Click

2 Activate StickyKeys

On the **Keyboard** tab, check the **Use StickyKeys** option to activate sequential-keystroke shortcuts with the **Ctrl**, **Shift**, and **Alt** keys. Then click the **Settings** button.

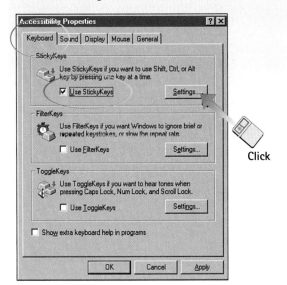

Click

3 Select StickyKey Settings

The **Options** section allows you to *lock* a modifier key (**Ctrl**, **Shift**, or **Alt**) by pressing it twice, and to disable **StickyKeys** by pressing any two keys at once. The **Notification** section provides options for sound signals to go along with modifier keys as well as a **StickyKey** icon on the taskbar. Activate any combination of these options and click **OK**.

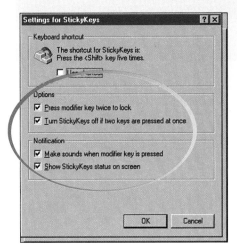

4 Activate FilterKeys

If you frequently press keys by accident, check the **Use FilterKeys** box. The **FilterKeys** option instructs Windows to ignore certain types of extraneous keystrokes. Click the corresponding **Settings** button to define this option further.

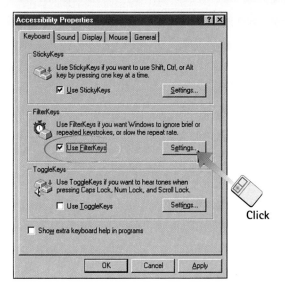

Click

5 Select FilterKey Options

Choose **Ignore repeated keystrokes** or **Ignore quick keystrokes**, depending on the kind of keystroke that typically gives you problems. In either case, click the **Settings** button to specify a range of keystroke speeds that Windows should ignore.

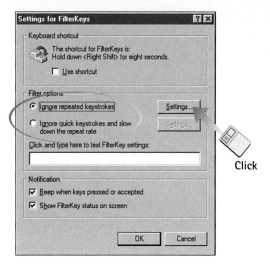

Click

6 Adjust the Speed Setting

Adjust the speed setting and click **OK** to confirm your selections for **FilterKeys**. Finally, click **OK** in the **Accessibility Properties** window to activate the keyboard features you've selected.

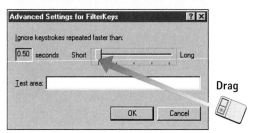

Drag

End

How-To Hints

Activating MouseKeys

For those who find the mouse impractical to use as a pointing device, the **MouseKeys** feature provides keyboard techniques that substitute for mouse actions. To activate this feature, click the **Mouse** tab in the **Accessibility Properties** window and check the **Use MouseKeys** option. Then click **Settings** to select additional options.

Using the On-Screen Keyboard

The **On-Screen Keyboard** is a new Windows Me tool that provides text input capability for users who find the keyboard impractical. The On-Screen Keyboard works in conjunction with a word processor or any other application designed for text input. Start this program by clicking **Start**, **Programs**, **Accessories**, **Accessibility**, and **On-Screen Keyboard**.

Task

Getting Connected for the First Time

*T*hese days, people everywhere are going online. From elementary school kids doing research for a science project, to teenagers chatting about their favorite new horror movies, to business people looking for good deals on computer equipment, to grandmothers keeping in touch with their far-flung families—everyone finds what they want on the World Wide Web.

If you're not online yet but want to be, you'll be glad to know that getting connected is easier than it's ever been before. You basically need three things:

- ✓ A *modem*, the hardware device that allows you to connect your computer directly to a phone line.

- ✓ A *browser*, the software that helps you organize your work online and find whatever information you need. Windows Me comes with Microsoft's browser, **Internet Explorer**.

- ✓ A personal account with an *Internet Service Provider* (also known as an ISP). You typically pay a monthly fee for this account. Using your account, you can access the Internet, send and receive email, and take advantage of any other features that your particular ISP makes available.

There are many ISPs to choose from. A few of them have names that are practically household words: America Online (AOL), Prodigy, and Microsoft Network (MSN). Although some major ISPs are more popular than others, they all offer essentially the same services.

In the tasks ahead, you'll use a Windows tool called the **Internet Connection Wizard** to explore your ISP options and—if you want—to open an account and go online for the first time. ●

How to Choose an Internet Service Provider

In today's Web-connected world, information about Internet Service Providers is everywhere. If you want an easy way to compare a variety of ISPs available to you, the **Internet Connection Wizard** is one good place to start. When you run this wizard, Windows dials out for a database of current information about available ISPs. In the subsequent list, you can read about these services and perhaps make a rational choice among them. After you've decided on an ISP, the wizard helps you get set up and connected.

Begin

1 Start the Internet Connection Wizard

Click the **Start** button, and then choose **Programs**, **Accessories**, **Communications**, and finally **Internet Connection Wizard**. (Alternatively, click the icon for this wizard if it appears on your desktop.) A Welcome window appears first on the desktop.

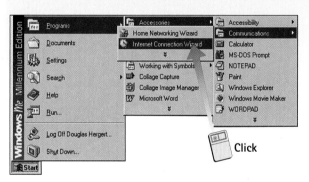

Click

2 Run the Tutorial

In the Welcome window, make sure that the first option, **I want to sign up for a new Internet account**, is selected. If you want some general information about the Internet and ISPs, click the **Tutorial** button. The wizard tutorial opens.

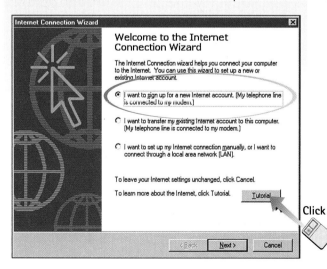

Click

3 Read Topics from the Tutorial

In the Tutorial window, select any topic you want to learn about and read the information presented. The tutorial is short, but contains some good introductory topics. Click the **Close** button when you're ready to return to the wizard.

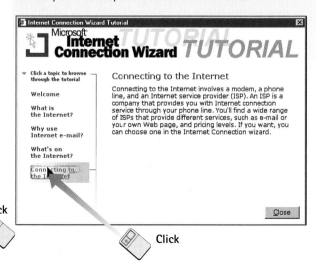

Click

4 Dial Up for ISP Information

Back in the Welcome window, make sure that your modem is connected to the phone line and click the **Next** button. Wait a few moments while the wizard dials out for current information about ISPs.

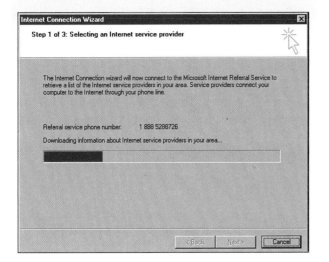

5 Read About the Available ISPs

The wizard presents you with a list of ISPs to choose from. You can read about each service in the list by clicking its name in the list on the left, and then scrolling through the **Provider information** box on the right.

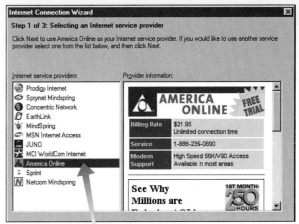

Click

6 Make a Selection

If you're ready to select an ISP, highlight its name and click **Next**. The next step depends on the ISP. In some cases, the wizard simply confirms your choice; when you click **Finish** (as shown here), the wizard places a new icon on your desktop. Click this icon to set up your account. For other services, the wizard guides you through entering the information required to establish your account.

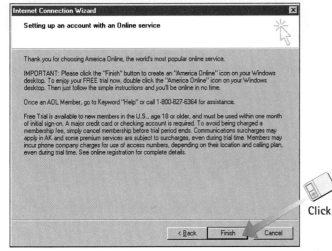

Click

How-To Hints

Using the Online Services Folder

If you see an **Online Services** folder on your desktop, try opening it to view icons for a selection of popular Internet service providers. Click any one of the icons to learn about a particular ISP—and to set up an account if you decide to do so.

Setting Up an Existing Account

You can also use the **Internet Connection Wizard** to set up an existing ISP account on a new computer. To do so, you'll need a few items of information from the account: your username, your access password, and the local phone number through which you dial up to the service. When you start the wizard, select the second option on the Welcome window (shown in Step 2), I want to transfer my existing Internet account to this computer.

End

How to Set Up an Internet Connection

When you've chosen an Internet Service Provider, there might be several ways to get started. In some cases, you can continue through the screens of the **Internet Connection Wizard** to set up your account. You'll have to supply certain predictable items of information: your name, address, and phone number; your billing preferences; and your credit card number. You'll also devise a *username* (by which you'll be identified in all online activity and in email messages) and a password to protect the privacy of your account. In this task and the next, you'll see generally how these steps can take place in the **Internet Connection Wizard**.

Begin

1 Enter Your Name and Address

For some ISP choices, the **Internet Connection Wizard** continues to guide you through the sign-up process. In the various fields of this first sign-up screen, type your name, address, and phone number. Click **Next** when you've entered and checked all the data.

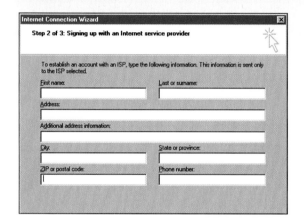

2 Select a Billing Plan

Most services have two or more billing plans to choose from. For example, you might be able to save some money if you're willing to prepay for a period into the future. (You can usually change this option after you've used the service for a while.) Make a selection and click **Next**.

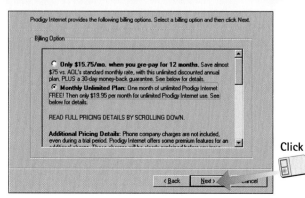

Click

3 Provide Your Credit Card Information

Enter all the information requested about your credit card, including the number, the expiration date, the name on the account, and the billing address. All this information will be sent to the ISP on a secure link. Click **Next** to continue.

4 Wait for a Connection

Wait while the wizard dials out to your selected ISP. Initially, you'll connect on an 800 number, but later you can select an appropriate local number for your account.

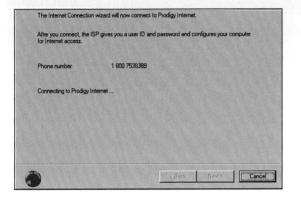

5 Enter a Username and Password

Enter the name you want to use online. Many people simply use their first initials and last name; others prefer made-up names, often whimsical. You must also devise a password and type it twice to confirm it. This password, along with your username, will identify you each time you sign on to the service. Click **Next** when you've completed this step.

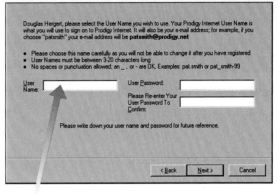

6 Select a Local Phone Number

To avoid long-distance charges when you sign on, select a phone number within your area code and exchange. Click **Next** when you've made your choice.

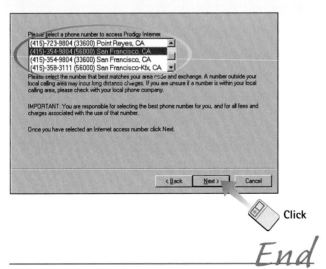

Click

End

How-To Hints

Choosing a Phone Number

If your service does not offer an access phone number that matches your area code and exchange, you might incur phone charges for your online time. These charges are *not* included in the monthly ISP fee; rather, they will add to your own cost of using the Internet. In some cases, a service might offer different phone numbers for different modem speeds.

Devising a Password

Create a password that is easy for you to remember but difficult for others to guess. If other people use your computer, they will be able to use your Internet account only if they know your password.

How to Connect to the Internet

After you've provided the **Internet Connection Wizard** with all the necessary account information, you're ready to sign on for the first time. The wizard continues guiding you through the process. You'll probably have to read and accept a membership agreement. (You might want to save or print this agreement for future reference.) After you confirm certain items of information that you've provided, you're ready to sign on. Once you're online, you can begin exploring the features of the service you've selected.

Begin

1 Accept the Member Agreement

The **Internet Connection Wizard** continues to guide you through the sign-up procedure. In the screen shown here, scroll through the text of the Member Agreement, and read its terms. Then choose the **I accept** option. Optionally, click **Save Copy** to keep a copy of the agreement on your hard disk. Then click **Next** to continue.

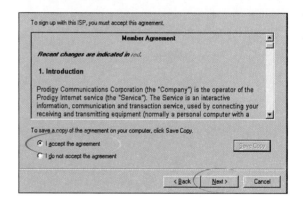

2 Confirm User Information

Carefully examine the user ID and password you've devised and the access phone number you've selected. If you want to change any of these, click the **Back** button to return to the appropriate windows. If not, click **Next** to confirm these fields.

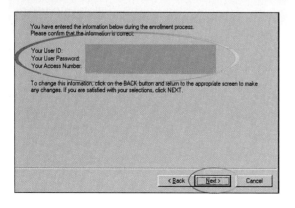

3 Wait for Configuration

The **Internet Connection Wizard** now configures your computer for signing on to your new ISP account. When everything is ready, you'll be notified. You might want to write down any initial instructions you receive at this point, including a service phone number or an online support site. Then click **Next**.

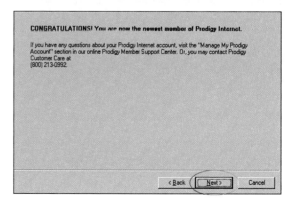

4 Complete the Wizard

You've now reached the final step of the wizard. Check the **To connect to the Internet** option if you want to sign on to your service right away. Then click **Finish**.

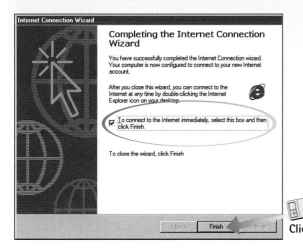

Click

5 Use Dial-Up Connection

The **Dial-up Connection** dialog box appears on the desktop. It shows the name of your service, your username, and your password (disguised as a string of asterisks). Check the **Save password** option if you want your password to be entered automatically each time you sign on. Then click the **Connect** button to go online.

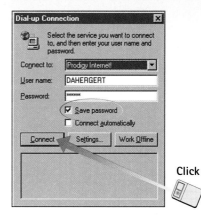

Click

6 Begin Exploring the Internet

When you first sign on to the Web, you're likely to find yourself on the *home page* of the service you've enrolled in. But the **Internet Explorer** browser software makes it easy to go anywhere you want on the Web. Begin by clicking links provided within the home page. Then turn to Part 6 to learn more about **Internet Explorer**.

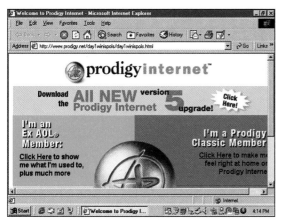

End

How-To Hints

Connecting Automatically

The **Dial-up Connection** box also has a **Connect automatically** option. If you check this option, the sign-on process becomes a one-click operation: You simply select the name of your service from the **Start** menu or click its icon on the desktop. No further confirmation is needed. Keep in mind, though, that your computer might sometimes attempt to sign on automatically when you are not present—for example, to update the content of a Web site. If you want to prevent this, leave the **Connect automatically** option unchecked.

Signing Off

To end an online session, pull down the browser's **File** menu and choose **Close**, or simply click the × button at the upper-right corner of the browser window. After the browser window is closed, you will be disconnected from the Web.

How to Connect to the Internet Through a Proxy Server

If you work in an office where everyone's computer is connected to a *local area network* (a LAN), you can ultimately go online and receive email through the intermediate services of the LAN. In other words, rather than setting up your own individual account with an Internet Service Provider, you connect to the LAN, which in turn provides access to the Web. The LAN is sometimes known as a *proxy server*. Your network administrator will give you specific instructions for connecting to the LAN and going online, or your office computer might already be configured appropriately when you first sit down at your desk. But if necessary, you can use the **Internet Connection Wizard** to help make the connection.

Begin

1 Start the Internet Connection Wizard

Click **Start**, and then choose **Programs, Accessories, Communications,** and **Internet Connection Wizard.** The Welcome window of the Internet Connection Wizard appears on the desktop.

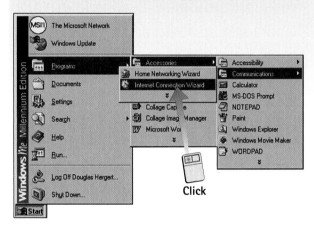

Click

2 Prepare to Connect Through a LAN

Select the third option, **I want to set up my Internet connection manually, or I want to connect through a local area network (LAN).** Then click **Next.**

Click

3 Select the LAN option

From the options presented on the next screen, select the second option, **I connect through a local area network (LAN)**. Then click **Next**.

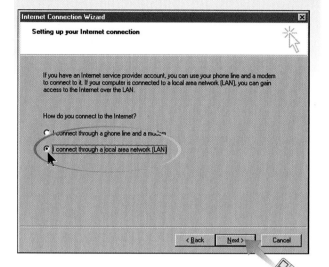

Click

4 Opt for Automatic Configuration

Unless your network administrator gives you other instructions, check the option labeled **Automatic discovery of proxy server (recommended)**. Then click **Next**.

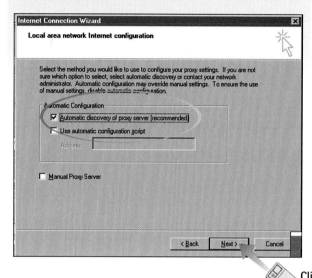

Click

End

How-To Hints

Making the Connection

After the wizard finds your LAN connection, it will guide you through the remaining steps to configure your computer. Before completing this process, make sure that you have received any necessary instructions from your LAN administrator.

Task

Using Internet Explorer

*I*nformation is the essence of the World Wide Web. Travel, weather, fine arts, government, books, commerce, food, technology, space, world news, geography, politics, social currents, scandal, humor, personal relationships, life styles, medicine, and every imaginable form of academic pursuit—all this and much, much more is covered on the Web. To make sense of this super-abundance of data, you need a *browser*, an application designed to help you find, view, and use the information you need.

Microsoft's Internet Explorer is one such browser. Its latest version, numbered 5.5, is part of the Windows Me package. It provides Web access and also helps define a variety of characteristic features on the Windows desktop. Thanks to Internet Explorer, you can easily coordinate online activity with the rest of your computer work.

When you use Internet Explorer to sign on to the Web, you'll find a number of ways to go to specific sites that interest you. A site might be organized into many different pages, the first of which is known as the *home page*. Many sites provide links to other related sites. Internet Explorer recognizes these links and efficiently moves you from one site to the next when you want to do so.

Web addresses are advertised almost everywhere these days. But even if you don't know a site's address, there are plenty of ways to find the information you're looking for on the Web. In the tasks in this part and the three parts to follow, you'll learn how to take advantage of the World Wide Web—and how to use Internet Explorer to ensure safe and efficient visits. ●

How to Sign On to Internet Explorer

Before connecting to the Web, you need to sign up for an account with an Internet Service Provider (ISP), as explained in Part 5. One such service is the Microsoft Network, shown here. Depending on the ISP you've chosen, the connect process may be slightly different in some details, but the basics are the same: To sign on to the Internet, you supply your username and password, and you click **Connect**. Once online, you're ready to explore the World Wide Web and to use the basic features of Internet Explorer—the toolbar, the address bar, and the menu commands.

Begin

1 Start Internet Explorer

To get started, click the **Internet Explorer** icon on the Windows Me desktop.

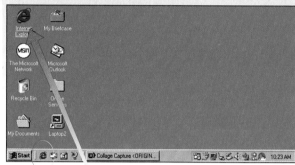

 Click

2 Sign On

Sign on by typing the name and password you established when you set up your account. Click **Connect**. When the sign-on process is complete, the **Internet Explorer** browser window displays the home page for your ISP (or whatever site you designate as your personal home page).

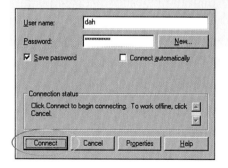

3 Examine the Browser Tools

At the top of the browser window you'll see a **menu bar**, a **toolbar**, and an **Address bar**, where you can enter the address of any Web site that you want to visit. (If these various tools do not appear initially, you can use commands in the **View** menu to display them. See the How-To Hints for details.)

Menu bar   Toolbar   Address bar

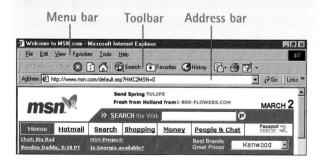

4 Click the Links Button

At the far right side of the **Address bar**, you'll see a button labeled **Links**. Click the button with the double-angle brackets >> to the right of the **Links** button to view a list of *quick links* to selected Web sites. Then click any entry in the list to jump directly to that site. (See the How-To Hints to learn about adding new entries to the **Links** list.)

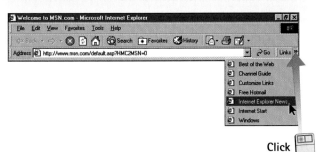

Click

5 Examine the Toolbar

The toolbar, located just above the **Address bar**, provides a collection of one-click buttons for some of the most important Internet Explorer operations. You'll learn to use several of these important tools in the tasks ahead.

End

How-To Hints

Checking Options in the Sign-On Window

Check the **Save password** option if you want the sign-on window in Step 2 to retain a record of your password. By doing so, you avoid having to re-enter your password each time you connect. (But note that anyone else sitting at your computer can also connect to your account without knowing your password.) Check **Connect automatically** if you want to further streamline the process; you can then connect with a single click on the desktop's **Internet Explorer** icon.

Changing the Browser View

Click the **View** menu and choose **Toolbars** to see a list of the toolbars you can display (or hide) at the top of the browser window. This menu also has a **Customize** command that you can use to modify the appearance of toolbars. If you want to hide toolbars temporarily and devote most of the screen to Web content, click the **Full Screen** command in the **View** menu, or press **F11** on the keyboard. Press **F11** again to toggle back to normal view.

Adding Links

You can add a new entry to the **Links** list by dragging any link directly from a Web page. To delete a link from the list, right-click the entry and choose **Delete** from the resulting shortcut menu.

How to Go to a Web Site

You can go to a Web site by typing its address in Internet Explorer's **Address bar**. (A site's address is also known as its *uniform resource locator*, or URL.) Another way to explore the Web is to use *links*. When you click a link, Internet Explorer takes you directly to the page that the link represents. The **Link** list is not the only place to find links; most Web pages contain links to related information located elsewhere online. On a Web page, a link typically appears as an underlined or uniquely colored reference to a specific topic.

Begin

1 Type the Address

If you know the address of the site you want to visit, type it in the **Address bar** and press **Enter**. Internet Explorer finds the site and goes directly to the page.

2 Click a Quick Link

To go to a page represented by a quick link, click the >> next to the **Links** button and choose any item in the list. (See the How-To Hints for more information about **Links**.)

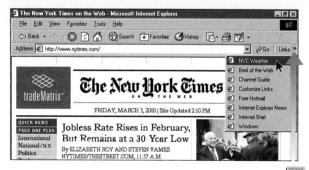

Click

3 Pull Down the Address List

To return to a site you've visited recently, pull down the **Address** list (click the arrow to the right of the **Address** box) and choose the page to which you want to return.

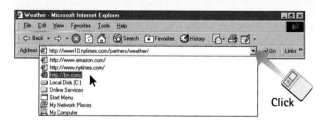

Click

4 Click Back or Forward

To go backward or forward among the pages you've visited during the current session, click the **Back** or **Forward** button on the toolbar. To return to your start page, click the **Home** button.

5 Jump to a Link

To jump from the current page to a related topic, move the mouse pointer over a link. The mouse icon turns into a pointing hand. Click to visit the site represented by the link.

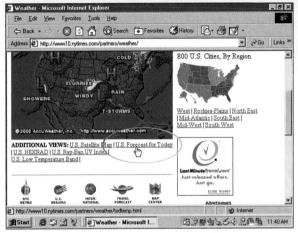

End

How-To Hints

Changing the View of the Address Bar

On the **Address bar**, you can change the relative width allocated to the address box and the links by dragging the vertical bar that separates these two elements. Alternatively, you can create a separate **Links** bar by dragging the **Links** button to a position below the **Address** bar.

Clicking Stop

If a site takes too long to appear on your screen—and you don't want to wait any longer—click the **Stop** button (the white × in the red circle) to cancel the link.

Clicking Back

When you click the **Back** button to return from a linked site to the page that contains the link, you might notice that the link reference has changed color. This indicates that you've already visited the linked site.

Using Back and Forward Lists

The **Back** and **Forward** buttons have attached lists of links that represent the sequence of sites you've visited. Pull a list down by clicking the corresponding down-arrow button, and choose any link in the list.

Adding a Quick Link

To add the current site to your personal list of quick links, drag the site's icon from the **Address** box to the **Links** button.

How to Search for a Site

You can often guess the address for a site just by combining the name of an organization with the appropriate "dot" suffix—**com** for commercial sites, **edu** for schools and universities, **gov** for government sites, and **org** for nonprofit organizations. But sometimes your search requirements might be more complex. Suppose that you want a list of sites that contain information about a particular topic—say, European cello makers, differential equations, the poetry of Afghanistan, or the twelfth-century sculptural ensembles at Chartres Cathedral. To find relevant sites, you can use powerful *search services* available on the Internet.

Begin

1 Start a Search

Click the **Search** button on the Internet Explorer toolbar. This click divides the browser window vertically into two parts: A **Search** bar appears on the left side of the screen, and the content area takes up a somewhat larger area on the right.

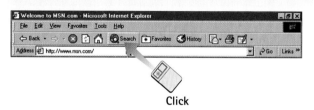

Click

2 Choose a Search Category

If necessary, click the **New** button at the top of the **Search** bar to clear away any previous search selections. You'll see a list of search categories; click the **Find a Web page** option if it is not already selected.

3 Start the Search

Type the text you want to search for and then click the **Search** button.

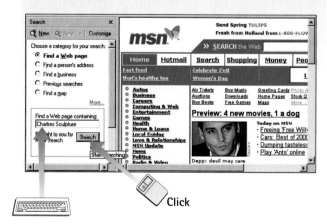

Click

4 Select a Site

The search results in a list of sites that contain the target words. Some of the sites might relate to your search, and others might not. Click the name of a site that you want to visit.

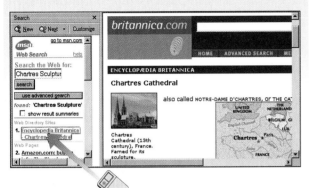

Click

5 Click a Link

The site might contain the information you're looking for, or it could contain one or more links that you'll want to investigate. Click any link to jump to another page or site.

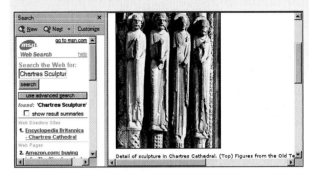

6 Customize the Search Settings

If you want to try a specific search service, click the **Customize** button at the top of the **Search** bar. In the **Customize Search Settings** window, select the **Use one search service for all searches** option and then select a name from the list of services. Click **OK**. Then try your search again.

Click

End

How-To Hints

Choosing a Search Service

Each search service has its own strengths and specialty areas. If you opt to work with a specific service (as in Step 6), you can go to the Web page for the service itself. There you'll be able to explore the various features available and also get help on conducting efficient and effective searches in the context of a particular service.

Searching Effectively

After you've performed a search, the Search bar displays a **Use advanced search** button (as shown in Step 4). Click this button if you want to refine the way the search is carried out. This option can be useful if the initial search results in too few—or too many—site links. For example, you can search for an exact phrase or use one or more words in your search text. You can also limit the search to sites modified within a range of dates that you specify.

How to Customize Internet Explorer

As you become familiar with the features of the Internet Explorer browser software, you might want to try customizing some of its operations. You can do so by opening the **Internet Options** dialog box. Using the tabbed pages in this dialog box, you can control many aspects of the browser's appearance and behavior. You'll examine a few of these settings in the upcoming steps, and others in Part 9, "Keeping Safe on the Internet."

Begin

1 Choose a New Start Page

Before you open the **Options** dialog box, consider whether you want to select a new home page or start page, the site that appears at the beginning of each new online session. If so, type the site's address in the **Address** bar and press **Enter**.

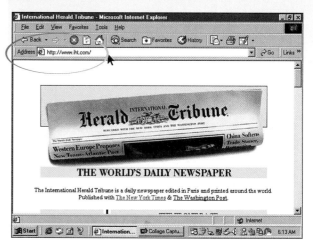

2 Open the Internet Options

When the site appears, pull down the **Tools** menu and choose **Internet Options**. A tabbed dialog box appears on the desktop.

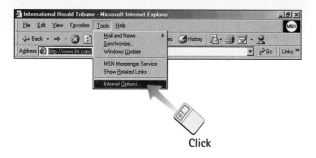

Click

3 Confirm the New Home Page

In the top portion of the **General** tab, you'll see the options that allow you to change your home page. Click **Use Current** if you want the current site to become your home page. Alternatively, type the address of any other site in the **Address** box.

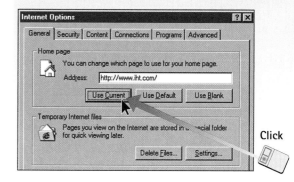

Click

4 Change the Browser's Colors

Click the **Colors** button, near the bottom of the **General** tab, to change the text and background colors that appear in the browser window. The resulting **Colors** box offers several options for specifying the colors of text, backgrounds, and link references.

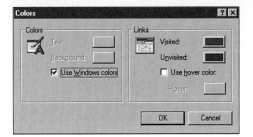

5 Select a New Color

Click any of the color buttons in the **Colors** dialog box to open a **Color** box that contains a selection of available shades; then click the color you want to associate with the selected feature. Click **OK** in both the **Color** and **Colors** boxes to confirm your selections.

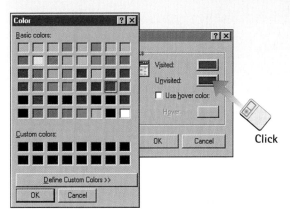

Click

6 Delete Temporary Files

Back on the **General** tab of the **Internet Options** box, you can click the **Delete Files** button to remove any temporary Internet content from your hard disk. Click **Clear History** to delete the list of sites you've visited in the current and previous online sessions. Then click **Apply** and **OK** to confirm any new settings you've selected.

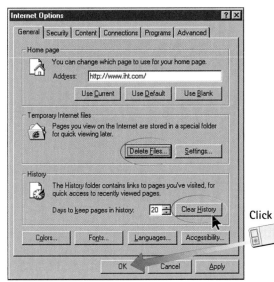

Click

How-To Hints

Setting Options Offline

If you prefer to set options when you are not online, you can do so from the Windows Me desktop. Right-click the **Internet Explorer** icon and choose **Properties** to display the **Internet Options** dialog box.

Select Advanced Options

The **Advanced** tab of the **Internet Options** box contains a list of check boxes and option buttons you can use to activate specific browser features. Although some of these options are for experienced users, others are simple and intuitive. Examine the list periodically to find options that will help you customize the behavior of Internet Explorer.

End

Task

Sending and Receiving Email

*P*eople everywhere are discovering the allure of email. For keeping in touch with colleagues, clients, friends, and relatives, email has become the medium of choice among people who spend time in front of a computer. Whatever message you need to send, email is often the simplest, quickest, and most convenient way to express your thoughts.

Outlook Express is the email application that comes with Internet Explorer. For the basic operations—sending and receiving messages and keeping track of previous communications—Outlook Express is intuitively organized. Messages are stored in folders, giving you convenient ways to read new correspondence and to review messages from the past.

After you've mastered the basics, you'll find many features that can improve your email experience. You can run a spell check on your message before you send it. You can use stationery formats to make your messages more lively and attractive. You can add a *signature*—an identifying block of text—to the end of every message you send. If you learn to attach files to messages, you can send entire documents over the Internet whenever necessary. Outlook Express also offers access to *newsgroups*, Internet locations where participants can exchange ideas with one another. When you find a newsgroup that interests you, Outlook Express shows you the list of messages that people have already written. You can browse through the messages, respond to any that you find engaging, and initiate new exchanges of your own. ●

How to Use Outlook Express

Whenever you want to check your email, you can start Outlook Express either from the **Internet Explorer** window or directly from the desktop. After connecting to your Internet account, Outlook Express tells you how many messages are waiting for you. The **Inbox** folder—with its list of new and old messages—is just a mouse click away. Below the message list, the preview pane displays the text of any message you select. To prepare an answer to any message, you simply click the **Reply** button.

Begin

1 Start Outlook Express

Click the **Outlook Express** icon on the desktop to start the application. If you are not already online, Outlook Express signs you on and connects to your email account.

Click

2 Click the Unread Mail Link

The front page of the **Outlook Express** window tells you how many email messages are waiting for you to read. To view the list of messages, you can click **Inbox** in the folder list at the left, or you can click the **unread Mail** link in the **Email** section of the window.

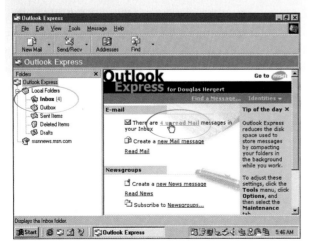

3 Select a Message

Newly arrived and unread messages appear in bold type and are preceded by a closed-envelope icon. Click to select the subject line of any message in the list. When you do so, the text of the message appears in the preview pane, just below the list of messages. Scroll through the text to read the entire message.

Attachment icon   Read message   Subject lines
Unread message   Preview pane

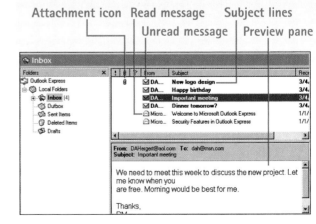

4 Reply to a Message

To reply to a selected message, click the **Reply** button on the toolbar, just above the folder list.

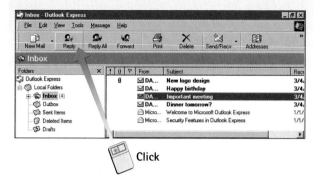

Click

5 Compose Your Reply

Outlook Express opens a reply window, with the name and address of your correspondent automatically recorded. Type the text of your reply. You can enter a new subject if you want, or you can keep the reference to the original subject.

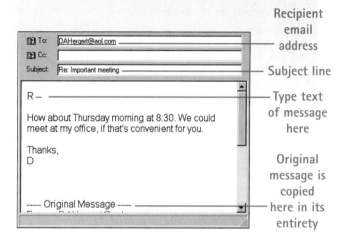

Recipient email address

Subject line

Type text of message here

Original message is copied here in its entirety

6 Send the Reply

Click the **Send** button at the upper-left corner of the reply window when you're ready to send your message.

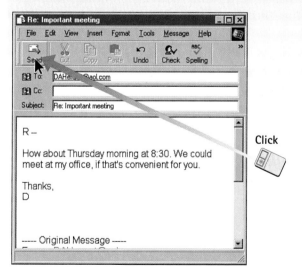

Click

End

How-To Hints

Email Tricks

To create a new message—not a response to an incoming message—click the **New Mail** button at the upper-left corner of the Outlook Express window.

To run a spell check before you send a message, press **F7** on the keyboard or click the **Spelling** button at the top of the message window.

To delete a message from the **Inbox** folder, select the subject line and click the **Delete** button on the toolbar. The message is moved to the **Deleted Items** folder and is deleted permanently when you exit Outlook Express.

Open any folder by clicking its name at the left side of the Outlook Express window. In particular, click **Sent Items** to review messages that you've sent in the past.

How to Set Options for Outlook Express

You can customize the operations of Outlook Express by choosing the **Options** command from the **Tools** menu. The available settings give you control over the way mail is sent and received on your account. In addition, you can use the **Signature** settings to place an identifying block of text at the end of each message you compose.

Begin

1 Open the Options Window

In Outlook Express, pull down the **Tools** menu and choose the **Options** command. The resulting **Options** box is organized into ten tabbed pages of options.

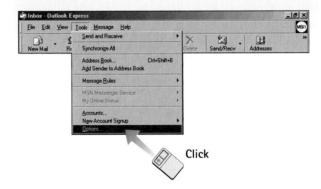

Click

2 Choose General Settings

Change any of the settings in the **General** tab. For example, choose a time interval for new message checks, turn the sound alert on or off for new messages, or opt to go directly to the **Inbox** folder when Outlook Express starts.

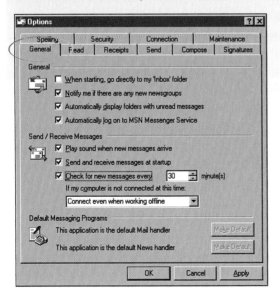

3 Choose Settings for Outgoing Mail

Click the **Send** tab for options related to outgoing mail. For example, you can save copies of your own outgoing messages in the **Sent Items** folder, include the original incoming message in your reply, and transmit replies as soon as you click **Send**.

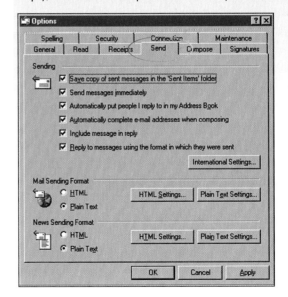

4 Choose Settings for Incoming Mail

Click the **Read** tab to set options for incoming mail. The first option determines how new messages are marked. By default, Outlook Express marks a new message as *read* several seconds after the text of the message appears in the preview pane. You can change this feature by entering a new time interval or by removing the check before the option.

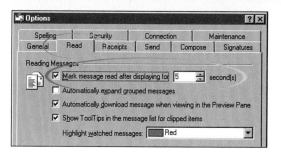

5 Add a Signature to Your Messages

Click the **Signatures** tab to create a "signature" text that will appear at the bottom of each message you write. If the **Signatures** box is empty, click the **New** button to create a first signature. Then check the **Add signatures** option at the top of the window.

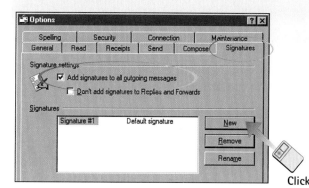

Click

6 Create the Signature Text

Enter the text of your signature in the **Text** box near the bottom of the window. Click **OK** to confirm this and any other settings you've changed in the **Options** box.

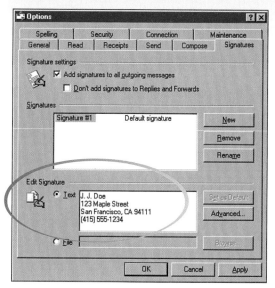

End

How-To Hints

Getting Help

For more information about any of the settings in the **Options** box, click the question mark button at the upper-right corner of the window and then click the option you want to read about. An appropriate tip box appears.

Checking for New Messages

If you disable the **Check for new messages** option in the **General** tab, you can still initiate a new message check at any time by clicking the **Send/Receive** button on the Outlook Express toolbar.

Using Stationery

For fancier outgoing email, you can place the text of your message in a predesigned stationery format. To choose from the available stationery options, click the down-arrow button to the right of the **New Mail** button and select one of the items in the resulting list. It's worth experimenting with these options to find just the right context for a given message.

How to Receive an Attached File

An incoming email message might include an *attachment*, which is a document file that the sender has included with the message. An attached file generally arrives in the format produced by the source application—for example, a word processed document, a graphic file, a photograph, or a spreadsheet. If you receive an attachment, you can easily open it, view its content, save it to disk, and modify it if appropriate.

Begin

1 Start Outlook Express

Start Outlook Express and click the **unread** Mail link to view your new messages.

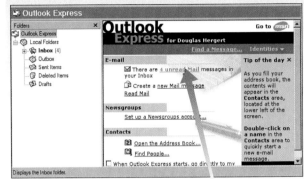

 Click

2 Find an Attachment

In the message list, a paper-clip icon indicates that a message contains an attachment. Click to select the subject line of the message to view its text in the preview pane. Notice that a paper clip button appears in the upper-right corner of the preview pane.

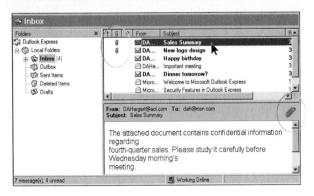

3 Select the Attached File

Click the paper-clip button. When you do so, a drop-down list shows the name of the attached file, or the list of files if more than one has been sent. Select an item in the list to open the file.

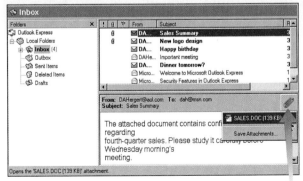

 Click

4 Open or Save the File

A dialog box offers you the option of opening the attachment immediately or saving it as a file on disk. If you choose the **Open it** option and click **OK**, Outlook Express opens the attachment in its own application window, assuming that a compatible program is available on your computer. (Carefully consider the virus warning that appears in this dialog box. In general, avoid opening an attached file unless you can be reasonably confident that the file is from a virus-free source.)

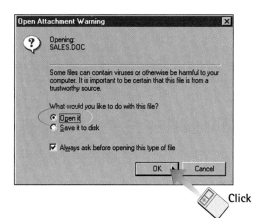

Click

5 Choose a Folder Location

If you choose the **Save it to disk** option, the **Save Attachment As** dialog box appears. Choose a folder location for the new file and click the **Save** button to complete this operation.

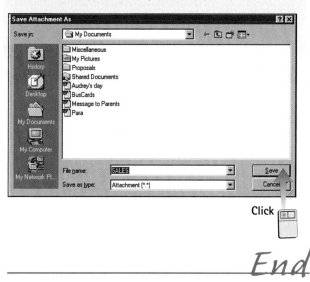

Click

End

How-To Hints

Receiving Multiple Attachments

It's possible to attach multiple files to a single email message. If two or more attachments arrive with an incoming message, all the files will be listed when you click the paper-clip button in the upper-right corner of the preview pane.

Working with Compressed Folders

For efficient handling, users sometimes use special "zip" software to *compress* large files—or collections of files—before sending them as attachments. If you receive a *zipped* file (often identified by a **ZIP** extension), Windows Me will save the file as a compressed folder. The folder icon will be distinguished by a vertical zipper down the middle. Conveniently, Windows can recognize and open a compressed folder—and the individual compressed files it contains—without the use of specialized *unzip* software. You'll learn more about this topic in Task 5, "How to Send a Compressed Folder."

How to Send an Attached File

To send a document by email, you can attach it to a new message and then simply send the message in the normal way. For example, you can send files that you've developed in your word processor, your spreadsheet application, or your paint program. You can even send sound files and digital photographs. To open your attachment, the recipient needs a compatible application that can recognize the format in which you send the file.

Begin

1 Create a File to Send

Start by developing the document you want to send and saving it to disk. In this example, the document is a bitmap file (BMP) created in the **Paint** program. For information about the Paint program, refer to Task 1 of Part 13, "Using the Built-In Windows Applications."

2 Start a New Message

Start Outlook Express and connect to the Internet. Click the **New Mail** button on the Outlook Express toolbar. A new message window opens on the desktop.

Click

3 Compose a Message

Type the address of the person to whom you want to send the message on the **To** line. (Alternatively, click the index card icon and choose the recipient from the built-in Address book. For clarity and convenience, the Address book might copy the recipient's actual name—and not the email address—to the **To** line; Outlook Express understands that the name stands for the recorded address.) Type a **Subject** line, and begin typing your message.

Click here to access the Address book

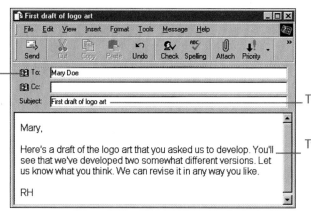

Type su
line h

Type me
text h

4 Attach the File

Click the **Attach** button on the toolbar. The **Insert Attachment** dialog box appears.

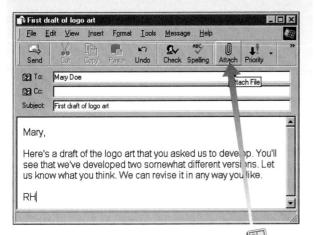

Click

5 Select the File

Navigate to the folder where you saved the target file in Step 1 and select the document you want to send as an attachment. Click the **Attach** button. To send more than one file with a single message, repeat Steps 4 and 5.

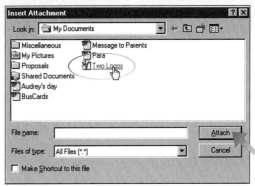

Click

6 Send the Message

Back in the new message window, notice that a new **Attach** line appears in the header section of the window. Verify that you have selected the correct file to send as an attachment, and click the **Send** button.

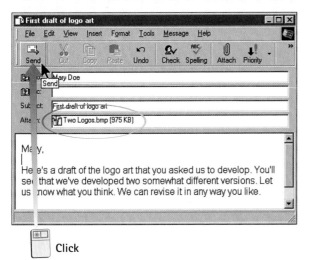

Click

End

How-To Hints

Starting a Message Directly from an Application

If you prefer, you might be able to open a new message directly from the application where you develop the attached document. From your word processor, spreadsheet, paint program, or other source application, pull down the **File** menu and look for the **Send** command. If the command is available, choose it. A new message window opens onto the desktop, with the current file already identified as an attachment. Write the message you want to send with the attachment and click the **Send** button to transmit the mail.

Using the Address Book

As you've seen, a useful Address book is included with Outlook Express. This feature can also be used as a standalone application. See Part 13 for an introduction to the Address Book program.

How to Send a Compressed Folder

Suppose that you want to send a group of files—including documents, graphics, and photographs—as an email attachment. But you can't conveniently send them individually in their original formats (there are too many or they're too big). Windows Me provides a solution: You can copy the files to a single *compressed folder*. In this folder, Windows reduces the total size of the files without compromising the content of your documents. In other contexts, a compressed folder is known as a *zip file*. Using one of several standard programs that are available to work with such files, the recipient of your compressed folder can *unzip* it and access the files you've sent.

Begin

1 Locate Files You Want to Send

In the **My Documents** window, open the folder containing the files you want to compress and combine into one zip file. In this example, the folder contains four files, originating from four different applications.

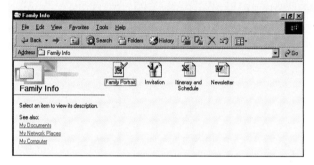

2 Create a New Compressed Folder

Right-click in an empty area of the folder window and choose **New** from the resulting shortcut menu. Then choose **Compressed Folder**. A new compressed folder icon appears in the window. A zipper graphic identifies this as a compressed folder, or a zip file.

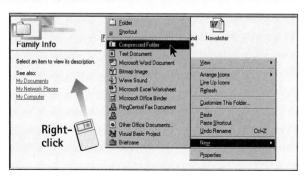

3 Rename the Folder

Initially the new folder's default name is highlighted, giving you the opportunity to enter a new name right away. Type a name that identifies the use you're planning for the folder and press **Enter** to confirm.

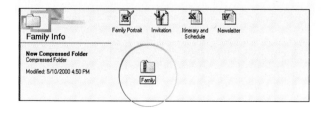

4 Drag Files to the Folder

Drag the target document files into the folder. You can drag files one at a time or as a group. (To select a group of files, hold down the **Shift** key as you point to each file in turn.) Windows copies each file to the folder and converts it to a compressed format.

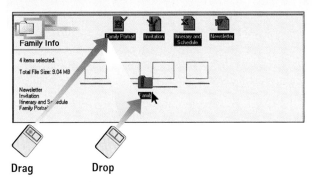

Drag   Drop

5 Confirm the Folder's Contents

Open the compressed folder by clicking its icon. Confirm that you've copied the correct files to the folder. Then close the folder and close the **My Documents** window.

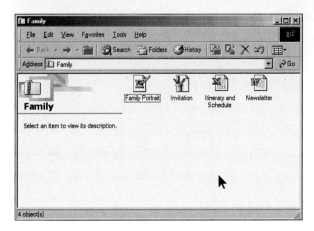

6 Send the Folder as a Zip File

Start Outlook Express and follow the steps outlined in Task 4 to send the compressed folder as an attached file. When you attach the compressed file to your message, you'll notice that Outlook Express correctly identifies it as a zip file (with a **ZIP** extension). Click **Send** to send your message and the zip file to the identified recipient.

How-To Hints

Opening a Compressed Folder

Compressed folders that you create in Windows Me are compatible with commonly available zip and unzip software. When you send a compressed folder attached to a message, the recipient can use standard software to unzip the file and access its contents, even in an operating environment other than Windows Me.

Restoring a File to Its Uncompressed Format

To restore a compressed file to its original uncompressed format, simply drag it out of the compressed folder into an ordinary folder. In response, Windows Me automatically converts the file; you can subsequently work with the document in its original application.

End

How to Use Newsgroups

A *newsgroup* is a set of online messages, listed together and ostensibly focused on a particular subject. Newsgroups are available for every imaginable topic, from actors to zookeepers, from parenting to paranormal phenomena. Messages can be written and posted by anyone who joins the group. Outlook Express links you to news servers so that you can join the newsgroups they provide. News servers are identified as folders at the left side of the **Outlook Express** window. Some newsgroups are monitored to maintain a particular focus and set of guidelines. Others are *un*monitored, which can result in unexpected content, both textual and photographic.

Begin

1 Select a News Server

Select a news server from the Outlook Express folder list at the left side of the application window. In this example, **netnews.msn.com** is the selection. (If no servers are listed, you'll have to set up an account. See the How-To Hints for details.) The first time you open a server, you'll have to download the list of newsgroups from its online source. Click **Yes** when you are so notified. A list of newsgroups appears in the resulting **Newsgroup Subscriptions** window.

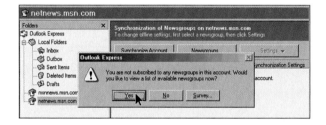

2 Type a Topic

In the text box above the newsgroup list, enter a word or two describing a subject you're interested in pursuing. Here, the entry **cooking** has resulted in a list of newsgroups devoted to food and recipes. Select a group you want to visit, and click **Go to**.

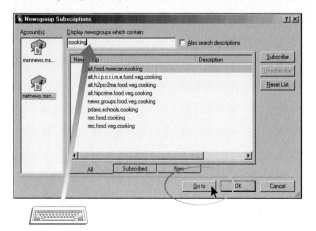

3 Read a Message

Scroll through the subjects that have been posted to the group and click the description of a message you'd like to read. The content of the message appears in the preview pane, just below the message list.

Newsgroup folder organization   Subject list

Preview pane

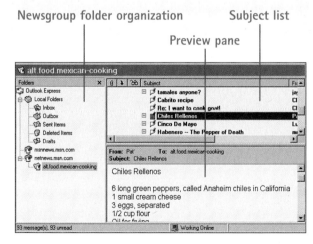

4 Reply to a Message

To reply to the selected message—that is, to post your own comments to the group—click the **Reply Group** button on the toolbar. Type your message in the resulting reply window.

Click

5 Post Your Response

To post your response to the group, click the **Send** button on the toolbar. Your response becomes part of the *thread* in this group topic.

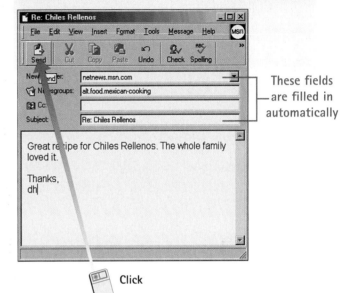

These fields are filled in automatically

Click

End

How-To Hints

Setting Up a Newsgroup Account

To set up a newsgroup account in Outlook Express, pull down the **Tools** menu and choose **Accounts**. Click the **Add** button and choose **News**. An **Internet Connection Wizard** guides you through the steps for setting up a new account. Supply your name and email address, along with the name of the news server you want to log on to. Check with your Internet service provider to find out what servers are available to you.

Replying to and Starting New Topics

To send a response directly to the author of a message, click **Reply** instead of **Reply Group** on the toolbar in Step 3. To start a new topic of your own, click **New Post**.

Supervising Access

The content of some newsgroups is clearly meant for adults. You'll want to supervise your children's access to newsgroups in general. To establish various levels of control over newsgroup content, pull down the **Tools** menu and choose **Message Rules** and **News**. In the resulting **New News Rule** window, you can arrange to exclude messages based on criteria that you specify. Be aware, though, that this solution might not protect you—or your children—from all content that you find unsuitable.

Task

Managing Your Work
on the Internet

*A*t the click of a button, you can divide the **Internet Explorer** window into two parts—displaying a specific list of links arranged vertically on the left and selected Web content on the right. The list on the left is sometimes known generically as the **Explorer** bar; it takes three forms: the **Search** bar, the **Favorites** bar, and the **History** bar. In all three cases, the selections you make among the links listed in the **Explorer** bar determine the Web content that you see on the right side of the browser window.

For example, you've already learned to use the **Search** bar to find specific topics on the Web. When you click a link in the **Search** bar, you jump immediately to the corresponding Web site. The site's content appears in the area at the right side of the browser window.

The **Search**, **Favorites**, and **History** buttons on the browser's toolbar each open a list of links at the left side of the browser window:

- ✓ The **Search** bar helps you find specific information on the Web. As you learned in Part 6, "Using Internet Explorer," the **Search** bar makes a variety of search services available to you. You use these services to make detailed searches for specific topics.

- ✓ The **Favorites** bar displays links to sites you've chosen as your own favorites. When you add a site to this list, you can also decide whether you want to make the site's content available when you're offline. If you choose the offline option, you can specify a schedule for *synchronizing* the site—that is, downloading the most recent content from the site so that you can later view the information offline.

- ✓ The **History** bar gives you a detailed look at the sites you've visited recently, organized chronologically, alphabetically, or by sites most often visited.

In the tasks ahead, you'll learn to use the **Favorites** and **History** bars and to synchronize your favorite pages for offline viewing. You'll also take a first look at a new **Internet Explorer** feature, the **Radio** bar, designed to give you access to local, national, or international radio station content, supplied directly from the Internet. ●

How to Set Up Your Favorite Sites

You can organize links to the sites you like best in the **Favorites** list. It's easy to add a site to this list. As you do so, you can also specify whether you want the site to be available for offline viewing, and you can arrange for scheduled downloads of the site's latest content. To jump to sites in your Favorites list, pull down the **Favorites** menu and choose a link; alternatively, click the **Favorites** button to display the list in the left pane of the browser window.

Begin

1 Find a Favorite Site

Log on to the Web and go to the site you want to add to your Favorites list.

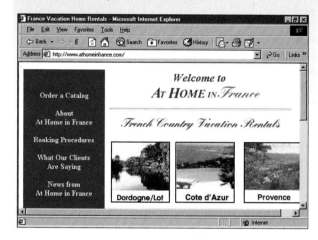

2 Add the Site to Your Favorites

Pull down the **Favorites** menu at the top of the browser window, and choose **Add to Favorites**. The **Add Favorite** dialog box appears on the desktop.

Click

3 Select the Offline Option

If you want this site to be available for offline viewing, click the **Make available offline** option. A check appears in the adjacent check box. Optionally, you can click the **Customize** button to select settings for this feature. (Refer to Task 2 for details.)

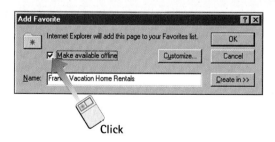

Click

4 Create a Folder in the Favorites List

If you want to store this link in a folder of its own in the Favorites list, click **Create in** and then **New Folder**. In the **Create New Folder** box, type a name for the new folder you're creating and click **OK**.

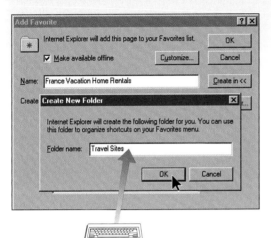

5 Confirm the New Favorites Item

The new folder appears in the Favorites list. Click **OK** to confirm that you want to store the new link in that folder.

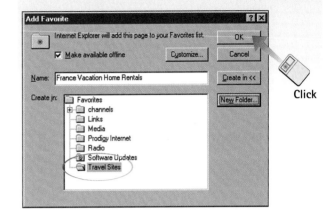

Click

6 Use the Favorites List

Whenever you want to jump to a site in your list, click the **Favorites** button on the toolbar. The **Favorites** bar opens on the left side of the browser window. Open the folder that contains the target link, and click the name of the site you want to visit. The site's content appears at the right side of the browser window.

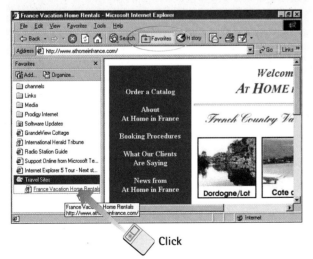

Click

How-To Hints

Deleting and Renaming Favorites

To delete or rename a link in the Favorites list, or to move a link to a new folder within the list, pull down the **Favorites** menu at the top of the browser window and choose **Organize Favorites**. The resulting dialog box shows all the folders and links in your list and provides command buttons for making changes in the list.

Creating a Favorite Shortcut on the Desktop

You can use either the **Favorites** menu or the **Favorites** bar to create a desktop shortcut for any link in your list. Right-click any item in the list; from the shortcut menu that appears, choose **Send to** and then **Desktop (create shortcut)**. A Web link icon appears on your desktop. To visit the site, simply click the icon.

End

How to Synchronize a Favorite Site

Following instructions that you provide, Internet Explorer can periodically download a favorite site's content to your hard disk. The download occurs on a schedule you specify or only when you request it. This process is known as *synchronizing* the site—that is, updating the site's current content from its online source. After this process, you can view the site's content at your convenience, online or offline. You can create a synchronize schedule whenever you add a site to your favorites list (click the **Customize** button on the **Add Favorites** dialog box shown in Step 3 of Task 1). Alternatively, you can select synchronize options for any item that's already in your favorites list, following these steps.

Begin

1 Choose a Favorite Site

Pull down the **Favorites** menu in the browser window and right-click the site whose options you want to change. From the resulting shortcut menu, choose **Make available offline**.

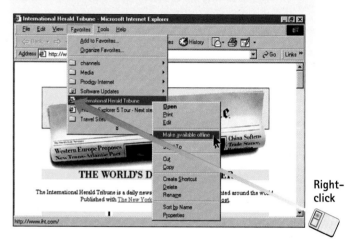

Right-click

2 Start the Offline Favorite Wizard

The first window of the **Offline Favorite Wizard** appears. Read the description it provides and click **Next** to proceed.

Click

3 Select a Download Option

The next window allows you to specify the extent of the download: the site's front page alone or the first page along with any linked pages the site might contain. Select **No** or **Yes**, depending on whether you want to download linked pages. Then click **Next**.

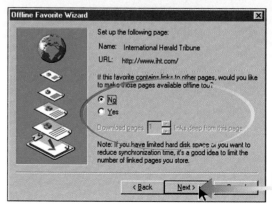

Click

4 Select a Synchronize Option

Choose from among three options for updating the site's content from the online source: synchronize on command, on a schedule you will create, or on an existing schedule you've already developed. (The third option does not appear if you've never set a schedule before.) To create a new schedule, click the second of these options and then click **Next** to set the schedule details.

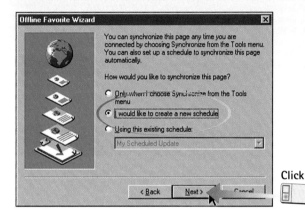

Click

5 Create a Schedule

Enter a numeric value in the **Every...days** box that specifies the frequency of the update; enter a convenient time during the day or night when you want the update to take place. If you want the update to be automatic, check the appropriate box. Then click **Next**. Finally, the wizard asks you to supply a password for the site if one is required. Click **Finish** to complete these steps.

Click

6 Review Your Synchronized Sites

Pull down the **Tools** menu and choose **Synchronize**. The **Items to Synchronize** box shows the name of each site, along with the date and time of the last update. To synchronize one or more of these sites on command, place a check next to each site you want to update and click the **Synchronize** button.

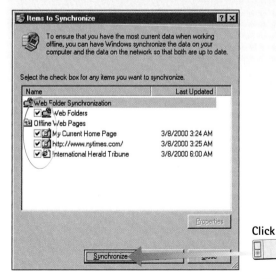

Click

How-To Hints

Updating Individual Sites

To update a scheduled site individually from the Favorites list without waiting for the scheduled update time, right-click the name of the site and choose **Synchronize** from the resulting shortcut menu.

Revising the Schedule

To revise the schedule for a site or to change the amount of information that will be updated, highlight the site's name in the **Items to Synchronize** box in Step 6 and click the **Properties** button. On the **Schedule** and **Download** tabs of the properties box that appears, you can change the update settings. If you want to remove this site from the **Items to Synchronize** list, remove the check from the **Make this page available offline** option on the **Web Document** tab.

End

How to Use the History List

Internet Explorer provides several techniques for returning to sites you've visited before. To go back to pages you've seen during the current session, click the **Back** button on the toolbar or select from the list of sites attached to the button. The **Address** bar has an attached list of names you've entered directly from the keyboard; pull down the list to view the addresses and select a site. The **Address** bar also has an elaborate **AutoComplete** feature, designed to streamline the entry of a previously visited address. But the ultimate place to go for a record of your recent online activity is the **History** list, which displays sites you've visited in current and previous sessions.

Begin

1 Open the History Bar

Click the **History** button on the toolbar. The **History** bar opens on the left side of the browser window.

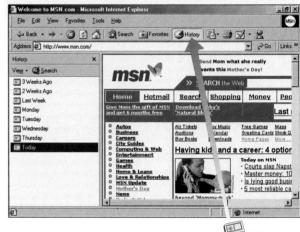

Click

2 Select a Day to Review

The History list is divided into calendar folders representing days and weeks of site links. Click the folder for the time period you want to review.

 Click

3 Open a Folder of Links

In the selected list, you'll find links organized in folders. Click a folder icon to open the folder and view its links.

 Click

4 Select a Link

Position the mouse pointer over a link that interests you. A small tip box shows you the name and address of the site. Click the link to go directly to the site; its content appears at the right side of the browser window.

Click

5 View the History Options

To increase or decrease the number of days in the History list, pull down the **Tools** menu and choose **Internet Options**. The **Internet Options** box appears on the desktop.

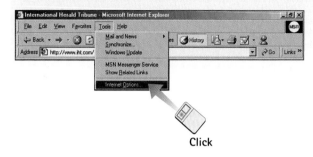

Click

6 Adjust the History Setting

In the **History** section of the **General** tab, click the up or down arrow button to increase or decrease the number of history days. Click **OK** to confirm the change.

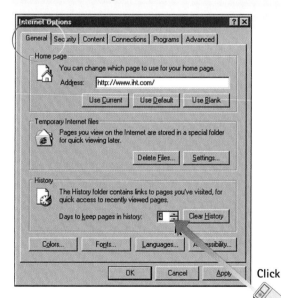

Click

End

How-To Hints

Changing the View of History

You can change the way the History list is organized by clicking the **View** button at the top of the **History** bar. The available options allow you to arrange the links by date (the default), by site in alphabetical order, by frequency of visits, or by today's order of visits.

Deleting History Entries

For convenience, you might sometimes want to clear the contents of the History list and start anew. To do so, click the **Clear History** button in the **Internet Options** box shown in Step 6.

Closing the History List

To close the History list, click the **History** button on the toolbar or click the small × in the upper-right corner of the **History** bar.

How to Use the Radio Bar

The **Radio** bar lets you listen to local, national, or international radio stations, streamed in from selected Internet sites. To use this feature, begin by displaying the **Radio** bar at the top of the browser window. A link takes you to a **Radio Station Guide** site, where you can select stations by categories. When you've found a station you like, you can start hearing its content at the click of the mouse. Thanks to the range of selections, you might find yourself listening in on today's election news from Sénégal, the latest music from France, or a talk show from Latvia.

Begin

1 Display the Radio Bar

Pull down the **View** menu at the top of the browser window and choose **Toolbars**. From the toolbar selection, click **Radio**. The **Radio** toolbar appears along with other browser toolbars at the top of the window.

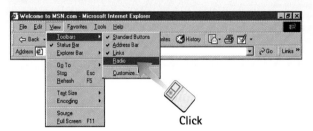

Click

2 Go to the Radio Station Guide

Click the **Radio Stations** button in the **Radio** toolbar and choose **Radio Station Guide** from the drop-down list of options. This is a link to a Microsoft site designed to get you started in online radio listening.

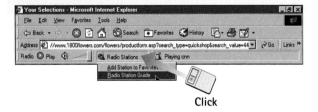

Click

3 Select a Radio Station

Click a link representing one of the featured stations. The selection of stations—and the organization of the page itself—will, of course, change over time on this Web site. Scroll through the page and survey the one-click links to radio stations around the world. Also keep an eye out for a search tool (for example, the text box and the **Go** button at the upper-right corner of this screen).

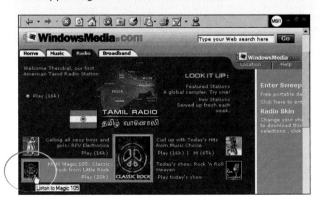

4 Wait for the Stream of Radio Content

The link you click in Step 3 will typically take you to the Web site of the selected radio station. Look for the link that starts the radio (the link might have words such as **listen**, **hear**, or **play**). Wait briefly while an initial stream of online audio content is downloaded to your computer. You should begin to hear the programming (music, news, talk, and so on) after a few seconds of waiting.

5 Use Controls on the Radio Toolbar

Use the volume slider on the **Radio** bar to increase or decrease the volume from the current radio station. To stop downloading content from the station site, click the **Stop** button on the **Radio** bar. To resume content from the same site, click **Play**.

6 Select a Favorite Station

As you use this feature over time, the **Radio** toolbar keeps a list of the stations you've tried. To go back to a favorite station, click the **Radio Stations** button and make a selection from the list.

Click

End

How-To Hints

Adding a Station to Your Favorites List

To add an online radio site to your Favorites list, click the **Radio Stations** button and choose **Add Station to Favorites**. In the **Add Favorite** dialog box, choose a folder for organizing this and other stations in the Favorites list and provide a name that identifies the station. Then click **OK** to add the station to the list.

Using the Radio Tuner Site

Look for a link to the **Radio Tuner** (or go directly to **http://windowsmedia. com/radiotuner**), an elaborate Microsoft site designed to help you search for international radio stations by categories such as language, location, format, and keyword.

Task

9

Keeping Safe on the Internet

*L*ike the world at large, the Internet has many sites you might consider inappropriate for your family. Some Web sites offer content that is unequivocally adult in nature. If your children use the Internet, you might be concerned about their exposure to this material. Other sites, although intended for a more general audience, can also contain topics you might find objectionable.

To help solve this problem, Internet Explorer's **Content Advisor** allows you to set rating levels for specific types of content, including language, nudity, sex, and violence. After you activate the **Content Advisor**, a rated site is blocked from use if it goes beyond the levels you've chosen. (An unrated site can also be blocked, depending on the options you set.) To maintain your selections in the **Content Advisor**, you create a private password. Only a person who knows the password can change or override your rating levels.

In addition to the **Content Advisor**, Internet Explorer offers other options related to security and safety on the Web. You'll explore some of these settings in the tasks ahead. Finally, in Task 4, you'll consider the safety issues involved in downloading application or data files from the Web. At the same time, you'll see an example of how the download procedure works.

How to Use the Content Advisor

The **Content Advisor** is designed to help you control access to the Internet in your household. There are several steps involved in using this feature. You begin by selecting rating levels in a variety of content categories, and then you establish a private password to protect your selections. Finally, you can activate or deactivate the Content Advisor, depending on who is using your computer to go online.

Begin

1 Open the Properties Window

Right-click the **Internet Explorer** icon and choose **Properties** from the shortcut menu to open the **Internet Properties** dialog box. (Alternatively, you can open the dialog box from within Internet Explorer: Pull down the **Tools** menu and choose **Internet Options**.)

Right-click

2 Open the Content Advisor

Click the **Content** tab. If this is the first time anyone has used the Content Advisor on your computer, click **Enable**; otherwise, click **Settings**. (If a password has already been established for this feature, you'll have to enter it in the **Supervisor Password** dialog box.)

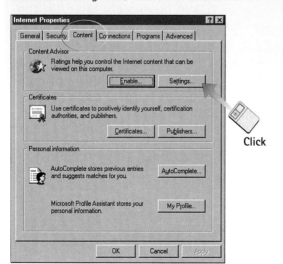

Click

3 Choose a Content Category

The **Content Advisor** box appears, with the **Ratings** tab selected. In the category list, choose one of the four content categories: **Language**, **Nudity**, **Sex**, or **Violence**.

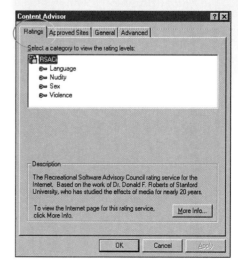

4 Select a Rating

Beneath the category list, drag the rating slider to the content level that's appropriate for your household. The **Description** box tells you what kind of content you can expect. Repeat Steps 3 and 4 for each of the remaining rating categories. In Task 2, you'll use the **Content Advisor** to establish a password and to activate your rating selections.

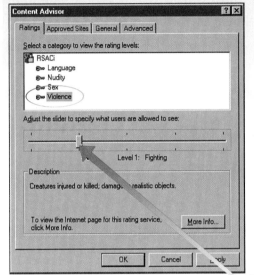

Drag

End

How-To Hints

Using the Rating Slider

To work the **Rating** slider in Step 4, use your mouse to drag the slider bar from one level to another.

Finding More Information

For more information about the rating service that governs the **Content Advisor**, click the **More Info** button. This button is a link to the rating service's Web site.

Changing the Password

To learn how to establish or change the password and activate the ratings you've chosen, refer to Task 2.

How to Activate the Content Advisor

After you've selected a set of Internet content ratings for your household, your next steps are to establish a supervisor password and to activate the Content Advisor. While the **Content Advisor** feature is in use, you'll encounter its characteristic warning message whenever you attempt to go to a restricted site. Unrated sites are another issue you'll have to deal with, as discussed in the How-To Hints.

Begin

1 Open the Content Advisor

Open the **Content Advisor** dialog box if it is not already open, following the steps outlined in Task 1. Click the **General** tab. Optionally, check one or both of the **User options** boxes regarding unrated sites and password-activated access to restricted sites. (See the How-To Hints for more information.)

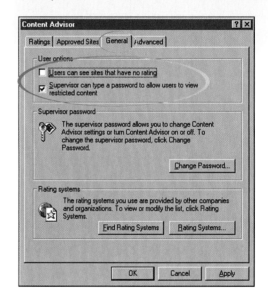

2 Change the Password

Click the **Change Password** button. In the resulting **Change Supervisor Password** dialog box, type the old password if one has previously been established. Type your new password twice in the boxes provided, click **OK** to confirm the new password, and then click **OK** to close the **Content Advisor** dialog box.

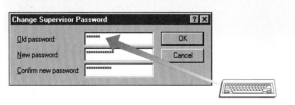

3 Activate the Content Advisor

In the **Content** tab of the **Internet Options** box, click the **Enable** button. (If the button's caption appears with the label **Disable**, the Content Advisor is already active.)

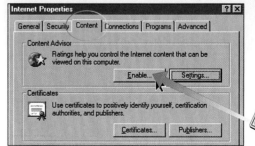

Click

4 Type the Password

In the **Supervisor Password Required** box, type the password you've defined for the Content Advisor and click **OK**.

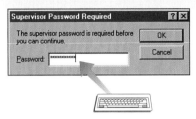

5 Confirm the Process

A message box notifies you that the Content Advisor has been enabled. Click **OK** to acknowledge the message. Then click **OK** to close the **Internet Properties** box.

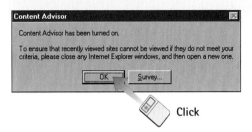

Click

6 Test the Advisor's Effect

When you next sign on to the Internet, the Content Advisor will monitor each new Web site you attempt to visit. If the site's ratings are not within the levels you've established for your household—or, optionally, if the site is unrated—access will be blocked. The message shown here is for an unrated site. Note that you can enter your **Content Advisor** password to view the site, thanks to the option selected in Step 1.

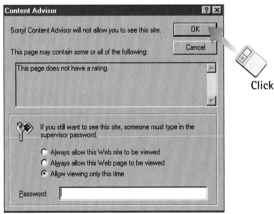

Click

End

How-To Hints

Disabling the Content Advisor

To turn the Content Advisor feature off, open the **Internet Properties** dialog box to the **Content** tab, click **Disable**, and supply your password.

Using General Options

Many Web sites are unrated—including some adult-content sites and many general-interest sites. On the **General** tab of the **Content Advisor** box, the **Users can see sites that have no rating** option gives you control over these sites. Leave the option unchecked to block unrated sites, or check it to allow access to these sites.

Select the **Supervisor can type a password to allow users to view restricted content** option if you want to be able to override the blocking feature by supplying your password as in Step 6.

Using Other Advisor Features

The **Approved Sites** tab of the **Content Advisor** dialog box allows you to develop a list of specific sites that can be blocked or allowed, regardless of their ratings or content. The **Find Rating Systems** button on the **General** tab takes you to a Web page that might list other rating systems available for your use.

How to Manage Security on the Internet

Internet Explorer is designed to issue warnings about potentially risky events as you move from one Web site to another. A suspect site might pose some danger to your computer or to the data stored on your hard disk. For this purpose, Internet Explorer divides sites into four zones, each with its own default security rating: **Internet**, **Local intranet**, **Trusted sites**, and **Restricted sites**. The **Internet** zone, which has a **Medium** security rating by default, contains all the sites you do not specifically assign to another zone.

Begin

1 Open the Options Box

In the **Internet Explorer** window, pull down the **Tools** menu and choose **Internet Options**. The **Internet Options** box appears on the desktop.

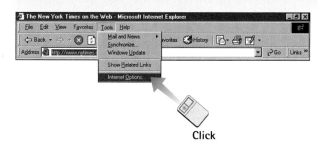

Click

2 Click the Security Tab

Click the **Security** tab to view information about security zones. The options on this page allow you to customize the security level for any zone you select.

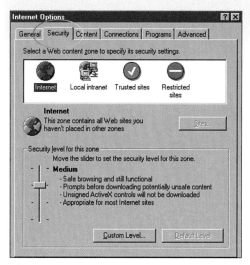

3 Choose a Zone

Click an icon for a zone that you want to change. The window gives a brief description of the zone, explaining its specific purpose.

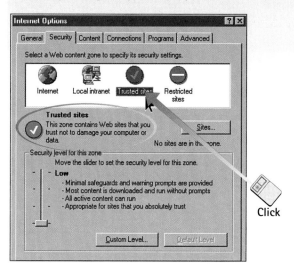

Click

4 Change the Security Level

Drag the **Security** slider up or down to change the security level you want for the current zone. Read about the features of the new level you've selected.

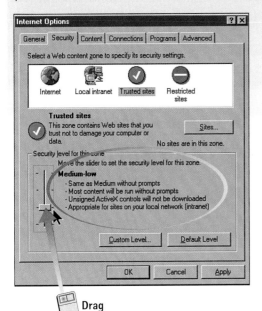

Drag

5 Add Sites to the Zone

Click the **Sites** button to assign your own list of commonly visited sites to this zone. In the resulting window, type the address of a site and then click **Add**. Repeat this step for all the sites you want to list in a particular current zone. Then click **OK** to confirm.

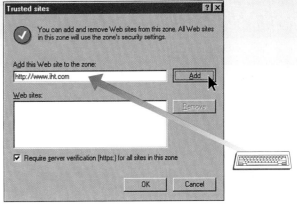

End

How-To Hints

Resetting the Defaults

To reset the default security level for a zone, open the **Internet Options** dialog box to the **Security** tab, select the zone, and click the **Default Level** button. Note that Internet Explorer issues a warning message when you set a security level that is below the default for a given zone. Click **Yes** if you're sure that you want to confirm the selected level.

Customizing a Security Level

The **Custom Level** button on the **Security** tab allows you to select specific settings to define the characteristics of a security level.

How to Download Safely

A *download* is a document or program file that you choose to receive from a source on the Internet. Many online locations offer tempting downloads that are free or nearly free. The question you must always ask yourself is whether the source is a reliable one. Can you be sure that the file you receive will be safe and efficient to use on your computer? In this regard, you should consider the range of negative possibilities, including malicious intent, inadvertent system incompatibilities, or just bad software design. Before you decide to download and install a program from the Web, learn what you can about the online source and then proceed with caution.

Begin

1 Find a Site

Connect to the Internet and use the resources of your browser to go to a particular download source. You might learn about a reliable site from a magazine article or from a friend or colleague. Alternatively, use Internet Explorer's **Search** bar to look for downloads by topics or functions. When you reach the target site, inspect the download offerings and select a category.

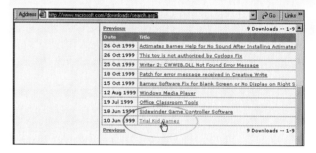

2 Select a Download

Click the **Download** link for the item you want to receive. Depending on the site, you might also have to complete additional steps, such as accepting a license agreement or completing a registration form.

3 Decide to Run or Save the File

In the **File Download** box, you can choose between running the program as soon as the download is complete, or saving the download file to disk for opening later. In the interests of caution, you should generally choose the **Save** option, if only to give yourself yet another opportunity to reconsider the merits of your source before you install and run the downloaded software.

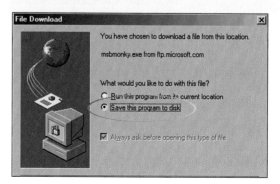

4 Designate a Disk Location

If you choose the **Save** option, you'll next need to designate a folder on disk where the download file should be saved. Some users like to create a special **Downloads** folder just for organizing files received from online sources. Click **Save**.

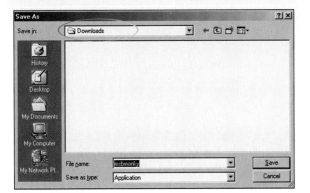

5 Monitor the Download Process

When the download begins, an information box appears on the desktop, charting the progress of the procedure. You'll be able to find out approximately how long the download will take. After the file is completely downloaded, click the **Open Folder** button to view the folder in which the file has been stored. You can now disconnect from the Internet if you want.

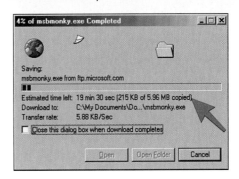

6 Install the Program

A software download is likely to arrive in the form of an EXE file designed to install the new program on your computer. When you're ready to perform the installation, click the file's icon and follow any instructions that appear on the screen.

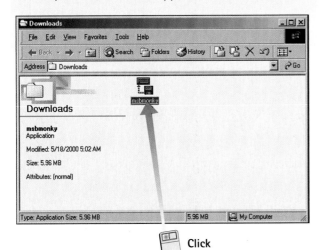

Click

End

How-To Hints

Downloading Shareware

One category of software downloads is known as *shareware*. A shareware publisher offers useful programs you can download and try out on your own computer. The implicit agreement is that you will eventually send a payment to the publisher if you decide to keep the software and continue using it.

Receiving Certificates

In some cases, you might have a chance to inspect a publisher's Web site certificate before you decide to download a file. This certificate represents a digital ID provided by a particular online authentication service. The certificate confirms that the site is secure and genuine, but does not necessarily ensure the quality of any software you might choose to download.

Task

PART 10

Working with a Windows Application

*A*pplications that run on the Windows desktop generally have certain basic features in common. As a result, each new application you undertake might seem easier to learn than the previous one. You never really have to start over again at the beginning of the learning curve. The more you work in Windows, the more intuitive each new step becomes.

In the tasks ahead, you'll look in detail at a handful of procedures that turn out to be important components of most Windows applications. These include starting an application and becoming familiar with its visual tools; choosing styles, fonts, and colors for textual information; formatting the content of a document; saving and printing files; using **Copy** and **Paste** commands; learning shortcuts for moving objects and changing their appearances; and accomplishing successful search-and-replace operations. In one way or another, you'll perform these same tasks in almost all major "productivity" applications, including spreadsheets, database management, graphics programs, and word processing.

As a useful context for exploring these universal tasks, you'll work with WordPad, the word processing program that comes with Windows. WordPad is simple enough to master in a short time, yet has the features you need for most day-to-day word processing tasks. Whatever you put on paper—letters, memos, reports, speeches, essays, stories, poems, plays, novels, recipes, grocery lists, homework assignments, term papers, dissertations, or the daily entries of your personal journal—WordPad can simplify your work and inevitably improve the result. Like other word processing programs, WordPad gives you tools to streamline every step along the way—from composing the initial draft, to revising and correcting the text, to producing attractive and readable copy on paper. ●

How to Get Started

To locate the applications that come with Windows, click the **Start** button, and then choose **Programs** and **Accessories**. When you're running a program on the desktop for the first time, you'll want to take a close look at the various shortcuts it offers for accomplishing specific tasks—including menus, toolbars, and other visual tools that can be arranged across the top of the application window. Then you should just plunge in and begin developing the content of a first experimental document. For example, in WordPad, you'll immediately see how the program manages the text you enter from the keyboard.

Begin

1 Start the Program

Click the **Start** button and choose **Programs** and **Accessories**. From the **Accessories** menu, choose the name of the application you want to run, in this case **Wordpad**. The program window appears on the desktop.

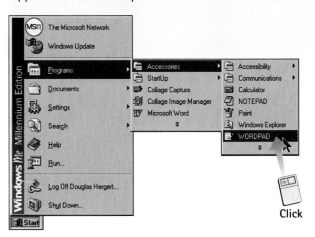

Click

2 Maximize the Application Window

If necessary, click the **Maximize** button on the right side of the title bar to expand the window to its largest possible size. The window's title bar initially displays a generic name—**Document** in the case of WordPad. After you save your work for the first time, the title bar will display the name you assign the file.

Document title   Minimize/Maximize Close

Restore

3 Examine the Toolbars

At the top of an application window, you typically see a menu bar, along with one or more rows of toolbars representing the program's features. The **WordPad** window includes a toolbar of buttons such as **Save**, **Print**, **Find**, **Cut**, **Paste**, and **Undo**; a *format* bar with a variety of text-formatting options; and a margin-setting tool known as the *ruler*. The **View** menu typically gives you options for hiding or viewing a program's toolbars.

Menu bar   Title bar   Format bar

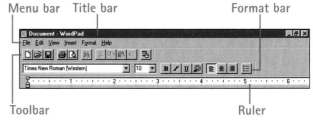

Toolbar   Ruler

4 Start a Practice Document

Try creating an experimental document. As you enter text into **WordPad**, you'll notice the flashing *insertion point cursor* (|) that marks your place. If you make a mistake, press the **Backspace** key to erase characters just to the left of the insertion point. To move the insertion point to a new place in the document, position the mouse pointer and click, or press arrow keys on your keyboard. Press the **Delete** key to erase a character to the right of the insertion point.

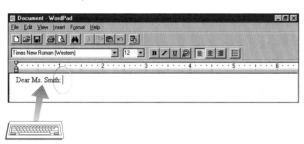

5 Experiment with the Document

Press **Enter** to start a new paragraph or to insert a blank line. Press **Tab** to indent. Then type a paragraph containing two or more lines of text. When you reach the end of a line, you'll see that WordPad automatically moves the insertion point to the beginning of the next line, a feature known as *word wrap*. In other words, you don't press **Enter** to start a new line within a paragraph; WordPad takes you to the next line automatically.

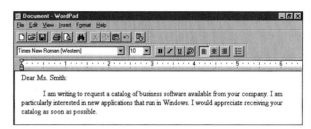

End

How-To Hints

Inserting Text

To insert new text in an existing part of your document, use the mouse or keyboard to move the insertion point and start typing. (If necessary, press the **Ins** key on your keyboard to toggle into *insert* mode, rather than *overwrite* mode.) Press **Enter** to create a new paragraph within the existing text.

Starting a New Document

To abandon the current document and start a new one, click **New**, the first button on the toolbar. Unlike more elaborate programs, WordPad allows only one open document at a time; on the other hand, you can run multiple instances of the WordPad application on the desktop concurrently.

Getting Help

Like all major Windows applications, WordPad has its own **Help** window. To open it, pull down the **Help** menu and choose **Help Topics**.

How to Apply Styles, Fonts, and Colors

Special typographical effects can enhance the appearance of documents you create in any application. To apply these effects to a document you've already developed, select the target text and then choose specific options, typically from a **Format** menu or format bar. In WordPad, you can apply boldface, italic, and underlining styles, individually or in combinations, to any selection of text. You can also increase or decrease the type size and change the font or typeface design in an entire document or a selected portion of it. As a final touch, you can add color to make the document even more attractive.

Begin

1 Select a Block of Text

Hold down the left mouse button and drag the mouse over the text to which you want to apply a style, size, font, or color. Your selection is *highlighted*—that is, displayed as white text against a dark background.

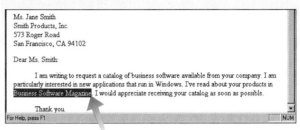

Drag

2 Apply New Styles

To apply styles to the selected text, click the **Bold**, **Italic**, or **Underline** button on the format bar. Note that you can apply a combination of styles to the highlighted text.

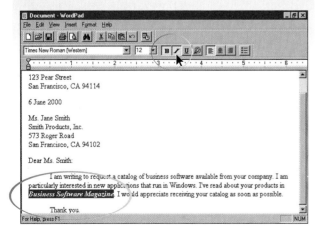

3 Increase or Decrease the Size

To change the size of the selected text, click the down-arrow button next to the **Font Size** box in the format bar and choose a new point size from the drop-down list.

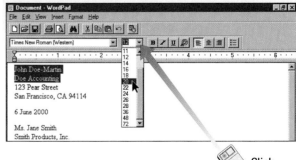
Click

4 Choose a New Font

To change the font of the selected text, click the down-arrow button next to the **Font** box on the format bar and choose the name of a new font from the resulting list.

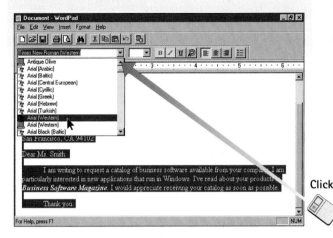

Click

5 Add a Color Selection

To change the color of the selected text in WordPad, click the **Color** button on the format bar and choose the color you want to apply. (Other applications might have different tools for selecting colors.)

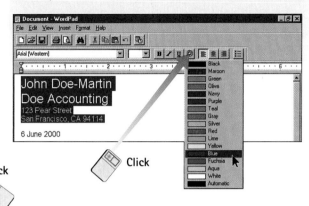

Click

6 Examine Your Document

Click the mouse pointer at the beginning of the document (or press **Ctrl+Home**) to deselect any highlighted text. Now you can see the results of your work.

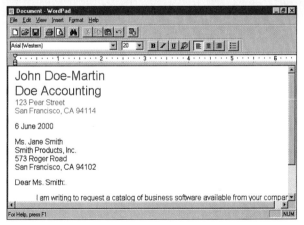

End

How-To Hints

Choosing Formats Before You Type

You can also select styles, fonts, and colors before you begin typing text. The selections are then applied to all new text you type.

Selecting Text with the Keyboard

You can use the keyboard to select text if the mouse seems inconvenient. Move the insertion point to the beginning or end of the text you want to select. Then hold down the **Shift** key and press the right- or left-arrow key repeatedly to select text within a line; hold **Shift** and press the up- or down-arrow key to select entire lines.

Selecting the Entire Document

Press **Ctrl+A** to select the entire content of the current document. To select a single line of text, click the blank white column just to the left of the line. Double-click at that location to select the entire paragraph.

How to Format Paragraphs

In WordPad, the format bar and ruler provide convenient tools for changing the alignment of text and for adjusting paragraph-indent settings. (Similar techniques are commonly available in other applications.) By default, text is left-aligned; each new line of text begins at the left margin. With a click of the mouse, you can center or right-align any line of text or all the lines of a paragraph. Changing the left- and right-indent settings of a paragraph is as simple as sliding markers to new positions along the ruler. Finally, you can add bulleted lists to a document by starting a new line and clicking the **Bullet** button on the format bar.

Begin

1 Change the Alignment

To change the alignment of one or more paragraphs, select the text, and then click the **Align Left**, **Center**, or **Align Right** button on the format bar. (Notice that a paragraph can consist of a single line of text ending with a return character.)

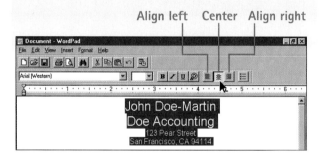

2 Adjust the Right Indent

To adjust the right-indent setting of one or more paragraphs, select the text and then slide the right-indent marker to a new position along the ruler.

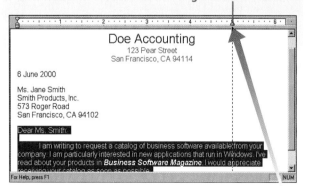

Drag

3 Create a Bulleted List

Click the **Bullets** button on the format bar. Type the first line in the list and press the **Enter** key to begin the next line. Each new line you type begins with a bullet. Click the **Bullets** button again to end the list.

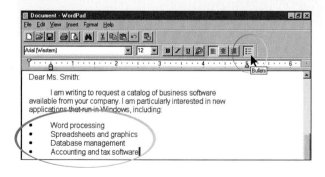

4 Change the Left Indent

To change the left-indent setting of a bulleted list, select the list, and then drag the square left-indent marker to a new position along the ruler.

Left-indent marker

Drag

End

How-To Hints

Using Indent Markers

At the left side of the ruler, the first-line indent marker and the left-indent marker are displayed as two triangles, one on top of the other. These markers can move independently; use your mouse to drag them to new positions along the ruler. To move both markers together, drag the small square marker displayed just below them.

Indenting an Entire Document

To change the indent settings for an entire document, pull down the **Edit** menu and choose the **Select All** command—or press **Ctrl+A**—to select all the text of the document. Then slide the indent markers to new positions along the ruler.

Setting Margins

Margins define the blank areas along the top, bottom, left, and right sides of the printed page. (In contrast, the indent settings represent paragraph offsets within the current margins.) To change the margins of a document, pull down the **File** menu and choose the **Page Setup** command. Then enter new measurement settings in the **Top**, **Bottom**, **Left**, and **Right** boxes.

How to Save a File

The more time you spend composing a document, the more frequently you'll want to save your work to disk. The first time you save, Windows gives you the opportunity to supply a meaningful name for the file. After that, each save operation updates the named file with the latest version of the document. Windows Me allows long, multiword filenames. For example, you can name a file **Smith Catalog Request**, instead of the less descriptive **SMITH.DOC**.

Begin

1 Save the Document

Click the **Save** button on the toolbar, or choose **Save** from the **File** menu.

 Click

2 Examine the Save As Dialog Box

If this is the first time you've saved this document, an application typically displays the **Save As** dialog box on the desktop. Here you see WordPad's **Save As** box.

3 Specify the Target Folder

If you want to save your file somewhere other than the current disk or folder, pull down the **Save in** list and make a selection. The **Save As** window displays the names of the folders stored in the location you've selected. Click a folder icon to open a folder for the current save operation.

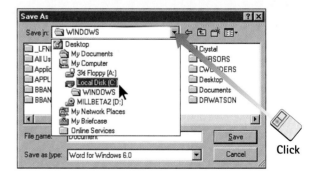 Click

4 Name the File

In the **File name** text box, type a name for the file you're about to create. Most applications have a default file format; in WordPad, for example, the **Save as type** box indicates a Word for Windows format by default. If you want to save your file in a different format, make a selection from the **Save as type** drop-down list. Click **Save** to complete the operation.

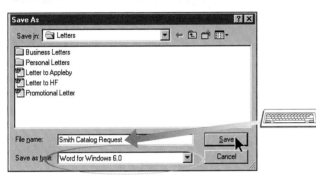

5 Update the File as You Work

As you continue to work on a document, save your work frequently. You can usually do so by any of three techniques: Choose **Save** from the **File** menu; press **Ctrl+S** from the keyboard; or click the **Save** button on the toolbar. No dialog box appears, but the file is updated with the current content of your document.

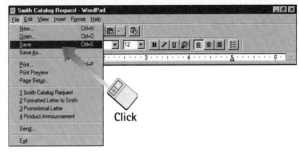

End

How-To Hints

Renaming a Saved File

To save a document under a new name—even if the document has already been saved—pull down the **File** menu and choose **Save As**. Type a new name in the **File name** box and click **Save**. (Note that this operation does not affect any previous versions of the file you've saved under different names.)

Reopening a File

To reopen a file that you've saved in a previous session with a program, click the **Open** button on the toolbar. In the **Open** dialog box, select the file and click the **Open** button. Alternatively, the **File** menu typically displays a short list of the most recent files you've worked with in an application. To reopen one of these files, pull down the **File** menu and choose the name of the document you want to work with.

Closing the Application

After you've saved the current file, you can quit the application by pulling down the **File** menu and choosing **Exit**. If you try the same action *before* saving changes in the current file, an alert box appears asking whether you want to save your document before quitting. Click **Yes** to save or **No** to quit without saving—that is, to abandon any unsaved changes.

How to Print a Document

Your final goal in any application is often to produce an attractive paper document that you can mail to a friend, distribute to colleagues, fax to a client, or duplicate for publication. When you think you're ready to print a document, many Windows applications allow you to examine a *preview* of its appearance on the screen; by previewing a document, you can avoid wasting paper until you're reasonably sure that the document looks just the way you want it.

Begin

1 Open the File

If the file you want to print is not open, click **Open** on the application's toolbar. In the **Open** dialog box, locate and open the folder that contains the target document, select the file, and click **Open**.

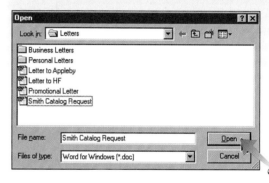

Click

2 Click Print Preview

Optionally, click the **Print Preview** button on the toolbar to see what your document will look like when you print it.

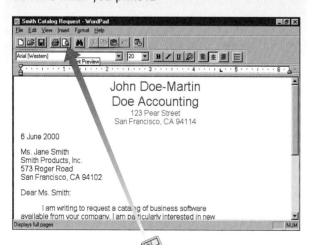
Click

3 Preview the Document

In the preview window, examine your document and make sure that it's formatted just the way you want it. Click **Close** to return to the normal view of your document. (Alternatively, click **Print** to initiate the printing operation directly from the preview window.)

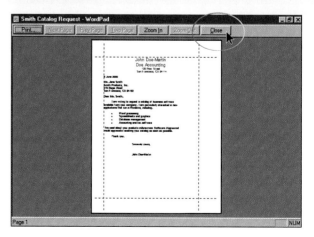

4 Print the Document

Back in the application's main window, pull down the **File** menu and choose the **Print** command. The **Print** dialog box typically gives you several important options: You can print the entire document or a specified range of pages; you can print multiple copies of your document; and you can opt to *collate* (to print all the pages of one copy before beginning the next copy). Click **OK** to begin.

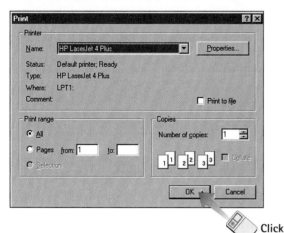

Click

5 Examine the Printed Document

Take a close look at your work. If you catch any errors, go back to the application to correct them. Then reprint the document.

End

How-To Hints

Printing with the Default Settings

To print a single copy of a document under the default settings, click the **Print** button on the toolbar. In many applications, this button immediately sends your document to the printer, bypassing the **Print** dialog box.

Printing a Portion of a Document

If you want to print only a particular passage from your document, select the text you want to print, choose **Print** from the **File** menu, and click the **Selection** option in the **Print Range** box. Click **OK** to begin printing.

Viewing Printer Properties

Optionally, click the **Properties** button on the **Print** dialog box to view or change the printer settings. The resulting dialog box shows an assortment of options, specific to the printer in use. See Part 11, "Printing," for more information about printing documents.

How to Copy and Paste

To copy information from one place to another in Windows, you perform a copy-and-paste operation. In the background, Windows uses the **Clipboard** to store the information you're copying. To carry out a copy-and-paste task, you first select the information and copy it to the Clipboard; then you select a destination and paste the information from the Clipboard. **Ctrl+C** is the standard shortcut for the **Copy** command; **Ctrl+V** is the shortcut for **Paste**.

Begin

1 Select the Target Information

To copy information from one place to another within a document, use your mouse or keyboard to select the information. Then hold down the **Ctrl** key and press **C** to copy the selection to the Clipboard.

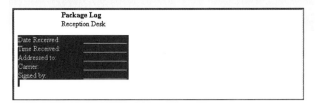

2 Paste the Information

Move the insertion point to the location where you want to copy the information. Hold down the **Ctrl** key and press **V**. If you want to make additional copies, repeat this step. In this example, the selection has been copied twice.

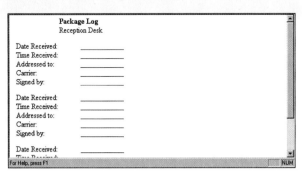

3 Copy Between Documents

To copy information from one document to another, first select the target information and press **Ctrl+C**, just as you would to copy within a single document.

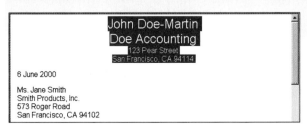

4 Paste to Another Document

Open the destination document and select the location where you want to insert the text. (In this example, it's a new document.) Press **Ctrl+V** to paste the information from the Clipboard.

> John Doe-Martin
> Doe Accounting
> 123 Pear Street
> San Francisco, CA 94114

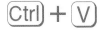

5 Copy from a Different Application

You can also copy information between documents you develop in different applications. First, select the information you want to copy from its source file. In this example, the source is a drawing created in the Paint program. Press **Ctrl+C** to copy the selection to the Clipboard. Then open the destination file in its own application, in this case a WordPad document.

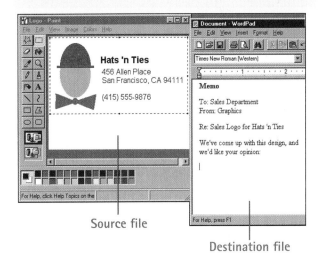

Source file

Destination file

6 Paste to the Destination

Select the target location and press **Ctrl+V** to paste the copy from the Clipboard.

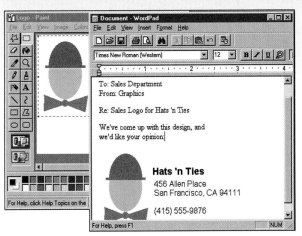

End

How-To Hints

Viewing the Clipboard

You can check the current contents of the Clipboard, using a program called Clipboard Viewer. Click the **Start** button and choose **Programs, Accessories, System Tools,** and finally **Clipboard Viewer.**

Cutting and Pasting

Unlike a copy-and-paste operation (which leaves the original information at its source), a cut-and-paste operation deletes the information from its source and moves it to a selected destination. The keyboard shortcut for the **Cut** command is **Ctrl+X.**

How to Use Text Shortcuts

Applications often provide shortcuts for making changes in the content of documents. Learning these shortcuts can streamline your work immeasurably. For example, WordPad (and other word processing programs) offer a variety of shortcut techniques for working with text. With a few quick mouse movements, you can select a line of text, move it to a new location in your document, and change its format. The clicking, dragging, and right-clicking techniques you practice in this task are also available for use in many other software contexts.

Begin

1 Select a Line of Text

To select a line of text, move the mouse pointer to the far left side of the application window. The pointer takes the shape of a white arrow pointing diagonally up and to the right. Click the line that you want to select. In response, WordPad highlights the entire line of text.

Click

2 Drag the Text to a New Place

To move the selected block of text, position the mouse pointer over the selection, hold down the left mouse button, and drag the mouse pointer to a new position. The pointer becomes a white arrow with a small attached box.

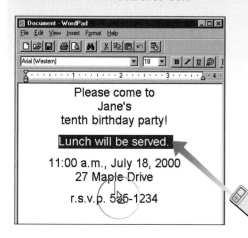

Drag

3 Complete the Move

Release the mouse button to complete the move. The text moves to the new position you've selected.

4 Change the Formatting

To change the format properties of a block of selected text, right-click the selection and choose **Font** from the shortcut menu.

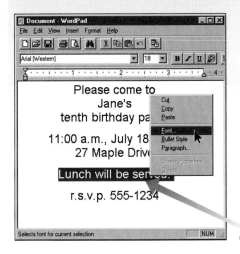

Right-click

5 Confirm the Changes

In the **Font** dialog box, select any new combinations of options, including the font, style, size, and color of the selected text. Click **OK** to confirm these changes.

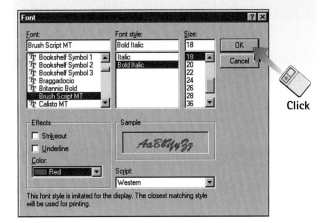

Click

6 Review Your Work

Click the mouse pointer elsewhere in the document to deselect the highlighted text. Now you can see the result of the formatting options you've selected.

End

How-To Hints

Using Shortcut Menus

As you've seen in several contexts, shortcut menus are available throughout Windows for changing the properties of objects on the desktop. To view a shortcut menu, simply right-click an object. The resulting menu always contains options and commands that apply specifically to the object you've selected.

Reversing the Mouse Buttons

Keep in mind that you can reverse the roles of the left and right mouse buttons so that the right button works for primary operations such as text selection, and the left works for secondary operations such as viewing shortcut menus. See Task 4, "How to Change the Mouse Settings," in Part 4, "Changing the Windows Me Settings," for details.

How to Search and Replace

As you develop a long document, you might sometimes need a quick way to find a particular passage in your work. Rather than scroll through many pages of content, you can use the **Find** command to search for the information you want to locate. Likewise, applications often have commands for making "global" changes throughout a document. For example, when you want to replace all instances of a word or phrase in a WordPad document, you can use the **Replace** command. Both the **Find** and **Replace** commands are located in the **Edit** menu.

Begin

1 Choose the Find Command

To search for information in a document, pull down the **Edit** menu and choose **Find**, or click the **Find** button on the toolbar.

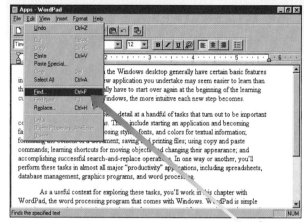

Click

2 Enter the Target Information

In the **Find** box, type the text you want to search for. Optionally, check **Match whole word only** to avoid searching for text embedded within a word; check **Match case** to search for the text in the exact uppercase/lowercase combinations you supply.

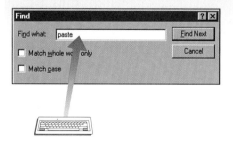

3 Start the Search

Click the **Find Next** button to search for the target text. As a result, the first instance of the text will be highlighted in your document. Click **Find Next** again to search further. When you're ready to close the **Find** dialog box, click **Cancel**.

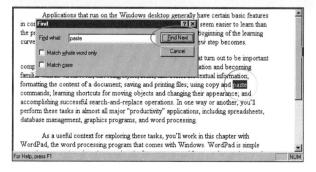

4 Replace All Text

To replace all instances of a particular word or phrase, press **Ctrl+Home** to move to the top of the document and then choose **Replace** from the **Edit** menu. The **Replace** box appears on the desktop. In the **Find what** box, type the text you want to replace. In the **Replace with** box, type the replacement text. Check **Match whole word only** to avoid changing text embedded within words; check **Match case** to replace only the exact text you've supplied. Then click **Replace All**.

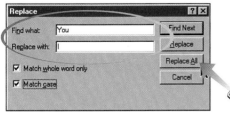

Click

5 Replace Text Selectively

To replace instances of the target text one at a time, click the **Find Next** button to highlight the next instance of the text, and then click **Replace** if you're sure that you want to carry out the replacement. (Alternatively, click **Find Next** again to skip this instance.) Keep clicking **Replace** for each appropriate replace operation.

Click

End

How-To Hints

Matching Whole Words Only

The **Match whole word only** option can be very important in search-and-replace operations. For example, if you're replacing **you** with **I**, you should check this option to avoid changing the embedded letters **you** in the word **youth**.

Adjusting Capitalization

After you complete a search-and-replace operation, you should manually go through your document and adjust capitalization in some instances of the replaced text. For example, the replacement text should be capitalized at the beginning of a sentence, but not within a sentence.

Undoing Revisions

Most applications, including WordPad, have an **Undo** command in the **Edit** menu and an equivalent **Undo** button on the toolbar. This feature is useful for restoring the original text whenever you change your mind about a revision you've made in a document. **Undo** is not always available, though; for example, you can't use **Undo** to restore all instances of a global replace operation in WordPad.

Task

Printing

When you print a document, Windows Me coordinates the software resources needed for the job—including the printer driver, the font selections, and the contents of the document itself. All this takes place in the background, without distracting you from your other activities on the desktop.

A printer icon shows up on the right side of the taskbar whenever you choose an application's **Print** command. Windows allows you to place multiple documents in line for printing—creating a *print queue*—and to continue your work while printing takes place.

At times, you might want to take more direct control over printing operations. One way to do so is to place an icon directly on the desktop to represent your printer. You can then form a print queue by dragging documents to the printer icon. To view the queue, simply click the icon; in the resulting window, you can issue commands to pause, resume, or cancel any print job. You can also change the order of the documents in the queue so that they print in a different order than the one in which they were sent to the printer. ●

How to Use a Desktop Printer Icon

You typically print a document directly from the application in which you created the file. Whether you're printing a letter from WordPad, a drawing from Paint, or a table of financial data from your favorite spreadsheet program, the steps are always the same: Start the application, open the file, edit it, and then choose the program's **Print** command to send the document to the printer. But suppose that you want a quick way to print several documents from a variety of source applications. You can create a shortcut icon to represent your printer on the desktop. You then use simple drag-and-drop to print.

Begin

1 Open the Printers Folder

Click the **Start** button, choose **Settings**, and then choose **Printers** to open the **Printers** folder.

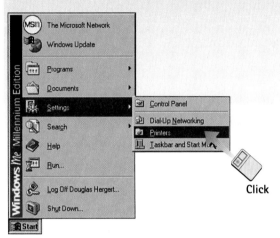

Click

2 Select a Printer Icon

The **Printers** folder contains icons for the printers you've installed on your system. Position the mouse pointer over the one you want to copy to the desktop.

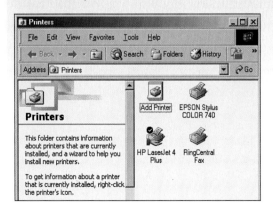

3 Drag the Icon to the Desktop

Using the right mouse button, drag the selected icon from the **Printers** folder to the desktop. Release the mouse button and choose **Create Shortcut(s) Here** from the shortcut menu. A copy of the printer icon appears on the desktop. You can now close the **Printers** folder.

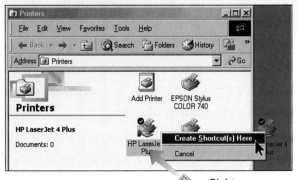

Right-drag

4 Open a Folder of Documents

Open the **My Computer** window and go to the folder containing the assortment of documents you want to print.

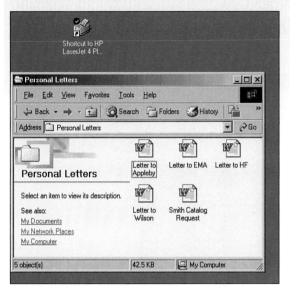

5 Print a Document

Drag any document from the open folder to the printer icon. Release the mouse button when the document icon is directly on top of the printer icon. Windows starts the application in which the file was created, opens the document, prints it, and then closes the application.

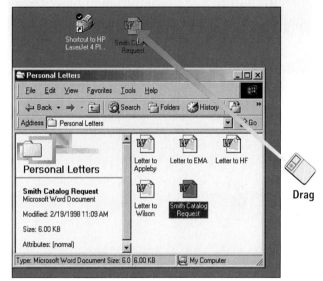

Drag

End

How-To Hints

Dragging Multiple Files

You can drag multiple document files to the printer icon in one operation. To select two or more files, press and hold the **Ctrl** key while you select the files in the source folder window. Then drag the entire selection to the printer shortcut icon.

Viewing the Print Queue

To open the print queue window and view any current print jobs, click the printer icon you've created on the desktop. When you open this window, you can manage the queue in a variety of useful ways. See Task 2, "How to Manage the Print Queue," for more information.

Identifying the File Type

If the document you've selected is not associated with a known application, Windows displays a message telling you so. In this case, the easiest way to print the file may be to open it in its source application and choose the **Print** command.

How to Manage the Print Queue

The *print queue* is the list of documents waiting to be printed. You can open a window that displays this queue by clicking the printer icon you've placed on the desktop. This window allows you to pause the current print operation, either for the entire queue or for individual documents in the queue. You can also cancel any print job in the queue.

Begin

1 Pause the Print Queue

Right-click the printer icon and choose **Pause Printing.** When you have several documents to send to the queue, the **Pause** status gives you the opportunity to form the entire queue before the printing begins.

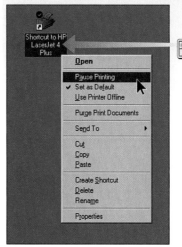

Right-click

2 Send Documents to the Printer

Send any number of documents to the printer, using the drag-and-drop operation described in Task 1.

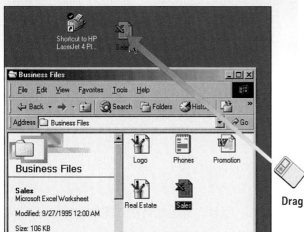

Drag

3 View the Print Queue

To view the print queue, click the printer icon on the desktop. The queue shows the name of each document waiting to be printed.

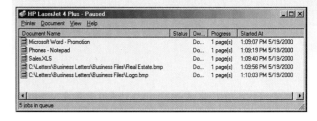

4 Pause an Individual Document

To change the status of any document in the list, right-click the document name. Choose **Pause Printing** to toggle the individual document into the **Pause** mode. (The selected document will subsequently remain in the **Pause** mode, even when you switch off the **Pause Printing** command in the **Printer** menu, as explained in the next step.)

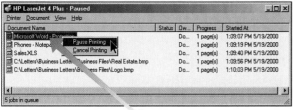

Right-click

5 Resume Printing Other Documents

To resume printing any documents that are not individually in the **Pause** mode, pull down the **Printer** menu and choose the **Pause Printing** option. The check mark next to this option means that the entire queue is in the **Pause** mode. When you choose the command, the check mark is removed, and the printing process resumes.

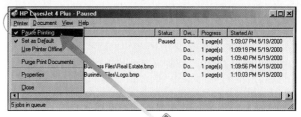

Click

6 Remove an Item from the Queue

To remove a document from the print queue, right-click the document and choose the **Cancel Printing** command. The name of the document disappears from the queue, and the document will not be printed.

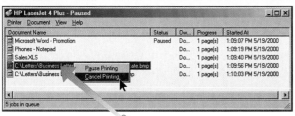

Right-click

End

How-To Hints

Pausing or Canceling a Print Job
Another way to pause or cancel the print operation for an individual document is to select the file in the print queue and then choose **Pause Printing** or **Cancel Printing** from the **Document** menu.

Changing the Order of the Queue
You can change the order of the items in the print queue by selecting a document and dragging it to a new position in the list.

Canceling the Entire Queue
To delete the entire print queue, pull down the **Printer** menu and choose the **Purge Print Documents** command. This action has no effect on the documents themselves; it simply cancels the print operations.

How to Install a Printer

At some time, you might want to connect a different printer to your computer—such as a newly purchased printer or one borrowed from a different system. To work successfully with a newly attached printer, you must generally install an important piece of software known as a *driver*. Windows Me comes with a large collection of drivers for the most popular printers on the market today. The **Add Printer Wizard** helps you select and install the appropriate driver for your printer.

Begin

1 Click the Add Printer Icon

Open the **Printers** folder by clicking the **Start** button and choosing **Settings**, and then **Printers**. Click the **Add Printer** icon in the **Printers** folder. The first window of the **Add Printer Wizard** appears on the desktop.

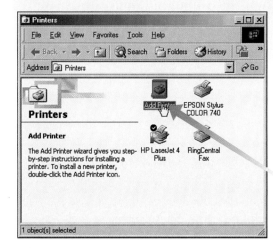

Click

2 Start the Add Printer Wizard

Click the **Next** button to begin the process of installing a new printer. (If you have installed a home network, the wizard next asks you whether this is to be a local or network printer. Make a selection and click **Next**. See the How-To Hints for more information.)

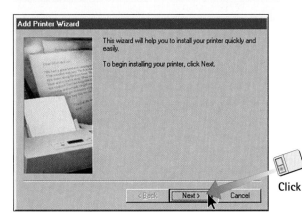

Click

3 Select the Make and Model

Select the manufacturer of your printer and then select the printer model you want to install. Click **Next** to continue.

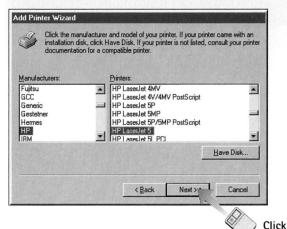

Click

4 Select the Port

Select the name of the port to which the printer is attached. In most cases, this name is **LPT1**. Click **Next** to continue.

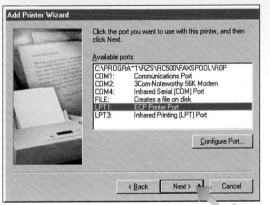

Click

5 Confirm the Printer Name

Click **Next** to accept the suggested printer name. This will become the name of the printer icon that Windows adds to your **Printers** folder.

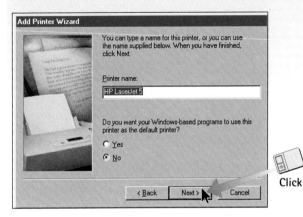

Click

6 Print a Test Page

Indicate whether you want Windows to print a test page on your printer. When you click **Finish**, the wizard may notify you to insert the appropriate Windows installation disk. Windows copies and installs the necessary driver to complete the installation process.

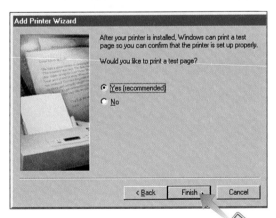

Click

End

How-To Hints

Changing the Default Printer

When two or more printers are installed on your system, the *default* is the one that's automatically used for printing unless you specify otherwise. To change the default printer, open the **Printers** folder, right-click a selected printer icon, and choose **Set as Default**. Notice that the **Add Printer Wizard** also gives you the opportunity to designate a new printer as the default, as shown in Step 5.

Installing a New Printer

If you're installing a printer you've just bought, the package probably includes a driver disk. When you reach Step 3 of the **Add Printer Wizard**, insert the disk and click the **Have Disk** button. Windows installs the driver for you.

Installing a Network Printer

On a home network, one computer can use a printer attached to a different computer. Turn to Parts 17, "Setting Up a Home Network," and 18, "Working on a Home Network," for more information about home networks.

Task

Combining the Resources of Applications

You might sometimes require the features of two or more Windows applications to produce all the elements of a single document. For example, you might want to incorporate a spreadsheet table or a graphic design into a word-processed report. One simple way to complete such a document is to use copy-and-paste operations to transfer information from one program to another, as described in Part 10, "Working with a Windows Application." But a more dynamic approach for sharing data between major applications involves special techniques known as *embedding* and *linking*.

Using these techniques, you can edit and update all the parts of a document you're developing, even if the information originates from different programs. For example, suppose that you're using WordPad or some other word processing software to prepare an expense report for a recent business trip. A central part of your document is a short table of expense data that you've compiled in a spreadsheet program. Halfway through your work, you notice that you've made a mistake in one of the entries in the expense table. With an embedded or linked spreadsheet document, you can revise your table quickly and easily, without leaving your word processor.

These techniques give you two different ways to combine data; your choice between them might depend primarily on how you decide to organize your work. An *embedded* document conveniently provides all the features and capabilities of the source application, but is independent of any existing file on disk. By contrast, a *linked* document is inserted into your current document and retains its connections with an original file on disk. If you make changes in the linked information, Windows transfers those changes to the source file. You'll see examples of both these approaches in the tasks ahead. ●

How to Combine Information in a Windows Application

As you develop the text of a document in your word processing program, you can easily insert information from other applications. If the insertion exists only as part of your word-processed document, not as a separate file on disk, it is known as an *embedded document*. A typical example is a worksheet table incorporated into the text of a business document. Whatever application you use to create the table (Microsoft Excel, Lotus 1-2-3, or some other spreadsheet), you'll have all the program's features at your disposal whenever you activate the embedded object.

Begin

1 Start Your Document

Start your word processing application and begin entering the text of a new document. This example shows how you might use WordPad to develop an expense report.

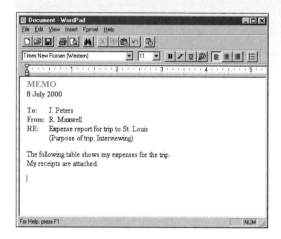

2 Choose the Insert Object Command

At the point in the document where you want to insert a worksheet, pull down the **Insert** menu and choose the **Object** command.

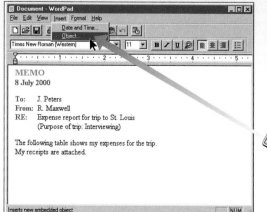

Click

3 Select an Application

In the **Insert Object** dialog box, make sure that the **Create New** option is selected. In the **Object Type** list, select the application you want to use to create a worksheet object in your document. Here, the selection is for an Excel worksheet. Click **OK** to create the embedded object.

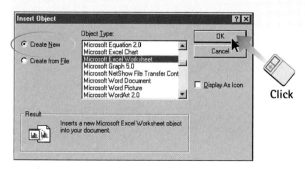
Click

4 Develop the Embedded Object

Windows inserts and activates a new embedded worksheet object into your document. The menus and toolbars at the top of your document are temporarily replaced by the features belonging to the embedded application. As you complete the worksheet, you can use all the features of the select-ed spreadsheet application to create a formatted table of values and formulas. When you finish your worksheet, click inside the word-processed text to deselect the embedded document.

The menus and toolbars are from the embedded application

An embedded Excel worksheet

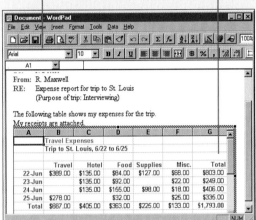

5 Save Your Work

The embedded worksheet appears as part of your word-processed document. You can now save your work to disk and print it if you want.

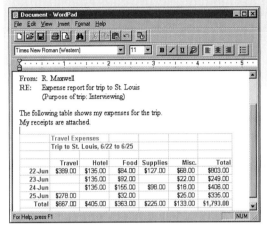

End

How-To Hints

Selecting an Object Type

If you do not have Excel (or any other spreadsheet application) installed on your computer, you won't be able to embed a spreadsheet document as shown in these steps. Try selecting a different application from the **Object Type** list in Step 3.

Activating Embedded Objects

You can activate an embedded document for further editing at any time by double-clicking inside the object. See Task 2, "How to Work with an Embedded Document," for more information.

Viewing an Object's Properties

To view the properties of an embedded document, deactivate the object and right-click it. Choose **Object Properties** from the shortcut menu. In the **Properties** dialog box, you'll find information about the embedded object, including its source application and size.

How to Work with an Embedded Document

An embedded object appears as part of another document, but is not linked to a separate file on disk. When you activate an embedded object, you can edit its contents using the tools and techniques available in the source application. The object can be activated directly in the host application window, or in a separate window that contains the source program.

Begin

1 Open a File with an Embedded Object

Open or create a document that contains an embedded object. (See Task 1 for details.)

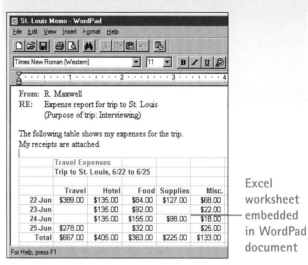

Excel worksheet embedded in WordPad document

2 Activate the Object

Double-click the embedded object to activate it. You can now edit its contents. At the top of the host application window, you'll see the menus and toolbars belonging to the object's source program.

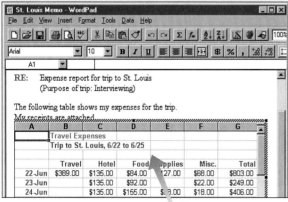

Double-click

3 Revise the Content

Make any changes in the content of the embedded object. The document behaves just as it would in its source application. In this example, changing a value in the worksheet table results in an instant recalculation of all the formulas that depend on that value.

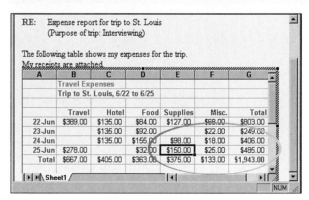

4 Save and Print the Document

To deactivate the object, click outside its borders in the host document. You can now save your work to disk and print the document if you want. The embedded object will be printed as part of the main document.

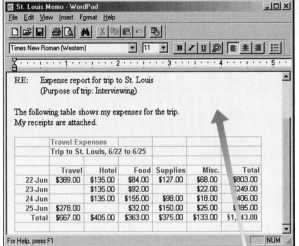

Click

5 Open the Object in Two Ways

To experiment, right-click the embedded object and choose **Worksheet Object**. The resulting menu contains two options for activating the object. Choose **Edit** to activate the object within the host document, as shown earlier in this example. Choose **Open** to activate the embedded object with a separate application window. Either way, all the features of the source application are available for your work.

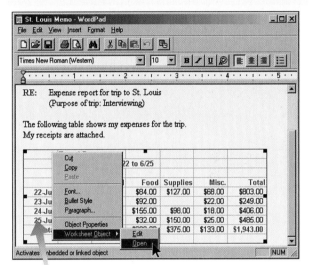

Right-click

End

How-To Hints

Inserting Existing Files

You can insert an existing file into a WordPad document as an embedded object. Choose the **Object** command from the **Insert** menu. In the **Insert Object** dialog box, click the **Create from File** option. Then type the name of the target file into the **File** box, or click the **Browse** button to look for the file. Leaving the **Link** option *unchecked*, click **OK** to embed the document into your current WordPad text. Because this embedded document is not linked to its source file, you can edit the information it contains without affecting the original file.

Using Copy and Paste Special

Another way to embed a worksheet into a word processed document is to select the worksheet information in its own application window and press **Ctrl+C** to copy the selection to the Clipboard. In your word processing application, choose **Paste Special** from the **Edit** menu. In the **Paste Special** dialog box, click **OK** to create the embedded object.

How to Work with a Linked Document

A *linked document* displays the content of an existing file as part of the document you're currently developing. When you activate the linked object and make changes in its content, Windows updates the source file to reflect the revisions. Conversely, if you edit the original file, the changes are transferred to the linked object in the document you're developing.

Begin

1 Create the File to be Linked

Create the document you plan to use as a linked object. In this example, the document is a worksheet table created in Microsoft Excel. Save the document and close the application.

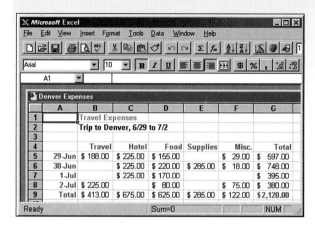

2 Create the Destination Document

Create the document in which you want to insert the linked object. Move the flashing insertion point to the position where you want to place the object.

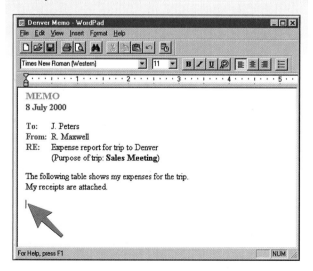

3 Link the Object

Pull down the **Insert** menu and choose the **Object** command. In the **Insert Object** dialog box, select **Create from File**. In the **File** box, type the full name of the file you want to link or click the **Browse** button to search for the target file. (See the How-To Hints for details.) Finally, check the **Link** option and click **OK**.

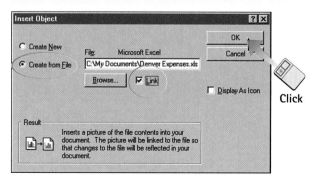

Click

4 Activate the Object

The new worksheet object appears in your word-processed document. Double-click the linked object to activate it.

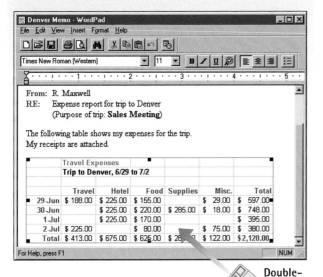

Double-click

5 Revise the Linked Document

A separate application window appears on the desktop to display the linked document. Make any changes you want. Then pull down the **File** menu and choose **Exit** to return to the original document.

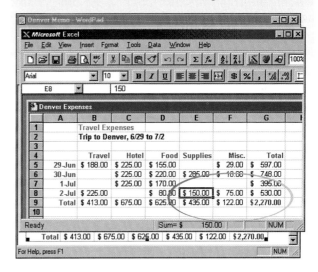

6 Save the Changes

In response to the **Save changes** prompt, click **Yes**. Your revisions are transferred to the linked object in your document, and are also saved to disk in the source file.

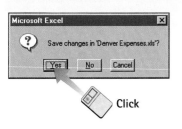

Click

End

How-To Hints

Browsing for a File

In the **Insert Object** dialog box, click the **Browse** button if you're not sure how to identify the file you want to link to your document. Then use the **Browse** dialog box to locate the file. When you've found and selected the file, click the **Insert** button to copy the file's name to the **Insert Object** dialog box.

Changing Properties

You can change several properties of a linked object. To do so, right-click the object and choose **Object Properties**. In the **Properties** dialog box, click the **Link** tab to view the characteristics of the link. The options in this dialog box allow you to change the way the link is updated (automatically or manually), to update the link immediately, or to break the link between the object and its source file.

Task

13

Using the Built-In Windows Applications

*S*tarting from its earliest versions, the Windows package has traditionally included a variety of small but gracefully designed application programs, some of which have become software classics in their own right. No one would claim that these "built-in" programs can compete with the features of the major productivity suites available in today's software market. All the same, programs like WordPad, Paint, and Calculator have their own special charms: They are easy to learn, they make only small demands on your computer's resources, and, within a context of circumscribed ambition, they are practical and completely reliable.

✓ The **Paint** program helps you create artwork that's engaging, educational, or just fun. Everything you need is close at hand: a palette of colors, an array of tools, and an empty canvas called the *drawing area*. All you add is a bit of inspiration.

✓ The **Calculator** gives you the equivalent of a multifunction handheld calculator right on your Windows desktop. You can perform quick calculations and copy the results to other applications using the Clipboard.

✓ **WordPad** is the enduring and familiar word processor that comes with Windows. You can learn much about the features of WordPad in Parts 10, 11, and 12. These parts discuss Windows applications generically, but often use WordPad as an example. By contrast, **Notepad** is a text editor, designed for creating and editing data files, listings, or system files.

✓ **Address Book** supplies email addresses for Outlook Express and is also a standalone application that you can run directly from the **Start** menu.

If any of these programs is currently unavailable on your computer, you can install it by clicking **Add/Remove Programs** in the **Control Panel,** and then selecting the **Windows Setup** tab. See "How to Add Windows Components" in Part 16, "Installing New Hardware and Software," for more information. ●

How to Use Paint

To begin a Paint picture, you select a tool and a color, and then start drawing with the mouse. Some of the tools are for freehand sketching, while others are designed to create specific shapes. You can move art around the drawing area or duplicate any part of your work. You can even add text. If you make a mistake, you can erase selectively or start over again. Note that, when you save a drawing to disk by selecting **File, Save**, Paint saves the file in the *bitmap* format with the extension **BMP**. Whether you're drafting a map, decorating an invitation, or—as in this task—designing a business logo, Paint provides an engaging medium for your creative efforts.

Begin

1 Start the Paint Program

Click **Start** and choose **Programs**, **Accessories**, and **Paint** to start the program. At the left side of the **Paint** window is a box of drawing tools. At the bottom is a box of colors. The empty drawing area takes up most of the rest of the window.

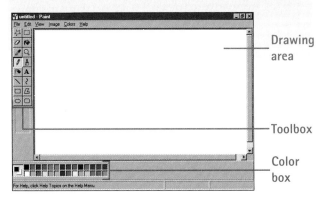

Drawing area

Toolbox

Color box

2 Draw Some Shapes

Select a color and a tool, then drag your mouse to form a shape in the drawing area. To set the *foreground* color, click a selection in the color box; to set the *background*, right-click a color. The options for a selected tool appear beneath the toolbox. Here you see the three *fill styles* for ovals and rectangles: outline only, outline and fill color, or color alone. In this step, draw two ovals and a thin rectangle as shown.

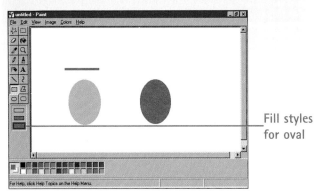

Fill styles for oval

3 Move a Shape

Click the **Select** tool at the upper-right corner of the toolbox. Drag the mouse around the shape you want to move. Then drag the selection to a new place, and click elsewhere to deselect. Try two moves here: First, move the top half of the red oval to a position just above the rectangle, forming a hat. Then select the hat and move it over the top of the gray oval.

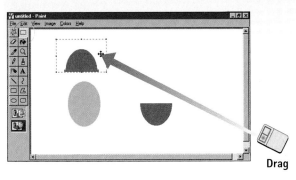

Drag

4 Copy a Shape

Click the **Select** tool and drag a rectangle around the shape you want to copy. Hold down the **Ctrl** key while you move the shape. A *copy* appears in the drawing area. Here, select the gray oval with its red hat; then press **Ctrl** and drag the mouse to create a second copy of the drawing. (Select the lower half of the red oval and press the **Delete** key to erase it.)

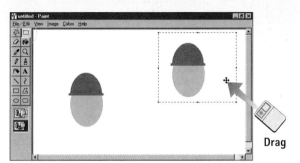

Drag

5 Experiment with Other Shapes

Use the **Polygon** tool to draw multisided shapes. Drag the mouse to draw the first side, then click the mouse at additional corner locations. Double-click to complete the shape. Here, use polygon shapes and a small circle to create a bow tie and a long necktie. Then move the ties below each face drawing.

6 Add Some Text

Use the **Text** tool to incorporate text into a drawing. Click the tool (the **A** button in the toolbox) and drag the mouse to form a text box in the drawing area. Then start typing text. Optionally, use the **Fonts** box to change the font, size, and style. Here, the text identifies the business in the new logo design.

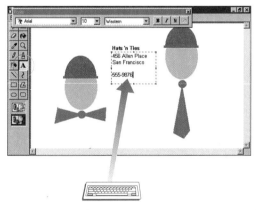

End

How-To Hints

Erasing Details in Your Drawing

To erase part of your drawing, select the **Eraser** tool and drag the mouse over the area you want to erase. If you've set a *background* color other than white (by right-clicking a color), the tool "erases" in the selected color.

Understanding the Select Tool Settings

When you click the **Select** tool, two options appear beneath the toolbox: *opaque* and *transparent*. When you click *opaque* and drag the selection, any existing shapes "beneath" the selection disappear from view. Click *transparent* if you want the existing drawing to remain in view behind the shape you are dragging. (In Step 3, you should use the *transparent* option.)

How to Use Calculator

With the **Calculator** program, you can perform quick arithmetic operations or find the results of complex mathematical functions simply by clicking buttons with the mouse or by entering numeric values and operators from the keyboard. For convenience, the application window appears in two versions. The one you choose depends on the complexity of the calculations you need to perform. A standard 10-key calculator provides the familiar arithmetic operations. A more elaborate scientific calculator has several columns of advanced mathematical functions.

Begin

1 Start the Calculator Program

Start Calculator by clicking the **Start** button, and then choosing **Programs**, **Accessories**, and **Calculator**.

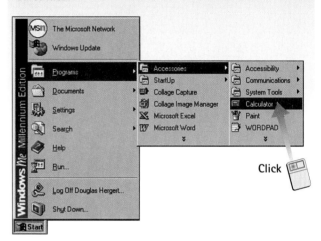

Click

2 Perform an Operation

Try performing an operation, just as you would on a handheld calculator. Click a sequence of digits with the mouse, or type them from the keyboard. Click an operator (**+**, **−**, *****, or **/**), and then enter a second number. Click the **=** button or press **Enter** from the keyboard to calculate the result.

3 Use the Clear Buttons

Try another calculation and experiment with the clear buttons. Click the **Backspace** button or press **Backspace** on the keyboard to erase the last digit you've entered. Click the **CE** (Clear Entry) button or press **Delete** to clear the most recent number you've entered. Click the **C** button or press **Esc** to clear an entire calculation.

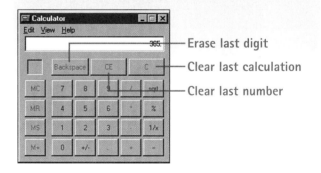

Erase last digit
Clear last calculation
Clear last number

4 Use the Memory Buttons

The memory buttons allow you to store and reuse intermediate results in a multistep calculation. Click **MS** to store the current value in memory. Click **MR** to copy the contents of memory to the display area, where the value can be used in the current calculation. Click **M+** to add the current display value to the number stored in memory. Click **MC** to clear the value from memory.

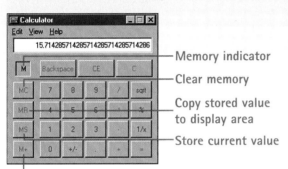

Memory indicator
Clear memory
Copy stored value to display area
Store current value

Add current value to value in memory

5 View the Scientific Calculator

To view the scientific calculator, pull down the **View** menu and choose **Scientific**. The various function keys are arranged on either side of the numbered buttons.

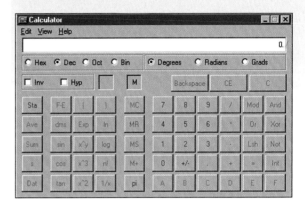

6 Paste a Result to a Document

To copy a displayed value to the Clipboard, pull down the **Edit** menu and choose **Copy** or press **Ctrl+C**. You can then switch to another application and paste the result into a document. Switch back to the Calculator program when you're ready to resume your work there.

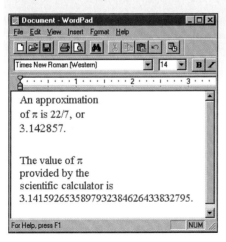

End

How-To Hints

Using the Statistics Box

The scientific calculator has an additional memory device called the **Statistics Box**, in which you can temporarily store a sequence of numeric values. To open this box, click the **Sta** button at the left side of the Calculator window. To copy a number to this box, type or calculate a value in the Calculator's display area, and then click the **Dat** button at the lower-left corner of the Calculator. To perform statistical operations on the values currently in the **Statistics Box**, click the **Sum** key for the total, **Ave** for the average, or **S** for the standard deviation. The result appears in the Calculator's display area.

How to Use WordPad and Notepad

WordPad is designed for producing attractive and readable documents. You can select fonts, styles, and colors; you can format your document; and you can even incorporate content from other applications. Read about these features in Parts 10, 11, and 12 of this book. By contrast, **Notepad** is a *text editor* for viewing, editing, or creating files that consist solely of text. Here the word *text* generally refers to characters you enter from the keyboard. A Notepad file does not contain formatting features that may be typical of a WordPad document.

Begin

1 Start the Notepad Program

To open Notepad, click the **Start** menu and choose **Programs**, **Accessories**, and **NOTEPAD**.

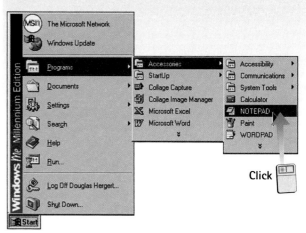

Click

2 Open an Existing Text File

To open an existing text file from disk, pull down the **File** menu and choose **Open**. In the **Open** dialog box, find the folder where the target file is stored, select the name, and click **Open**. Note that text files are usually stored on disk with a **TXT** extension.

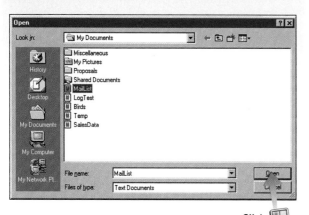

Click

3 Revise the File

The text of the file appears in the work area. You can now revise the text in any way. For example, delete characters by positioning the cursor and pressing **Backspace** for a previous character or **Delete** for the next character. Insert a new line by moving the cursor to the end of an existing line and pressing **Enter**.

4 Save and Print Changes

To save the changes you've made, pull down the **File** menu and choose **Save**. To print a copy of the current file, choose **Print** from the **File** menu.

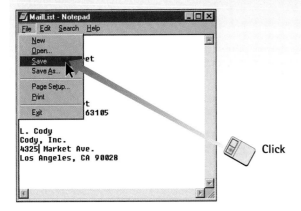

Click

5 Start a New File

To clear the current file from the Notepad window and start a new file, pull down the **File** menu and choose **New**. You can then begin typing new lines of text. Press **Enter** at the end of each line.

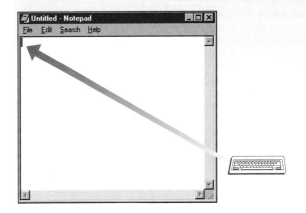

6 Use Word Wrap

If your text file contains long individual lines of text, pull down the **Edit** menu and choose the **Word Wrap** command. Notepad will break the text into smaller lines that you can view within the dimensions of the application window. This option affects the display only. No actual line break is added to the text unless you press the **Enter** key.

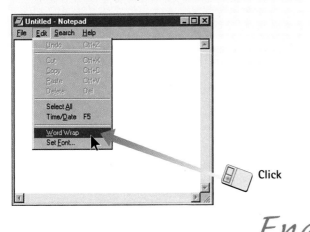

Click

End

How-To Hints

Entering the Time and Date

To enter the current time and date into a text file, pull down the **Edit** menu and choose the **Time/Date** command; alternatively, press **F5**.

Creating a Log File

To create a *log file*, in which the current time and date are automatically entered as a new line of text each time you reopen the file, type **.LOG** (starting with a period) on the first line of the file.

Using the Search Menu

The **Search** menu contains commands that enable you to find specific sequences of text in an open Notepad file. Choose the **Find** command and type the text you want to search for. Then click **Find Next** one or more times to search for all the occurrences of the target text.

TASK 4

How to Use Address Book

Address Book is officially part of the Outlook Express package; in this context, its role is to keep track of email addresses for your online correspondence. To open it, click the **Address Book** button on the Outlook Express toolbar or choose **Address Book** from the **Tools** menu. But Address Book is also available as an independent program you can run directly from the **Start** menu. It can store a great deal more than email addresses. You can use it for all kinds of personal data, including home and business addresses; multiple phone, fax, and pager numbers; job information; and miscellaneous notes.

Begin

1 Open the Address Book

To open the Address Book from the **Start** menu, choose **Start, Programs, Accessories,** and **Address Book.**

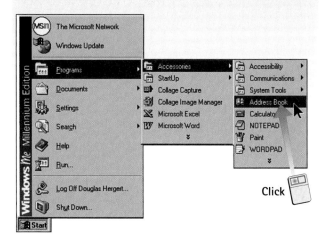

Click

2 Add a New Contact

Click the **New** button on the toolbar and select **New Contact** to add a new entry to the Address Book. In the **Name** tab of the **Properties** box, type the name and email addresses for this entry. You can store multiple email addresses and choose any one of them as the default. (See the How-To Hints for details.)

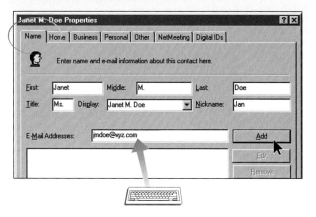

3 Enter a Home Address

Click the **Home** tab and type the person's home address. There is room for three phone numbers, labeled **Phone, Fax,** and **Mobile.** You can also record a personal Web page address on this tab.

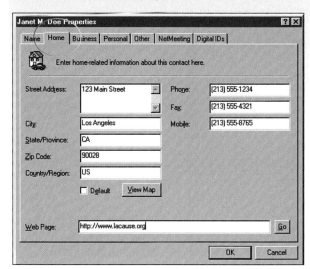

4 Enter Job Information

Click the **Business** tab to enter detailed information about this person's job, business location, title, work phones, and corporate Web page.

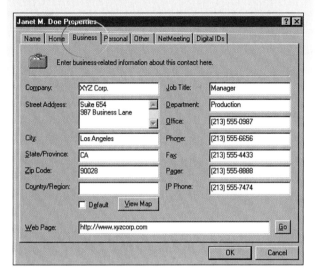

5 Record Any Other Information

Click the **Personal** tab to enter information about the person's family, birthday, and anniversaries. Click **Other** if you want to record other notes, such as food preferences or reminders from recent business meetings. Finally, click **OK** to confirm this new entry and save it in the Address Book.

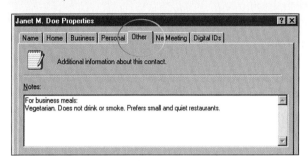

6 View a Person's Data

Back in the main Address Book window, position the mouse pointer over the name of any person to view complete information recorded in that entry. A pop-up box shows all the data.

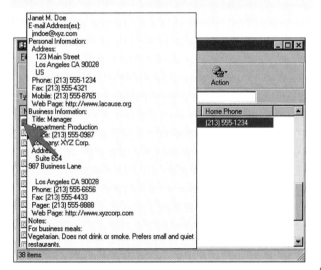

End

How-To Hints

Storing Multiple Email Addresses

To create a list of two or more online addresses for a given person, type each new address in the **E-mail Addresses** text box shown in step 2 and click **Add**. The addresses are listed in the scrollable box below. To set a default address, highlight the address in the list and click the **Set as Default** button.

Printing Your Address Book

You can print selected entries from your Address Book for use when you are away from your computer. Select the entries you want to print and click the **Print** button on the toolbar. In the **Print** dialog box, select a format for the printed output; the style options are **Memo, Business Card**, or **Phone List**. (Select the **All** option to print your entire address book.) Click **OK** to start printing.

Task

14

Experiencing Multimedia in Windows Me

*A*s personal computers have become ever more powerful and sophisticated, multimedia applications—combining video, sounds, photographs, and color images—have become an important part of the computing experience. Windows Millennium Edition provides several important tools designed to enhance your enjoyment of multimedia:

✓ The Windows **Media Player** plays video and sound from local and online sources. You can use the Media Player to watch movie clips, news, and any variety of entertainment features from selected Web sites; you can also use it to load and play video files stored on disk.

✓ **Windows Movie Maker** is a specialized application environment designed for *capturing* and *editing* video content. If you're interested in creating digital movies—to view on your computer or to share with others online—this is a program you'll want to explore.

✓ The **Imaging for Windows** application is a versatile tool for working with images transmitted from scanner devices or digital cameras. The Imaging program collaborates with device-specific software to help you view, edit, annotate, transfer, and save scanned images or photographs.

✓ The new **My Pictures** folder is a convenient place to store, view, and even modify image files on your computer.

As you explore these features in the tasks ahead, you'll find a variety of practical illustrations and examples. ●

How to Use the Media Player

The **Media Player** application presents video and sound on the Windows desktop. Whether the source is a compact disk, a file on your computer, or an online media site, this versatile program is designed to recognize and work with a wide variety of formats and to present you with the clearest video and audio possible on your computer system. When you receive media content from the Internet, the Media Player uses a streaming media technology that allows you to view one part of the video while other parts are still being transmitted.

Begin

1 Start the Media Player

Click the **Start** button, choose **Programs**, **Accessories**, and **Entertainment**, and then click **Windows Media Player**. Alternatively, click the application's icon on the desktop or in the Quick Launch section of the taskbar, if these tools are available. The **Media Player** window appears on the screen.

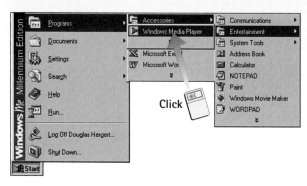

2 Switch Between Full and Compact Mode

The **Media Player** application window has two display formats, known as **Full Mode** and **Compact Mode**. You can use keyboard commands to switch between these two formats: Press **Ctrl+2** to view the **Compact Mode**; press **Ctrl+1** to return to the **Full Mode**, as shown here.

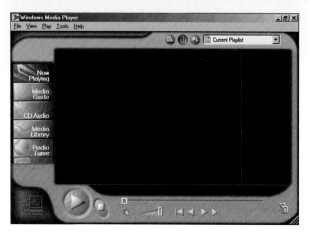

3 Play a Music CD

Click the **CD Audio** button in the vertically arranged taskbar at the left side of the application window. Then insert a music disk in your CD-ROM drive. **Media Player** automatically starts playing the music recorded on the disk and displays a list of tracks and play lengths.

Click

4 Open a Video File

To view a video, begin by opening its file from disk. In the **Full Mode**, pull down the **File** menu and choose **Open**. Navigate to the folder where the video file is stored, select the name of the file, and click **Open**. In this example, the selected file is a sample video from the Windows disk.

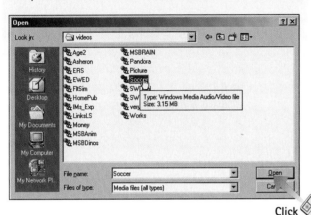

Click

5 Watch the Video

After a few seconds, the video content begins appearing in the **Media Player** window. You can use commands in the **Play** menu or the controls arranged along the lower portion of the application window to stop or pause the video or to change the volume level of the accompanying sound.

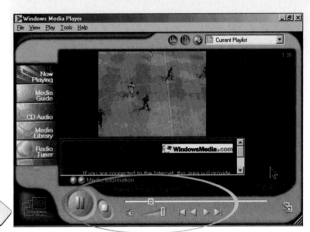

6 Go to the Media Guide

To visit the Microsoft Media Guide site on the Internet (**WindowsMedia.Com**), click the **Media Guide** button in the vertical task bar. Sign on to the Web in your usual way. When the Media Guide appears, explore its content and make a selection from the list of categories (for example, **Movies**, **Art**, or **News**). You'll find a variety of video clips that can be viewed in the Media Player.

 Click

How-To Hints

Changing the Media Player Skin

In the **Compact Mode**, Media Player can appear on your desktop in any of several dramatically distinct graphic designs, known as *skins*. To view the available skins and to choose the one you want to use, click the **Skin Chooser** button in the Full Mode's vertical task bar. (Alternatively, pull down the **View** menu, choose **Task Bar**, and then click **Skin Chooser**.) You'll see a list of skins and a preview box where you can view an image of any skin you select. To switch to a new skin, click the **Apply Skin** option. To return to the standard **Full Mode**, press **Ctrl+1**.

Changing the Media Player Settings

To make adjustments in the appearance and function of the Media Player, pull down the **View** menu and choose **Options**.

End

How to Use Windows Movie Maker

In Windows Movie Maker, you combine collections of video and audio content to produce a digital movie file. You begin by *capturing*, or transferring, video and audio material from installed recording devices or from existing media files on disk. When you do so, the Movie Maker divides the material into *clips*, convenient lengths of content that can serve as the building blocks of a movie. In the *workspace*, you combine selected clips and arrange and edit them to suit your movie plan. Finally, you can show the finished product on your desktop in Windows Media Player, or you can share the movie over the Internet.

Begin

1 Start Windows Movie Maker

Click the **Start** button, then choose **Programs**, **Accessories**, and **Windows Movie Maker**. At the left side of the Movie Maker window is the *collections area*, where captured videos and their clips are listed. At the right is the *monitor*, where you can preview a movie project in progress. At the bottom (out of view in the figures of this task) is the *workspace*, where you arrange and edit the clips of your movie project.

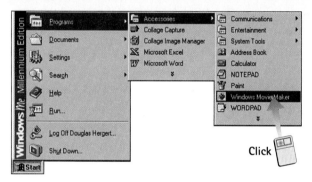

Click

2 Record from a Video Device

To capture a new video or audio sequence from a recording device that's attached to your computer, pull down the **File** menu and choose **Record**. In the resulting **Record** dialog box, select the device and the relevant settings. Then click the **Record** button.

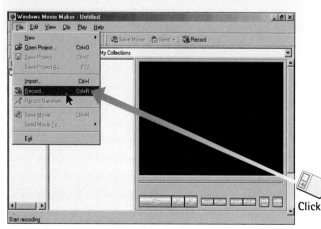

Click

3 Import a Video File

To capture a video or audio sequence from an existing file on disk, pull down the **File** menu and choose **Import**. Navigate to the target disk and folder and select the media file you want to capture. Then click **Open**.

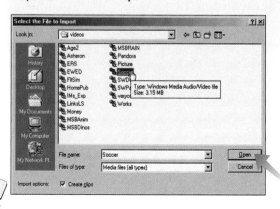

Click

4 Wait for Clips to Be Created

By default, the Movie Maker program divides an imported video file into *clips*, distinct sections or events in the video content. In some files, clip markers may be part of the media file itself; otherwise, Movie Maker starts a clip whenever a new video frame appears in the content. Wait for the program to complete clip detection in the file you're currently capturing.

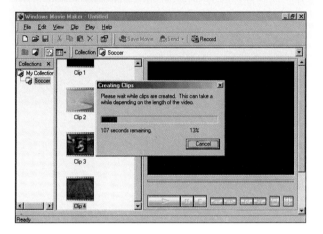

5 Try Playing a Clip

The clips are represented as a scrollable list of images at the right side of the collections area. To preview a clip, click its image in the list. Then pull down the **Play** menu and choose **Play/Pause**, or click the **Play** button located below the monitor.

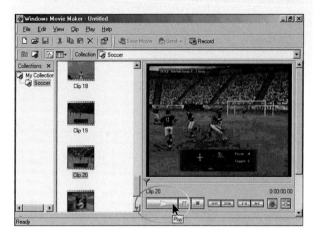

6 Step Frame-by-Frame Through a Clip

To step frame-by-frame through the currently selected clip, click the **Previous Frame** or **Next Frame** button located below the monitor (or choose **Previous Frame** or **Next Frame** from the **Play** menu).

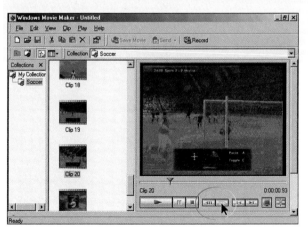

End

How-To Hints

Understanding Collections

A *collection* is a container for video or audio clips. When you capture material from a video camera or other device—or when you import material from an existing media file—the Movie Maker lists the content as a new collection. Click the name of any collection to view the clips it contains. To create a movie, you combine clips from any number of collections you have added to your collections area.

Getting Help with Movie Maker

Movie Maker comes with excellent help material. Choose **Help Topics** from the **Help** menu to read much more about the program. You can also choose **Tour** for a complete introduction to the application.

How to Create a Movie Project

After you've used Windows **Movie Maker** to capture collections of video and audio material, you can begin building a movie project by selecting and combining clips from your collections. The horizontal workspace at the bottom of the Movie Maker window shows the clips you've selected for your movie. The workspace has two views: the **storyboard** shows the sequence of clips, and the **timeline** shows their duration and timing. In the workspace, you can easily rearrange and edit the clips to produce your movie project. Preview your project at any time by playing it in the monitor.

Begin

1 Capture Collections of Videos

Using the **Import** or **Record** command in the **File** menu, capture the video and audio materials you want to include in your movie project. (See the previous task for details.)

Click

2 Add Clips to Your Project

Click a collection and then click the clip you want to add to your project. Pull down the **Clip** menu and choose **Add to Storyboard/Timeline** to copy the clip to the workspace. Repeat this step for each new clip you want to add. Select **Storyboard** or **Timeline** from the **View** menu to change the view of your clips in the workspace.

Click

3 Arrange and Edit the Clips

To rearrange the order of clips, drag any clip to a new position in the workspace. To reduce the length of a clip, select the clip in the storyboard and click **Play** to begin playing the clip. Select **Set Start Trim Point** and then **Set End Trim Point** from the **Clip** menu to mark the beginning and end of the reduced clip length.

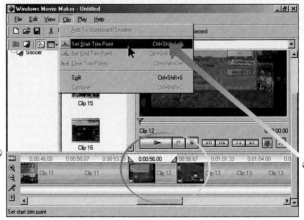

Click

4 Add an Audio Narration

Pull down the **File** menu and choose **Record Narration**. In the resulting dialog box, click **Record** to begin recording a narration track for your movie project. Click **Stop** when the recording is complete. Save the recording as a file on disk. The new sound track is represented in the workspace, just below the sequence of video clips.

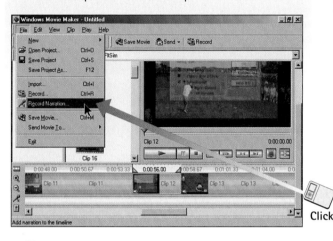

Click

5 Try Playing the Project

To preview the movie project you are developing, click in a gray area of the workspace (to deselect any single clip in the project); then choose **Play/Pause** from the **Play** menu.

 Click

6 Save the Project as a Movie

Continue adding, editing, and arranging clips until the project plays just the way you want it to play. Then pull down the **File** menu and choose **Save Movie**. Select a **Setting** option in the **Save Movie** dialog box, and fill in the fields of the **Display information** section. Then click **OK**. In the **Save As** box, supply a name for the movie file and click **Save**.

 Click

How-To Hints

Changing the Transition Between Clips

You can create a *cross-fade* transition between two clips in your movie project. In the timeline view of the workspace, select a clip and drag it into the length of the clip just to the left. The overlap between the two clips represents the transition. During the transition time, the frames of one clip fade out while the frames of the other fade in.

Playing the Finished Movie

When you choose the **Save Movie** command, Movie Maker creates a file that you can subsequently view in Windows Media Player. Alternatively, you can send the movie file as an attachment to an email message or publish the file on the Web.

End

How to Use Digital Cameras with Windows

With a digital camera attached to your computer, you can view, modify, and print photographs, merge digital pictures into text documents, and transmit photos to others using email. Many digital cameras are available on the market today; but regardless of the camera you use, the **Imaging for Windows** application provides a consistent environment for working with your digital photos. The **Imaging** program collaborates with your camera's software to acquire photos and make them available on the screen. Then you can save the photos to disk, where they'll be available for other applications.

Begin

1 Start the Imaging Program

Click the **Start** menu, choose **Programs** and **Accessories,** and then click **Imaging.** The **Imaging** application window appears on the desktop.

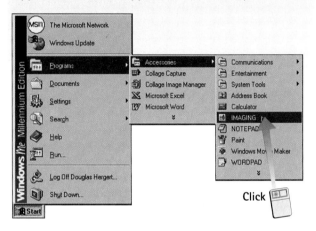

Click

2 Select an Image Source

If more than one imaging device is connected to your computer, you must identify the source for the images you want to work with. Pull down the **File** menu and click the **Select Scanner** command. In the resulting dialog box, select the name of the camera you've installed and connected to your system. Click **OK.**

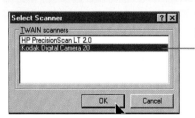

Select the camera from which the image file will come

3 Acquire the Photographs

Pull down the **File** menu again and choose **Scan New.** In response, Imaging launches the software designed to acquire photos from your camera. (This software is stored on your computer at the time you install the camera itself, and is designed specifically to work with your camera.)

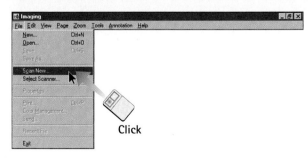

Click

4 Send the Photos to Imaging

Use the camera software to load the photographs, select the ones you want to work with in the Imaging program, and give the command to begin the transfer. In this figure, a set of photos has been selected for transfer to the Imaging program.

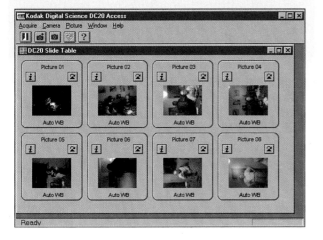

5 View the Photos

When the selected pictures have been sent to Imaging for Windows, pull down the **View** menu and choose **One Page** to see one photo at a time, choose **Thumbnails** to view photos in rows of reduced images, or choose **Page and Thumbnails** to see a column of thumbnail images at the left and a single enlarged photo on the right, as shown here. These options are also available as buttons on the toolbar.

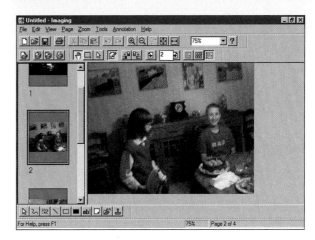

6 Save the Photos to Disk

If you want to save your photographs to disk, pull down the **File** menu and choose **Save As**. In the **Save As** dialog box, type a name for the file. Note that the default file type is **TIFF Document**, a format that saves the entire collection of photographs in a single file. Click **Save** to complete the operation.

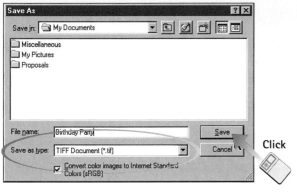

Click

End

How-To Hints

Rotating Images

If the vertical or horizontal orientation is incorrect for the current photograph, pull down the **Page** menu, choose **Rotate Page**, and then select a direction. Alternatively, click the **Rotate Right** or **Rotate Left** button on the **Imaging** toolbar.

Zooming Images

To change the view size of the current photograph, pull down the **Zoom** menu and choose any one of the options presented. You can increase or decrease the size to a percentage of the actual, or you can select one of the "best fit" options.

How to Use a Scanner with Windows

A *scanner* produces a digital image of a paper document. The document itself can contain any kind of content, including color graphics, photographs, text, or any combination of these. The scanner quickly transmits an image to your computer, where you can make changes in the graphics, select a portion for copying, add the image to a word-processed document, or send it out in an email message. The **Imaging for Windows** application is a versatile tool for editing scanned images and saving them to disk.

Begin

1 Start Imaging and Select a Scanner

Click the **Start** button and then choose **Programs, Accessories**, and **Imaging**, as shown in the previous task. When the **Imaging** window appears on your desktop, start your work by pulling down the **File** menu and choosing **Select Scanner**. Highlight the name of the scanning device you want to use and click **OK**.

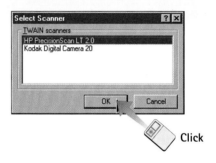

Click

2 Start the Scanning Software

Pull down the **File** menu again and choose **Scan New**. In response, the Imaging program launches the scanning software that works with your scanner. (This software is stored on your computer at the time you install the scanner itself, and is designed specifically to work with your scanning hardware.)

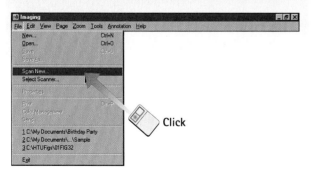

Click

3 Scan the Image

Insert a document in your scanner and use the scanning software to start the scan. The amount of time required to complete the scan depends on the hardware itself. When the process is complete, the image appears in the application window.

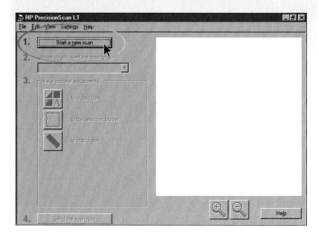

4 Send the Scan to the Imaging Program

Choose the command (or click the button) that sends the new scan to the Imaging application. You might have to wait a few seconds for this transfer to be accomplished. When it is complete, the scanned document appears in the Imaging window.

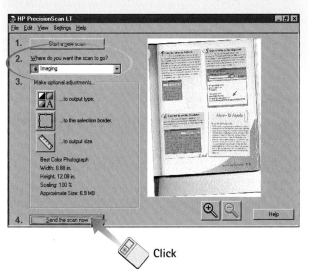

Click

5 Choose a Zoom Level

Pull down the **Zoom** menu and choose a viewing option. You might want to experiment with different Zoom levels to see which one best suits your work with this image.

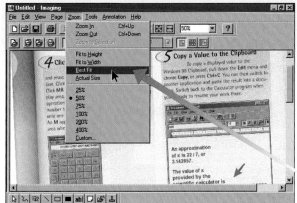

Click

6 Save the Scanned Image

Pull down the **File** menu and choose **Save As**. Type a name for the new file and choose a file type. Then click **Save**.

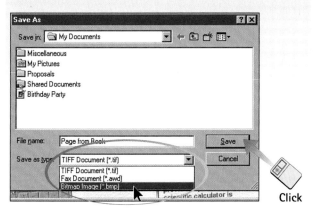

Click

End

How-To Hints

Adding Pages to the Document

An Imaging for Windows file saved in the **TIFF** format can consist of multiple images from sources such as a scanner, a digital camera, or individual image files already stored on disk. Each image is a page in the **TIFF** document. Pull down the **Page** menu and choose **Insert** to add a page at the current position in the document; choose **Append** to add a page to the end of the document. From the **Insert** or **Append** submenu, choose **Scan Page** if you want to perform another scan to produce the content of the new page; choose **Existing Page** if you want to open an image file on disk as the new page.

Scanning Text Documents

Your scanner software can include the capability to convert a scanned text image into editable text. This conversion process is sometimes known as *optical character recognition*, or OCR. Send the text to your word processing application (WordPad, for example), and not to the Imaging for Windows program.

How to Work with Images

Whether you're working with a photograph, a scanned image, or a graphics file from disk, the **Imaging for Windows** program provides tools for editing and enhancing the content. You can select a portion of the image for copy-and-paste operations. Using this procedure, you can create a new Imaging document that contains a pasted selection of an existing image. You can also annotate the image in a number of interesting ways. For example, in the task ahead you use the **Attach-a-Note** tool to produce a text annotation for a scanned image.

Begin

1 Open an Image

Start the **Imaging for Windows** program as in the previous two tasks. In the application window, pull down the **File** menu and choose **Open**. Select the Imaging file you want to work with and click **Open**. The image appears in the application window. Scroll through the image to locate the portion you want to work with.

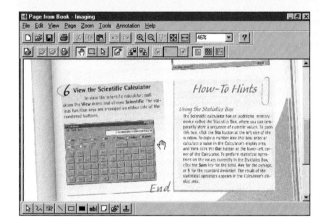

2 Copy a Selection

Pull down the **Edit** menu and choose **Select Image**, or click the **Select Image** button on the Imaging toolbar. Move the mouse pointer into the work area and drag around the area you want to select. A dotted rectangular border appears around your selection. To copy this selection to the Windows Clipboard, pull down the **Edit** menu and choose **Copy** or press **Ctrl+C** at the keyboard.

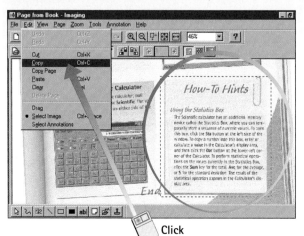

Click

3 Open a New Image Document

Pull down the **File** menu and choose **New**, or click the **New** button on the standard toolbar. In the **New Blank Document** dialog box, select a file type and click **OK**. Select the **TIFF** format to create a multipage graphic document; select **Bitmap Image** to create a single graphic file. See the How-To Hints for more information.

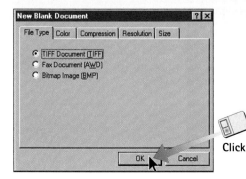

Click

4 Paste the Selection

In the new blank document, pull down the **Edit** menu and choose **Paste**, or press **Ctrl+V** at the keyboard. A copy of your image selection appears in the work area. You can drag the image to any position you like within the page. Click any blank position in the work area to deselect the image.

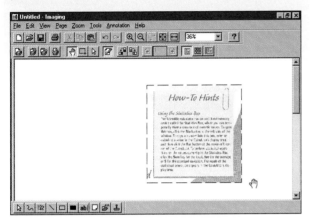

5 Attach an Annotation Note

From the **Annotation** menu, choose **Attach-a-Note** or click the **Attach-a-Note** tool in the **Annotation** toolbar, located at the bottom of the application window. Inside the work areas, drag the mouse pointer to define the rectangular area where you want to display an attached note. Release the mouse button, and a yellow note sheet appears in the work area.

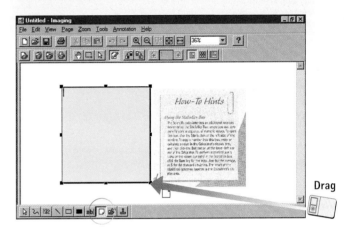

Drag

6 Type Text into the Note

Inside the attached note, you can now type a block of text that explains or otherwise annotates the image. When you're finished, save the file and its annotation.

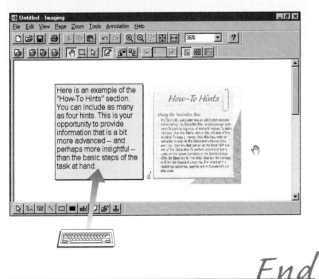

End

How-To Hints

Changing Attach-a-Note Properties

The **Attach-a-Note** tool has a default background color and font properties for the text you type into the note. If you want to change these properties, right-click the **Attach-a-Note** tool in the **Annotation** toolbar. In the **Attach-a-Note Properties** window, you can select a new background color or click **Font** to change the text properties.

Saving Annotated Documents

If you store an annotated document in the TIFF format, annotations are saved as an overlay that can later be edited or removed. (You can change this status by choosing **Make Annotations Permanent** from the **Annotations** menu.) By contrast, annotations become a permanent part of the image when you save a document in one of the other file formats: BMP or AWD.

How to Use the My Pictures Folder

The My Pictures folder is a convenient new Windows Me location, designed to provide easy access to all kinds of image files, including photographs, drawings, and other graphics. To use the tools it provides, simply save any new image files in the My Pictures folder, or copy existing files to the folder from elsewhere on your system. Then open the folder to preview, modify, or print any file you select. You can even view a *slide show* of all the image files currently stored in the folder.

Begin

1 Open the My Pictures Folder

Click the **Start** button and choose **Documents**. Then click **My Pictures**. The My Pictures folder opens onto the desktop.

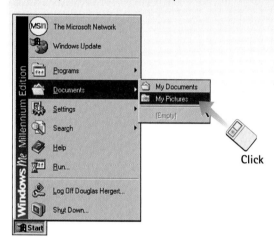

Click

2 View Thumbnail Images

As in other Windows Me folders, you can view file collections as icons, lists, or thumbnail previews. If you don't initially see thumbnails in the My Pictures folder, pull down the **View** menu and choose the **Thumbnails** option.

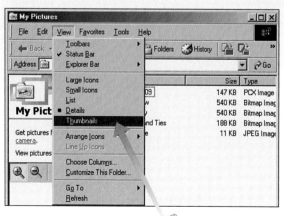

 Click

3 Select an Image for Previewing

Position the mouse pointer over an image you want to focus on. The image appears in the preview area at the lower-left corner of the folder window.

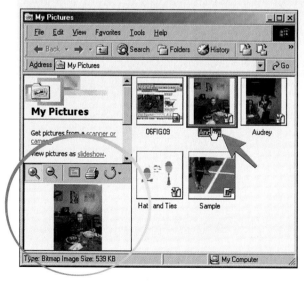

4 Use the Preview Tools

Use the icons in the preview toolbar to modify or print the current image: Click **Zoom in** or **Zoom out** and then click inside the image to change the viewing size. Click **Print** to print a copy of the image. Click **Rotate** and then select a rotation direction to change the orientation of the image.

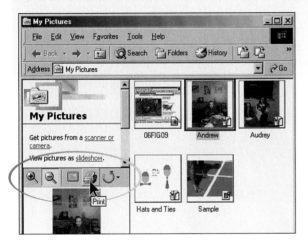

5 Open an Image in the Preview Window

Click the **Image Preview** button in the toolbar to open the current image in an image window of its own. This new window's toolbar provides zooming, sizing, printing, and rotating functions. Close the window by clicking the × in the upper-right corner of the title bar.

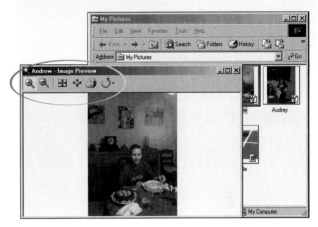

6 Start a Slide Show

Back in the **My Pictures** folder, click the **Slideshow** link to start a full-screen slideshow of all the images currently stored in the folder. Use the icons in the slideshow toolbar to start or pause the sequence, to jump forward or backward among the images, or to close the slideshow and return to the **My Pictures** folder.

Click

How-To Hints

Creating a New Image File

The **scanner or camera** option in the **My Pictures** folder is a one-click link to the image-capturing software associated with any camera or scanner device installed on your computer.

Viewing Picture Files in Other Folders

Although the **My Pictures** folder has a number of unique features, other folder windows may provide different ways to view image files in Windows Me. Typically, any folder window provides a thumbnail image of the currently selected image file. In addition, you can click the icon for an image file to open the picture in a special previewing version of the Imaging for Windows application.

End

Task

Playing Games in Windows Me

*A*fter a stretch of serious computer activity, a game program provides a calming and salutary break from your work. Play a couple of hands of cards or solve a challenging puzzle on your computer screen; you'll return to your work with a fresh point of view and an alert mind.

Windows Me offers a collection of familiar game programs along with some very new approaches to gaming. Among the classic amusements, you'll find the ever-popular **Solitaire**, a fast-moving version of everyone's favorite one-person card game. The computer shuffles and deals the cards for you and sets up the playing table. You move quickly through the game by dragging and clicking your cards with the mouse. Other one-person card games include **FreeCell** and **Spider Solitaire**. In contrast, **Minesweeper** is an entertaining test of logical skills and deductive powers.

But if solitary programs are not your style, you can now play online with people who share your enthusiasm for a particular game, and whose skills match your own. You can choose from a variety of entertainments, such as **Checkers**, **Backgammon**, **Hearts**, and other games that may require two or more players. There are two ways to play online. The simpler way is to click the **Start** button and choose an Internet game from the **Games** menu. The selected program signs you on to the Web and searches the **Microsoft Gaming Zone** for another person who wants to play the same game and whose skill level is the same as yours. When a match is found, you can start playing. Alternatively, you can sign on to the Internet yourself and to go directly to the Gaming Zone (**www.zone.com**), where you'll find a large selection of games and many participating players.

You'll explore all these approaches to gaming in the tasks ahead. In addition, if you are an *action* game enthusiast, Windows Millennium Edition makes it easier than ever before to install and use game hardware devices such as joy sticks, game pads, and other controllers. You'll learn about this topic in Task 4. ●

How to Select a Game

When you click **Start** and make your way to the **Games** menu, you'll find the games that are included in the Windows Millennium package. Each game comes with a set of explanations, rules, and tips, which you can read by choosing **Help Topics** from the **Help** menu in the game window itself. If any games are missing on your computer, install them by using the **Add/Remove Programs** utility in the Control Panel. (See "How to Add Windows Components" in Part 16, "Installing New Hardware and Software," for details.)

Begin

1 Choose an Item from the Games Menu

To launch a game, click the **Start** button and choose **Programs** and **Games**. Then click the name of the game program you want to try.

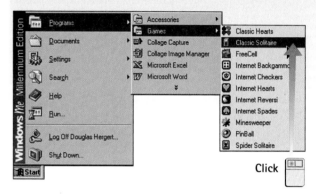

Click

2 Try Solitaire

The **Solitaire** program deals seven *row stacks* across the playing area, leaving the remainder of the deck face down at the upper-left corner. To win the game, you'll attempt to build suit stacks in the four spaces at the upper-right corner. A *suit stack* is a sequence of cards in a given suit, arranged in ascending order from ace to king. The object of the game is to move all 52 cards to their respective suit stacks.

Row stacks   Suit stacks

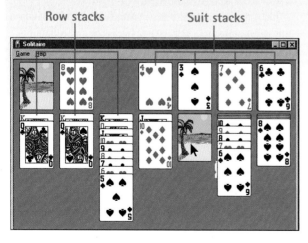

3 Try FreeCell

Your goal in **FreeCell** is to move all 52 cards, in ordered suits, to the *home cells* in the upper-right corner of the playing area. Along the way, you can make use of *free cells*, located in the upper-left corner, as intermediate placeholders for cards that cannot yet be moved to their correct positions in the home cells.

Free cell   Home cells

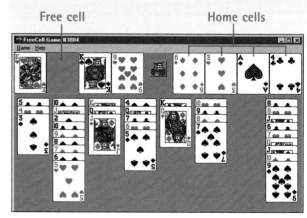

4 Play Pinball

In **3D Pinball for Windows**, the game controls for the plunger and the flippers are represented by keys on your keyboard. Press **F8** to view or change the current controls. Press **F2** to begin a game; choose **Launch Ball** from the **Game** menu to start the action.

5 Try Spider

Spider is a solitaire game that uses two decks of cards. The program begins by dealing 10 stacks of cards across the play area, each with one card face up. Five additional stacks of cards, shown at the lower-right corner, remain to be dealt. You must attempt to rearrange the 10 stacks in suit order, king to ace. Each time you complete a suit, the entire stack of cards is moved away, leaving you more room to work with. Click **Deal!** to receive the next row of cards.

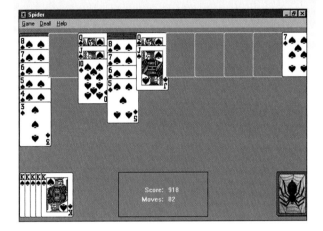

6 Play Minesweeper

In **Minesweeper**, the game window is a field containing mines you have to identify and mark within a limited length of time. When you click a given square in the field, you may uncover a number that tells you how many mines exist in the surrounding squares. If you uncover a mine, you lose. You win by successfully uncovering all the squares that do not contain mines and marking all those that do.

How-To Hints

Choosing Options for Play

All these games offer options that change the rules or appearance of the game. For example, in Solitaire, you can choose among different scoring systems and card-draw options. You can also change the picture or design shown on the backs of the cards. In Minesweeper and Spider, you can select different levels of difficulty. In FreeCell, you can choose a specific game (that is, a deal of the cards) by number, in case you want to try the same game more than once. You can also keep track of your wins and losses in most of these games.

End

How to Play Internet Games

The Windows Me **Games** menu offers a list of Internet games—including Backgammon, Checkers, Hearts, Reversi, and Spades—that you can play online with appropriately matched opponents. When you choose one of these games, the program signs you on to the Web and searches the **MSN Gaming Zone** for one or more other players who are waiting to play. A game of Hearts or Spades requires a total of four players; the other games require only two. When an opponent matching your level of expertise is available,—you are linked together and the game begins. During the game, you can communicate with your opponent (politely, please) by exchanging chat messages.

Begin

1 Choose a Game

Click the **Start** menu and choose **Programs** and **Games**. Then click the name of an Internet game from the **Games** menu. In the resulting **MSN Gaming Zone** window, click **Play** to connect to the Internet. Depending on how you've set up your browser, you may have to type your name and password and click **Connect** to go online.

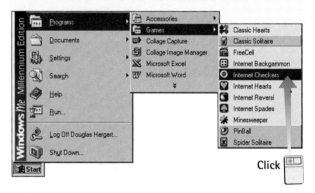

Click

2 Wait for an Opponent

The game server begins searching for another player. The length of the search depends on the number of players who happen to be waiting when you sign on, and may vary according to the time of day and the day of the week. (If you get tired of waiting, click **Quit**. Alternatively, you can use the wait time to review the rules of the game; click **Help** to open the **Help** window.)

3 Begin the Game

When the game server finds an appropriately matched opponent, a game window appears on your desktop, and you can begin playing. In the example of Checkers, you and your opponent take turns moving your red or white pieces up or down the game board.

4 Chat with Your Opponent

Optionally, you and your opponent can chat with each other during the game. If you want to chat, select the **on** option in the **Chat** box. Your opponent will be notified and may also select the **on** option. If both players agree, you can enter a chat message into the text box at the bottom of the game window and click **Send** to begin a conversation.

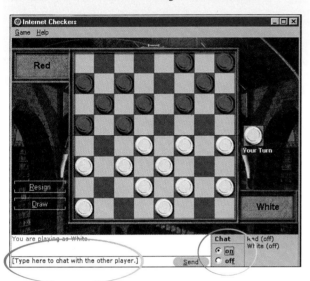

5 Interrupt the Game

At any point, you can interrupt the current game and search for a new opponent. To do so, pull down the **Game** menu and choose **Find New Opponent**. Optionally, change your own skill level before you search for a new opponent. Click the **Skill Level** command and choose a new setting.

 Click

6 Finishing the Game

The current game ends when one of the players is declared the winner. At this point, you are offered the opportunity to play another game with the same opponent. If you both agree, a new game begins.

End

How-To Hints

Using Chat Abbreviations

Experienced online chat enthusiasts tend to use and recognize a list of abbreviations that reduce the amount of typing in messages. For example, **ASL?** is a request for personal information about an opponent—age, gender, and location. You can find a selection of chat abbreviations in the **Help** window.

Avoiding Personal Information

Game opponents are not automatically identified to each other. The only information another player will know about you is what you supply in the Chat window. If you want to maintain privacy, avoid giving out your name, email address, location, or other identifying information.

How to Sign On to the Gaming Zone

The Internet options in the **Games** menu give you the opportunity to play a variety of games online against individual opponents. When you start one of these games, you are matched automatically with another player who is waiting online to play the game you've selected. A different way to play games on the Web is to go directly to Microsoft's Gaming Zone site and make your own choices from a large selection of available games, game-room levels, and individual players. The first time you visit this site, you go through a brief signup process to establish a personal zone name and password. Then you can play online whenever you want.

Begin

1 Visit the Gaming Zone Site

Start your browser, sign on to the Web, and go directly to the Microsoft Gaming Zone site at **www.zone.com**. When you see the site's home page, click the **Free Signup** link to set up your membership in the Gaming Zone.

2 Complete the Signup Process

Follow the instructions that appear in your browser window to sign up for the Gaming Zone. You must make up a name that identifies you as a member of the Gaming Zone, and a password that you'll supply each time you want to visit. There will be a brief download of Gaming Zone software to your computer. When you complete these one-time-only steps, you'll see a **Welcome** page.

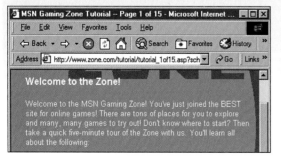

3 Select a Game

When you're ready to play, go back to the Zone's home page and scroll down to the list of available games. Click the name of the game you want to play.

4 Give Your Name and Password

A **Sign In** window appears next. Supply the zone name and password you established for yourself in Step 2 and then click **OK** to enter the Zone. You'll see a list of game rooms available for the game you've selected. Rooms are generally arranged by levels of expertise. Click a room that is appropriate for your skill level in the game.

5 Choose a Game Table

After you enter the game room, you can scroll through the various tables in the room. If you want to play, click an empty chair. If you just want to look over the shoulders of existing players, click an existing player at any table.

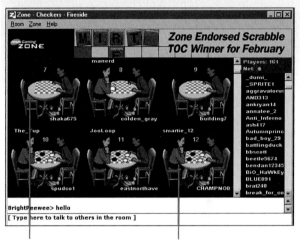

Click to play   Click to observe a game

6 Watch or Play the Game

Regardless of whether you're playing or watching, you'll see the game board for the table you've chosen. Now you're ready to play or to observe a game in action.

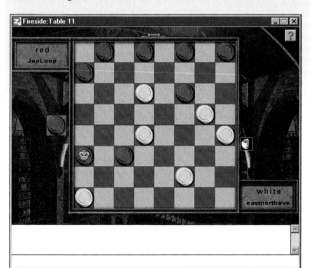

End

How-To Hints

Using the Gaming Zone Programs

After you complete the initial signup process for the Gaming Zone, you'll find a new folder of **MSN Gaming Zone** programs in your **Start** menu. (Click **Start** and choose **Programs** to find the **MSN Gaming Zone** menu.) The first option in this menu is simply a link to the Gaming Zone itself. The second opens the **ZoneFriends** window, which you can use to create a list of friends within the Zone. You can also use this window to set up your own preferences for participating in the Zone and to establish a level of privacy.

Chatting and Sending Messages

While you're in the Zone, you can chat with other players or send messages to individual players. To do so, double-click a member's name and select options in the resulting **ZoneMessage** box.

How to Set the Properties of a Game Controller

Action games represent yet another category of entertainment software. You can purchase any number of increasingly sophisticated fast-action game programs to install on your computer. You'll probably also want to buy a special-purpose *game controller* to attach to your computer, for use with these games. These devices generally include their own installation software, which you'll run at the time you first attach the controller to your computer. Alternatively, the **Gaming Options** utility in the Windows **Control Panel** provides tools you can use to adjust the properties of a game device.

Begin

1 Open the Control Panel

Click the **Start** button, choose **Settings**, and then click **Control Panel**. In the **Control Panel** window you'll find an assortment of icons you use to set options and properties on your computer.

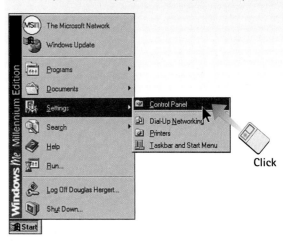

Click

2 Open the Game Options Window

Scroll through the **Control Panel** window and look for the **Gaming Options** icon. Click the icon to open the properties window for game devices.

Click

3 Add a Game Controller Device

In the **Controllers** tab, you'll find a list of any game controllers that are already installed on your computer. Click **Add** to include a new item in the list.

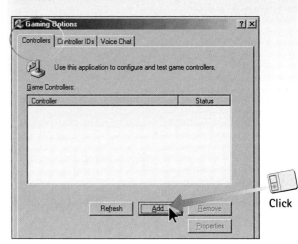

Click

4 Select a Device

In the **Add Game Controller** box, scroll through the list of known game devices and select the one you want to add to your list of installed game hardware. Click **OK**.

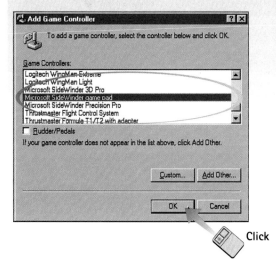

Click

5 Test the Device and Set Properties

Back in the **Game Controllers** list, select the name of the device you want to test or adjust and click the **Properties** button. The resulting **Properties** box shows a variety of testing, diagnostic, and property-setting tools, depending on the device you've selected. In this example, the **Test** tab allows you to try out the various buttons and controls on a device. Click **OK** when you've confirmed that the device is working appropriately.

Click

End

How-To Hints

Using Plug-and-Play Devices

Some game controllers are designed as *plug-and-play* devices. This means that Windows will detect the device as soon as you attach it to your computer and will automatically install the necessary driver software. Other devices require specific installation steps, which are outlined in the instructions you receive in the device package. The **Gaming Options** dialog box is always available for changing the properties of devices you've already installed.

Identifying the Game Port

Before you purchase a particular device, take a close look at the back of your computer and make sure that you have an appropriate and available port to which the device can attach correctly. You should examine the device itself and learn to recognize the way it will plug into your computer.

Task

Installing New Hardware and Software

*A*s your computing needs change over time, you might find yourself acquiring new hardware and software for your personal computer. Thanks to Windows Me, expanding your system has never been easier. No matter what you decide to add—a new pointing device, an additional disk drive, a digital camera, a scanner, the latest spreadsheet program, this year's tax software, or a video game for the kids—Windows ensures a simple and reliable installation process.

In the tasks ahead, you'll focus on two sets of tools, both located in the Control Panel. The **Add New Hardware Wizard** helps you complete the installation of the most common types of hardware you're likely to add to your computer; the **Add/Remove Programs** tool guides you through the steps of installing new applications or adding uninstalled Windows components to the desktop. You can use this same utility to *un*install software that you don't use any longer, thereby liberating disk space for other uses. Finally, you'll learn to create a special startup disk, designed to help you recover gracefully from system failure should anything ever go wrong with your installation of Windows Millennium Edition. ●

How to Use the Add New Hardware Wizard

When you add a new piece of hardware to your computer system, you'll want to make sure that Windows recognizes the new device and uses it successfully. The **Add New Hardware Wizard** will help you complete the installation process. If your new hardware package includes a *driver* disk, keep the disk handy as you begin these steps.

Begin

1 Open the Control Panel

Click the **Start** button and choose **Settings** and then **Control Panel**.

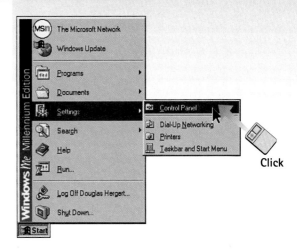

Click

2 Click the Add New Hardware Icon

Click the **Add New Hardware** icon in the **Control Panel** window to open the **Add New Hardware Wizard**. (If your Control Panel is currently displaying only the commonly used options, you'll have to click **View all Control Panel options** to find the **Add New Hardware** icon.)

Click

3 Start the Wizard

The first wizard window appears. If any other programs are currently running on the desktop, close them now before continuing. Click **Next** to begin installing your new hardware.

Click

4 Search for the Hardware

The next window refers to *Plug-and-Play* devices, a category of hardware that Windows recognizes and installs without special instructions from you. When you click the **Next** button on the window shown here, Windows searches for such devices and presents a list of any that are discovered. If the list does not include the device you are currently trying to install, select the **No** option and click **Next** again.

 Click

5 Select the Hardware Category

The next window gives you the option of letting Windows continue the search for your new hardware. If you prefer to identify the hardware yourself, select **No** and click **Next**. A list of hardware categories appears in the next window. Scroll through the list and select the type of hardware you want to install, and then click **Next**.

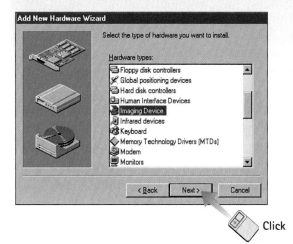

Click

6 Select the Make and Model

The next window lists manufacturers and hardware models. Make selections from both lists. If you have a disk containing the driver for the hardware, click **Have Disk**; if not, click **Next** and be prepared to insert your original Windows disk to complete the installation. The wizard guides you through any remaining steps.

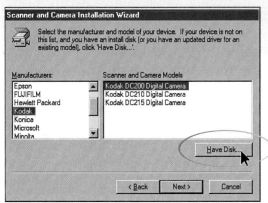

How-To Hints

Installing a Printer

If the new device is a printer, click the **Start** button, choose **Settings**, and then choose **Printers**. In the **Printers** window, click the **Add Printer** icon. See "How to Install a Printer" in Part 11, "Printing," for more information.

Changing Modem Properties

To change the properties of an installed modem, click the **Modems** icon in the **Control Panel**. In the **Modems Properties** box, select the **General** tab and click **Properties**. The resulting window allows you to change the general properties of the modem and the parameters of a standard connection.

End

How to Add Windows Components

Windows Me has many components and applications, some of which might not be included in your system's default installation. To avoid taking up space on your hard disk with options you don't plan to use, Windows lets you decide which elements to install. Some features described in this book—and others not covered here—might be missing from your **Start** menu or desktop. If you want to use those components, you must begin by installing them from the original Windows Me disk.

Begin

1 Open the Control Panel

Click the **Start** menu, choose **Settings**, and click **Control Panel**.

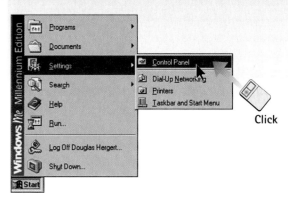

Click

2 Click Add/Remove Programs

In the **Control Panel** window, click the **Add/Remove Programs** icon. The **Add/Remove Programs Properties** box appears on the desktop.

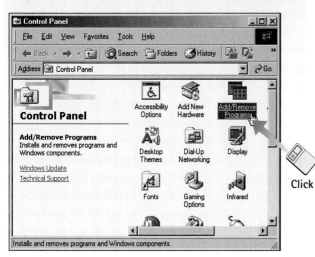

Click

3 Select a Component

Click the **Windows Setup** tab. Select the category of the item you want to install from the **Components** list. The **Description** box provides a brief description of the category you've selected. Click the **Details** button to install specific items from this category.

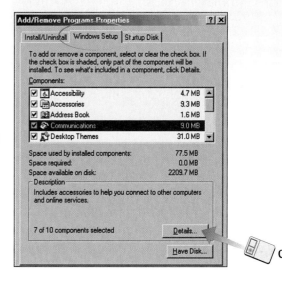

Click

4 Select Items to Install

A new window shows the items available in the category you've chosen. Select each option that you want to install, placing a check mark in the corresponding box. Click **OK** to close both windows. You might be prompted to insert your original Windows Me installation disk or CD-ROM; do so, and then click **OK** to complete the process.

Click

End

How-To Hints

Creating New Menu Items and Shortcuts

After installing a new component, Windows updates the shortcuts to the new feature. This might mean that a new entry appears in the **Accessories** list or some other part of the **Start** menu. For other components, a new icon might appear directly on the desktop.

Recognizing an Incomplete Installation

In the **Components** list of the **Windows Setup** tab (shown in Step 3), a gray check box indicates an incomplete installation in a particular category. In other words, some items have been installed, and others have not.

Opening the Control Panel

Another way to open the Control Panel is to click the **My Computer** icon and click the **Control Panel** icon.

How to Install and Uninstall Software

When you buy a software package for your computer, your first step is to install the new application. Unless the package gives you other specific installation instructions, the **Add/Remove Programs** utility is one simple way to carry out this process. Furthermore, you can use this same tool to *un*install a program you no longer use. Windows applications typically install files in multiple disk locations, and often share software components with other programs. Attempting to remove an application manually by deleting files directly from folders can therefore be risky. The **Remove** feature does the job safely and systematically.

Begin

1 Click Add/Remove Programs

Click the **Start** button and then choose **Settings** and **Control Panel**. In the **Control Panel** window, click **Add/Remove Programs**.

Click

2 Click Install

On the **Install/Uninstall** tab of the dialog box, click the **Install** button to install new software.

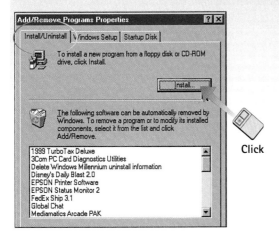

Click

3 Insert the Disk

When the **Install Program From Floppy Disk or CD-ROM** message appears, insert the disk for the new application and click **Next**. Windows locates the disk and prepares to start the installation.

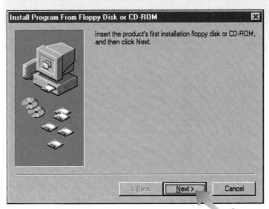

Click

4 Complete the Installation

Click **Finish** and follow the instructions to complete the installation process. If the program is delivered on multiple disks, you'll be notified when it's time to swap disks.

Click

5 Uninstall an Application

To remove an existing application from your hard disk, select a name from the list of removable programs in the lower half of the **Install/Uninstall** tab, and then click the **Add/Remove** button. Follow the instructions that Windows provides.

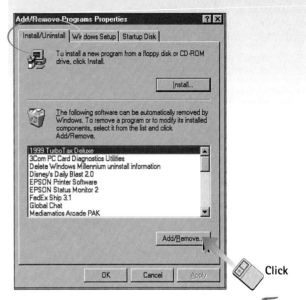

Click

End

How-To Hints

Using the Run Command

Some applications instruct you to use the **Run** command to start the installation. To do so, insert the installation disk and choose **Run** from the **Start** menu. Type the path and filename of the installation program and click **OK**. Alternatively, if a program is delivered on CD-ROM, the installation process may begin automatically as soon as you insert the disc. In this case, you need only respond to any installation options that are offered.

Closing Other Programs

As a general rule, you should close any programs that are running on the desktop before you try to install a new application.

Choosing Installation Options

Many applications offer multiple installation options, allowing you to install all or a selection of features from a software package—depending on your specific needs and expectations. If you initially choose to install only a selection of features, you can later add other components by running the installation program again. Click **Add/Remove** in the **Install/Uninstall** tab to begin.

How to Create a Startup Disk

Windows Me is a reliable operating system, but unpredictable problems sometimes occur. As a safeguard, you should always have a startup disk that you can use to boot your computer in the event that something goes wrong with Windows or your hard disk. You might have created a startup disk when you first installed Windows on your computer. If not—or if you have misplaced the disk—you can use the **Add/Remove Programs** utility to create a new one.

Begin

1 Open Add/Remove Programs

Click the **Start** menu, and then choose **Settings** and **Control Panel**. In the **Control Panel** window, click **Add/Remove Programs**. The **Add/ Remove Programs Properties** box appears on the desktop.

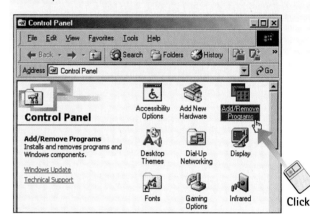

Click

2 Click Create Disk

Select the **Startup Disk** tab, and then click the **Create Disk** button.

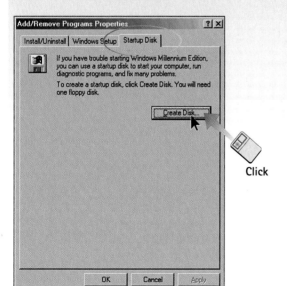

Click

3 Insert a Blank Disk

Follow the instructions on the **Insert Disk** box: Insert a floppy disk into the appropriate drive and click **OK**.

Click

4 Complete the Startup Disk

As the disk is created, Windows shows you what percentage of the process is complete. When it's done, remove the floppy disk, label it, and put it in a safe place where you'll find it if you ever need it.

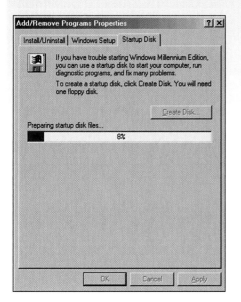

End

Task

Setting Up a Home Network

*I*n Windows Millennium Edition, a *home network* consists of two or more computers connected in a way that allows them to share resources. For example, each connected computer might be able to send documents to a single network printer, access Web sites using a shared Internet connection, or read document files located on other computers in the network.

Your own goals in creating a network will depend on how your home computers are used, and who uses them. A home network may simply be a convenient way to share a major piece of equipment such as a printer, or to provide access to important business files across the network. If you access the Internet over a single phone line, the network may become a way for two or more people to go online at the same time. But even if you work alone in front of multiple computers, a home network can streamline your work with documents and other resources.

Thanks to Windows Me, setting up a home network requires no specialized understanding of network software or hardware. An elegant tool called the **Home Networking Wizard** guides you through the entire installation process. Specifically, this wizard helps you make a series of decisions regarding the characteristics of your own network and then provides the resources for adding other computers to the network. Even if some of your computers are running on previous versions of Windows (95 or 98), the wizard gives you the tools necessary to add them to the network.

Before you run the Home Networking Wizard, you must install a *network adapter* (also known as a *network interface card*) on each computer that will ultimately become part of your network. For a desktop computer, this might mean inserting a card into an available slot inside the computer; for a laptop, you can simply install a PCMCIA card in an empty socket at the side of the machine. (External network adapters are also available.) You'll also have to install the driver software supplied with the hardware. The network adapters are typically connected to each other by cable, in an arrangement that is sometimes known as a *peer-to-peer* network. If you are connecting only two computers, you'll need a *crossover* cable that successfully handles the signals between the two network adapters. For more than two computers, you may need another piece of equipment called a *hub*, to which you connect cables from each computer in your home network. All this off-the-shelf hardware is easy to find at your local computer store and is simple to install. ●

How to Use the Home Networking Wizard

After you install the appropriate network adapter hardware and connect your computers by cable, the **Home Networking Wizard** gives you the options and information you need to add each computer to your network. When you first run the wizard on your Windows Me computer, you'll choose a *workgroup name* for your network and another name to identify the computer itself. For this first computer, you'll select options to begin defining the characteristics of your network. Then you'll run the wizard again on each additional computer—even computers that use Windows 95 or 98—and choose a unique name and a set of network properties for each.

Begin

1 Start the Wizard

Click the **Start** button and choose **Programs, Accessories, Communications**, and finally **Home Networking Wizard**.

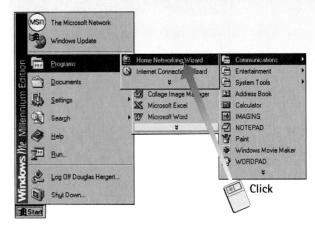

Click

2 Begin the Steps

The **Welcome** window is the first of a dozen or so dialog boxes that guide you through the steps of defining your network. Read the information it contains and click **Next** to begin the process.

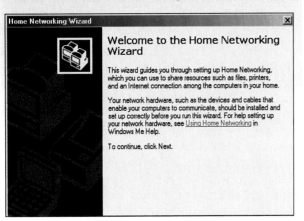

3 Choose the Initial Setup Option

As you'll learn later, the wizard can accomplish different tasks in different situations; for example, it can store a setup program on a floppy disk so that you can add non-Millennium Edition machines to your network. But for now, you want to begin setting up a home network on your Windows Me computer. Choose the first option and click **Next**.

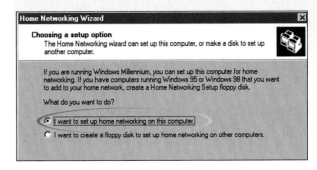

4 Identify Your Internet Connection

In the next window, select the option that correctly describes this computer's Internet connection. Then click **Next** to make more decisions related to Web use.

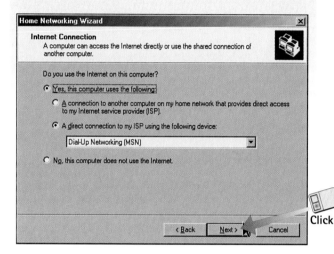

5 Choose Internet Connection Sharing

Next you decide if you want to activate *Internet Connection Sharing*, allowing computers on your network to sign on to the Web on a single line. Click the first option if you want this feature to be part of your network, or the second option if you do not. Then click **Next**.

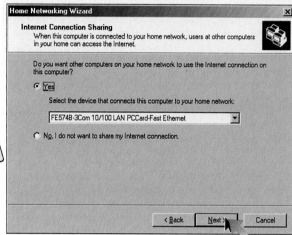

Click

6 Create a Name for This Computer

Each computer in your network must be identified by a unique name. In the **Computer name** box, type the name you want to assign to the current computer. You also need a *workgroup* name, which must be the same for all computers in the network. The wizard suggests **MSHOME** as the default name for the workgroup. If you want to use a different name, select the second option and type the name in the text box. Then click **Next** to continue.

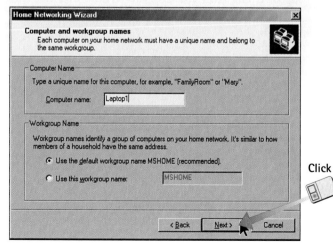

Click

How-To Hints

Understanding the Hardware Setup

As described in the introduction to this part, the hardware for a home network is simplest when you are connecting only two computers. Each computer needs a *network adapter card*, which you can install in an available slot inside your desktop computer or in an empty PCMCIA socket in a laptop computer. You then run the setup software for these adapter cards to install the appropriate drivers on each computer. Use a *crossover* cable to connect the two computers correctly through their network adapters. (Unlike the cable you would use to connect an individual computer to an existing LAN, a crossover cable handles the signals correctly between two computers in a *peer-to-peer* network.)

Continues

How to Use the Home Networking Wizard Continued

In the first steps of the **Home Networking Wizard**, you defined a network name for the current computer and activated Internet Connection Sharing. In the next steps, you'll see how to define file sharing for your network and establish a password to protect your documents. You'll also choose a network printer. Finally, the wizard produces a setup program on a floppy disk so that you can add other computers to your network—even machines that are running Windows 98 or Windows 95.

7 Choose a File-Sharing Option

The next wizard window presents options for sharing files and printers on the current computer. Check the first option if you want to share your **My Documents** folder on the network. Click the **Password** button to establish a password for the security of shared files.

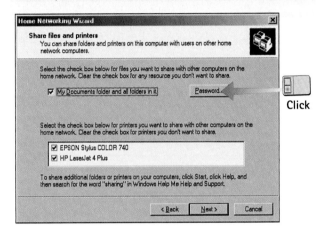

Click

8 Create a Password for File Sharing

Decide on the password that you want to use for file sharing. To confirm, type it twice in the **Password** dialog box; alphabetic case is significant. Click **OK** to return to the **Share files and printers** options.

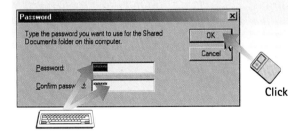

Click

9 Choose a Network Printer

If the current computer has a printer that you want to share on the network, check the name of the printer in the list. Clear the check boxes for any listed devices that you do not want to share on the network. Then click **Next**.

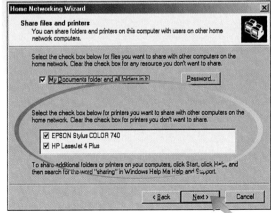

Click

10 Prepare a Disk for Other Computers

Now the wizard is ready to prepare a Home Networking Setup disk that you can use to add any Windows 98 or Windows 95 machines to your network. To create the disk, select **Yes** and click **Next**.

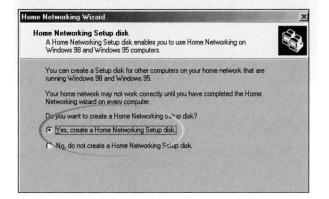

11 Insert a Disk and Wait for Setup

The wizard instructs you to insert a blank formatted disk in your floppy disk drive. Click **Next** again, and the wizard stores the setup program on the disk.

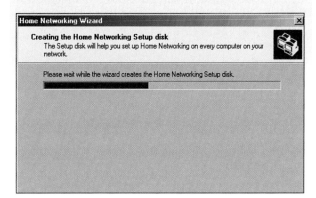

12 Install the Network

Now the **Home Networking Wizard** is ready to install the network properties you've selected. Before you go forward, you can click the **Back** button to review or change any of these properties. Click **Finish** to confirm the properties and set up the network. The next step is to run the Home Network Setup program on a second computer. You'll see how this process works in the next task.

Click

End

How-To Hints

Using the Wizard to Change Properties

The **Home Networking Wizard** is also designed to help you change the characteristics of an existing network—for example, to select a new network printer or to change the options you've selected for Internet Connection Sharing or file sharing. You'll learn more about this topic in Task 3, "How to Change Properties for the Network."

Changing the File-Sharing Properties

After you've defined and installed your network, you can change file-sharing properties at any time for a selected folder on your hard disk. In the **My Documents**, **My Computer**, or **Windows Explorer** window, right-click the folder whose properties you want to change and choose **Sharing** from the resulting shortcut menu. The **Sharing** tab of the resulting dialog box allows you to specify how the contents of the folder will be shared on the network.

How to Add Computers to Your Network

After you define the properties of the first computer on your network, you need to repeat the process for each additional computer. If other computers are running Windows 98 or Windows 95 rather than Windows Millennium Edition, you'll use the Home Networking Setup to install the **Home Networking Wizard** on each computer. Then you'll proceed through the steps of the wizard. Typically, your Windows Me computer provides services such as an Internet connection and a network printer. When you install each subsequent computer, you select the network services you want to use.

Begin

1 Run the Setup Program

If the next computer is running Windows 95 or 98, insert the Home Networking Setup disk in the floppy disk drive. Then click **Start** and choose **Run**. In the **Run** dialog box, type the path and name of the Setup program (for example **a:\setup.exe**) and click **OK**.

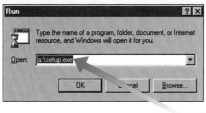

2 Install the Wizard

A **Welcome** window appears on the desktop, providing brief instructions about the process ahead. Click **Next** to install and run the **Home Networking Wizard** on the current computer. The next window charts the progress of the wizard's installation and lets you know when it is complete. Click **Next** again to continue.

3 Choose a Connection Option

In the next window, specify whether the current computer uses an Internet connection on the home network or a direct connection. Click **Next** to continue.

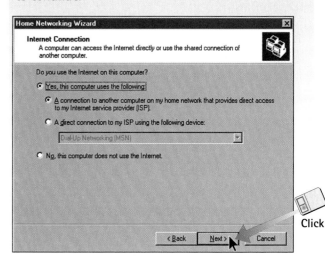

Click

4 Create a Name for This Computer

Create a unique name to identify this new computer on the network. Type the name in the **Computer name** box. Make sure that the **Workgroup name** is the same for all new computers you add to the network. Click **Next** to continue.

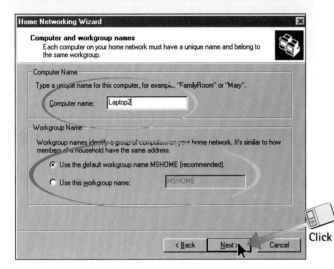

Click

5 Select Other Options

In the next wizard windows, you continue defining properties for the current computer, including file sharing and printer sharing. Make selections and click **Next** to proceed.

Click

6 Complete the Setup

When you come to the window shown here, click **Finish** to complete installation. The **Home Networking Wizard** lets you know when setup has been accomplished on each computer. To gain access to shared folders and other shared resources, click the **My Network Places** icon on the desktop of a Window Me machine; click the **Network Neighborhood** icon on the desktop of a Windows 95 or 98 machine.

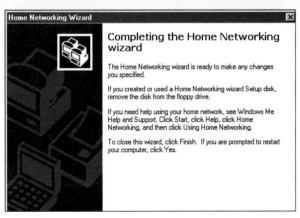

End

How-To Hints

Installing Windows Me Computers

If all the computers you want to include in your network are already running Windows Millennium Edition, you do not have to create the Setup disk. Instead, you can simply run the **Home Networking Wizard** directly from each computer in turn. Click **Start** and choose **Programs, Accessories, Communications**, and **Home Networking Wizard**.

Understanding Peer-to-Peer Resource Sharing

The **Home Networking Wizard** allows you to identify shared resources on *any* networked computer. For example, you may have different printers attached to different computers, and you may want to make all the printers available on the network. If you follow the steps carefully, the wizard is versatile enough to set up shared resources in any way you want to use them.

How to Change Properties for the Network

After you set up your home network, you can run the **Home Networking Wizard** again at any time to modify the properties of the network on any computer. In some cases, a change in one computer will require changes on other networked computers. The wizard guides you through the steps. In addition, another Windows tool is available for a quick view of network properties on the current computer: the **Network** properties box, which you can open from the Windows **Control Panel**.

Begin

1 Open the Network Properties Box

Click the **Start** button and choose **Settings** and **Control Panel**. In the **Control Panel** window, find the **Network** icon and click it to open the **Network** properties box. The content of the resulting properties box is divided into three tabs: **Configuration**, **Identification**, and **Access Control**.

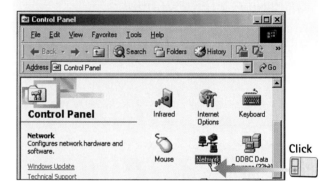

Click

2 Read About Network Components

In the **Configuration** tab, you'll find a scrollable list of *network components* that have been installed on the current computer. These include software components, communications protocols, hardware devices that connect computers, and other services. For an overview, click the **?** button at the upper-right corner of the properties box, and then click inside the components list.

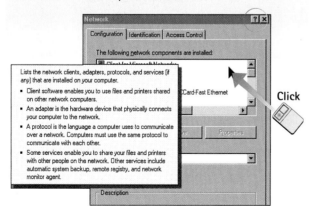

Click

3 Identify Specific Components

Select any component in the list for a more specific description, which appears in the box at the bottom of the properties box.

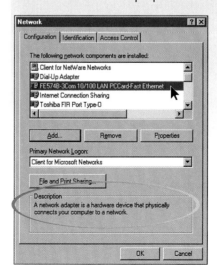

4 Change the File and Print Sharing Options

Click the **File and Print Sharing** button if you want to change the settings for resource sharing on the current computer. In the resulting dialog box, you can select or clear options for file sharing and printer sharing. Click **OK** to close the dialog box and return to the **Network** properties box.

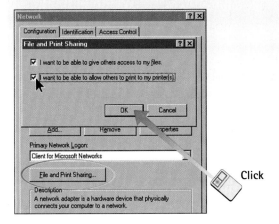

Click

5 Change the Computer Name

Click the **Identification** tab to view the network names for this computer. If you need to change the name of the current computer, or modify the Workgroup name for your network, you can do so on this page of the properties box.

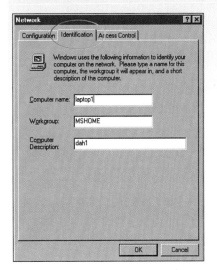

6 View the Access Options

Finally, click the **Access Control** tab to view two options for protected resource sharing. The first option allows individual password protection for shared resources; the second option gives group access to shared resources. Click **OK** to confirm any changes you've made in any tabs of the **Network** properties box.

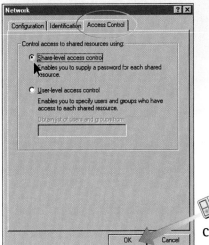

Click

How-To Hints

Making Changes in the Network

When you select new options in the **Network** properties box, you may be instructed to restart your computer before these changes can take effect. In most cases, you'll probably prefer to use the **Home Networking Wizard** instead of the **Network** properties box to make important changes in your network characteristics. But the **Network** properties box provides an overview of the network components, along with important information about shared resources.

End

Task

18

Working on a Home Network

*A*n individual computer on your home network potentially has access to a variety of resources, including the network printer, the shared Internet connection, the documents stored on other computers, and even the applications installed on shared disk drives. But with all this extra access, operations on a network computer remain almost identical to the familiar Windows tasks you've learned to perform on a standalone computer.

This is perhaps the most remarkable aspect of network computing: After a while, you hardly realize you're working on a network. Whatever the task, the steps are always familiar. If the network printer is your default printing device, your documents are routed there whenever you choose a **Print** command in any application. Going online to visit your favorite Web sites is as simple as it's always been, even if your own computer uses an Internet connection that physically resides elsewhere on the network.

Likewise, viewing and revising documents from another computer is the same as working on files stored on your own computer. To locate specific documents on the network, you simply open the **My Network Places** folder. You'll find an icon for this folder directly on your desktop. You'll also see it in the list of **Look in** documents in any **Open** dialog box, and even in other Windows tools such as the **Search** program. This folder gives you access to the documents and applications stored on other network computers. From **My Network Places**, you can open the folder for a computer's hard disk and then look for other folders and documents stored on the target disk.

As you explore these and other network operations in the tasks ahead, you'll have the chance to experiment with a couple of tools designed specifically for the network. The **Net Watcher** application gives you an overview of the network and allows you to monitor the use of resources belonging to your own computer. **WinPopUp** is a small but useful program designed for sending quick messages from one computer to another across the network. ●

How to Share Files and Printers

On your home network, you'll get used to seeing the **My Network Places** folder listed alongside other, more familiar folders such as **My Documents** and **My Computer**. In a variety of contexts, **My Network Places** gives you access to documents stored on other computers in the network. For example, if you want to open a network document in an application that's running on your own desktop, simply look for **My Network Places** in the **Open** dialog box. From this folder, you can open files stored on other computers, revise the files, and then save them back to their original locations. You can also print documents to a network printer directly from an application running on your desktop.

Begin

1 Look in My Network Places

Start an application (WordPad in this example) and choose the program's **Open** command from the **File** menu. At the top of the **Open** dialog box, pull down the **Look in** list and choose **My Network Places**. Depending on how your network is organized, you might have to open additional locations (for example, **Entire Network** followed by the name of your network and the name of the individual computer you want to access) before you find an icon for the hard disk drive.

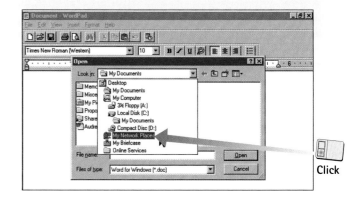

Click

2 Open the Hard Disk on a Network Computer

In the list of files and folders, click the name of the hard disk for the target computer.

 Click

3 Open a Folder and Select a File

Navigate to the folder that contains the file you want to open. Then click the name of the file. The document appears in the work area of your application.

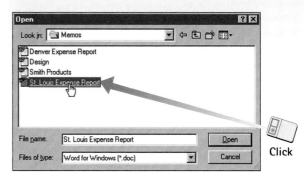

Click

4 Revise and Save the File

You are now looking at the content of a file that is stored on another computer in the network. Make any necessary revisions in the document. Then choose **Save** from the **File** menu, or simply click the **Save** button on the application's toolbar. The file is saved back to its original location on the hard disk of the selected network computer.

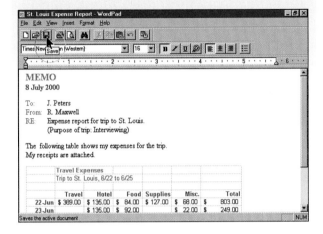

5 Print to the Network Printer

To send a document to the network printer, pull down the **File** menu and choose **Print**. In the **Print** dialog box, make sure that the network printer's name is selected in the **Name** box. (If the network printer is the default on your computer, as shown in this illustration, you do not have to make any changes in the **Name** box.) Then click **OK**. The document is sent across the network to the appropriate computer and from there to the network printer.

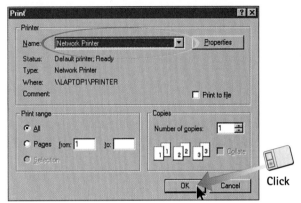

Click

End

How-To Hints

Working in Windows 98 or 95

If you are working on a Windows 98 or Windows 95 computer, the network folder is called **My Network Neighborhood**, not **My Network Places**.

Working with Shared Folders

Depending on how you've set up your home network, some folders may require a password for access to their contents. If so, the user on another computer must know the password to open the folder. To create a *shared folder* on your own computer, right-click the target folder icon in the **My Documents** or **My Computer** window and choose **Sharing** from the shortcut menu. In the **Sharing** tab of the resulting dialog box, you can specify an access level for the folder (**Read-Only** or **Full**), and you can create a password that will be required for access. The icon for a shared folder displays a blue-sleeved hand just beneath the folder itself.

Opening a Document That's Already in Use

If you attempt to open a document that someone else is working on elsewhere on the network, you may receive a notice that the file is already in use. Depending on the application, you may be denied access to the file temporarily. Alternatively, you might be offered a read-only version of the file to view or a copy of the file (separate from the original file) to work on.

How to Share an Internet Connection

If you've set up *Internet Connection Sharing* as a feature of your home network, individual computers on the network can go online at any time using the shared connection. The computer where the connection resides is sometimes known as the *ICS host*. By design, the host and other computers on the network can use the shared connection concurrently. In other words, each individual user on the network is free to visit any sites on the Web, regardless of the online activity taking place on other network computers.

Begin

1 Start Internet Explorer

On a computer that is set up to use your network's shared Internet connection, click the **Internet Explorer** icon on the desktop to go online. When you do so, a sign-on window may appear on the ICS host computer, and may require a response before you can make your own connection.

Click

2 Connect on the ICS Host

If the host computer is not set up to connect automatically, the user at the host computer must type the correct name and password, and then click **Connect**. (If the host computer is already online, this step does not occur.)

Click

3 Visit Any Web Site

Back on the non-host computer, you can visit any Web sites you want, just as you would if your own computer were connected directly.

4 Visit Different Sites on the Host

The person sitting at the host computer can also open **Internet Explorer** and use the shared connection to visit any sites on the Web. In other words, two (or more) distinct but concurrent online sessions can take place on a single shared connection.

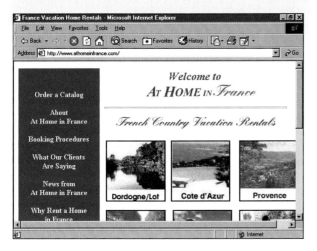

5 Get Email

The person sitting at either computer can also open a mail server to receive email.

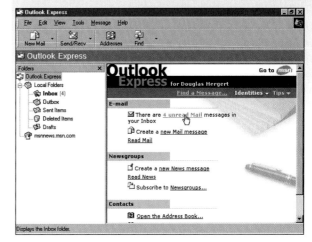

End

How-To Hints

Viewing the ICS Properties

To view the properties of Internet Connection Sharing on your computer, begin by opening the **Internet Properties** window. You can do this by right-clicking the Internet Explorer icon on your desktop, and choosing **Properties** from the resulting shortcut menu. Then click the **Connections** tab and click the **Sharing** button at the bottom of the window. The **Internet Connection Sharing** dialog box shows the details of the Internet connection and the home network connection.

How to Use Net Watcher and WinPopUp

The **Net Watcher** application is a system tool that allows you to monitor activity on your home network. You can find out who is connected, what resources are shared, and which files from your own computer are in use on other network computers. Another useful network tool is **WinPopUp**, which sends messages from one computer to another across the home network. Each computer on the network can send and receive messages, as long as WinPopUp is running on every desktop.

Begin

1 Start Net Watcher

Click the **Start** button and choose **Programs, Accessories,** and **System Tools.** Then click **Net Watcher.** The **Net Watcher** application window appears on the desktop.

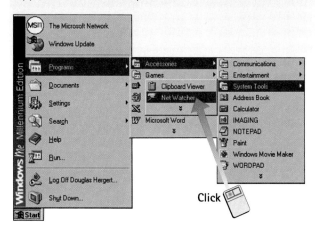

Click

2 Examine Current Network Activity

In the Net Watcher toolbar, click any of the **Show** buttons (the last three icons on the toolbar) to specify the information you want to see. **Show users** gives a list of all the computers and users on the network. **Show shared folders** displays a list of shared resources available from the current computer (as in this illustration). **Show files** provides a list of files from the current computer that are open somewhere on the network. (You'll find equivalent commands in the **View** menu.)

Show users   Show shared folders   Show files

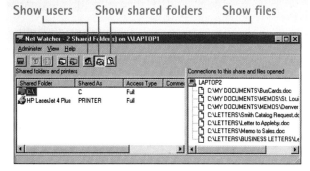

3 Disconnect a User

If you want to disconnect a user from resources on your own computer, click **Show users,** select the name, and then click **Disconnect user** on the toolbar. A message box asks you to confirm that you want to disconnect the user. If you click **Yes,** any open files from your own computer will be closed on the target computer.

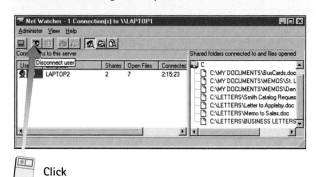

Click

4 Start WinPopUp

Click the **Start** menu and choose **Run**. Type the name and path of the WinPopUp program (generally, it's **\windows\winpopup.exe**) in the **Open** box and click **OK**. WinPopUp appears on the desktop. (Note that other network computers must also be running WinPopUp in order to receive messages.)

5 Send a Message

Click the **Send** button on the WinPopUp toolbar. In the **Send Message** dialog box, select the destination of your message: a particular user or computer, or the entire network (identified as the **Workgroup**). Type the name of the user, computer, or workgroup to which you want to send a message. In the **Message** box, type the text you want to send. Click **OK** to send the message.

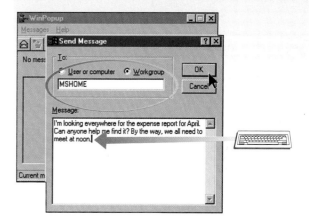

6 Receive a Message

When a new message arrives from someone on the network, you'll hear a beep. Click the **Next** button (►►) to scroll forward through existing messages until you find the one you want to read. Click the **Previous** button (◄◄) to review old messages. Click the **Delete** button to erase the currently displayed message from the WinPopUp window.

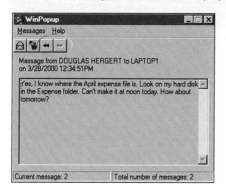

End

How-To Hints

Refreshing the Net Watcher Display

If you suspect that Net Watcher is not accurately keeping up with current network activity, pull down the **View** menu and choose **Refresh** (or simply press **F5** at your keyboard).

Changing the Options of WinPopUp

To change the way WinPopUp notifies you when a new message arrives, pull down the **Messages** menu and choose **Options**. The **Options** dialog box has three check boxes. Select the **Play sound** option if you want to hear a beep whenever a new message arrives from another computer on the network. Select the **Pop up dialog on message receipt** option if you want the WinPopUp window to pop up and display any new message. Select the **Always on top** option if you want the WinPopUp to be visible all the time.

Task

Restoring, Backing Up, and Customizing

In the three tasks ahead, you'll explore a miscellany of tools that offer specialized ways to control your system. The first two tools, **System Restore** and **Backup,** give you options for maintaining the integrity of your system and protecting information you store on your computer. The third, **Desktop Themes,** is a novelty program that customizes the visual and sound environment of your desktop.

The new **System Restore** program gives you the unique opportunity to return your system to a previous state, undoing changes that have unexpectedly produced impaired results. For example, you might use this program after installing a new piece of software or hardware that ends up damaging normal operations on your computer. The System Restore tool makes an attempt to return your system to its previous state—that is, to recover the working conditions you enjoyed before the ill-fated installation.

Backup provides a simple and reliable way to keep backup copies of your most important files. You can use this program to produce major system backups on special-purpose recording devices such as tape drives; or you can simply keep smaller data backups on disk. Note that Microsoft Backup might not be installed automatically on your computer as a part of Windows Me; if not, you'll have to search for it and install it from your original Windows program disk.

After two heavy-hitting tools like System Restore and Backup, the third task in this part strikes a lighter note. The **Desktop Themes** utility offers an outrageous variety of sight-and-sound motifs, designed to add a bit of levity to your desktop environment. You can choose subject matter such as art and travel, science and nature, and historical periods. Each theme includes visual elements for a variety of desktop properties, including wallpaper, icons, window colors, fonts, and mouse pointers—as well as distinct sound effects. Whether all this variety suits your own professional work environment—not to mention your sense of good taste—is up to you to decide. ●

How to Use System Restore

At specified moments while your computer is on, the **System Restore** program automatically registers *restore points*–date-and-time markers to which you can eventually "roll back" your system if necessary. In the event that something goes wrong with your computer–after a new software installation, a download, or some other operation that has caused unpredictable damage–you can start **System Restore** and select a particular restore point in the program's calendar. As a result, your system returns to its state at the date and time you select. Note that you can also use System Restore to create manual restore points, which are markers you define yourself before initiating a potentially hazardous operation.

Begin

1 Start System Restore

Click the **Start** button and choose **Programs, Accessories,** and **System Tools,** then click **System Restore.** The program's **Welcome** window appears on the desktop.

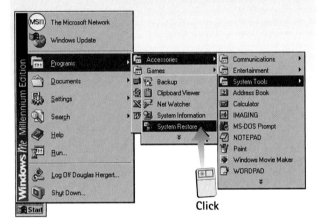

Click

2 Choose the Restore Option

To restore your computer to a previous state, choose the first option, **Restore my computer to an earlier time.** Then click **Next.**

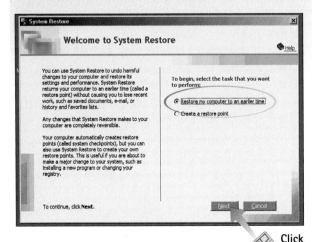

Click

3 Select a Restore Point

On the restore point calendar, click a date that you believe to be just before the harmful event that you now want to undo. A list of timed restore-point descriptions appears just to the right of the calendar. Choose the restore point to which you want to return and click **Next.**

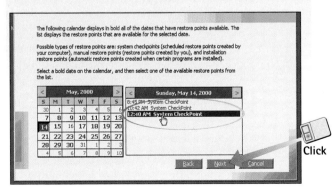

Click

4 Confirm Your Choice

A warning box appears next, reminding you to close all programs and files before proceeding; click **OK**. Then the **Confirm** window shows the restore point you've selected. If you are sure that this is the correct choice, click **Next** to restore your computer.

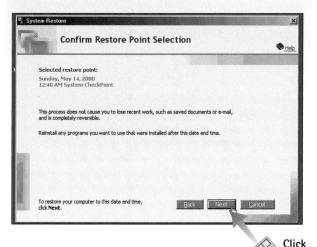

Click

5 Create a Restore Point

If you want to create a *manual* restore point—that is, a point that you define and describe yourself for future reference—select the second option in the **Welcome** window, shown in Step 1 above. Click **Next** to view the **Create a Restore Point** window. Enter a description for the restore point you want to create and click **Next**.

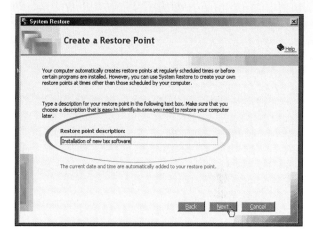

6 Confirm Your Manual Restore Point

The next window shows the date, time, and description of the new restore point. To confirm this information and register the restore point, click **OK**. (If you want to revise the definition, click **Back**.)

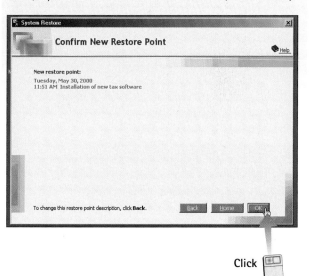

Click

End

How-To Hints

Understanding Restore Points

System Restore creates several types of restore points to register different events on your computer. A restore point is automatically created whenever you install a new application that uses the latest installer technologies (known as *InstallShield* or *Windows Installer*); or when automatic Windows updates are downloaded and installed on your system. In addition, *scheduled* restore points are registered periodically while your system is on.

Maintaining Document Files

When rolling back your computer to a restore point, **System Restore** leaves your document files alone, even if you created them after the selected restore point. This exception applies to any files you've stored in the **My Documents** folder and to files that have common extensions such as DOC and XLS.

How to Use Microsoft Backup

To protect the data you store on your hard disk, you might periodically want to create backup copies of important files or folders—or even of your entire system. The **Backup Wizard** simplifies this procedure. You begin by selecting the information you want to save, and then you choose a destination for the backup set. If you subsequently lose information on your system, the **Restore Wizard** allows you to restore selected files to your hard disk and gives you easy ways to control the outcome of the restore operation.

Begin

1 Start Microsoft Backup

Click the **Start** button and choose **Programs, Accessories, System Tools**, and then click **Backup**. In the **Welcome** window, keep the default selection—**Create a new backup job**—and click **OK**.

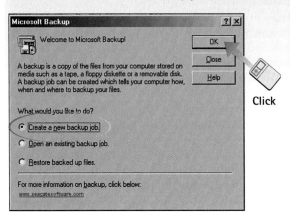

Click

2 Select Files to Include in the Backup

In the first window of the **Backup Wizard**, choose **Back up My Computer** or **Back up Selected files, folders, and drives**. If you choose the second option, the wizard gives you the opportunity to specify the objects to back up, as shown here. Use the list on the left to open folders and drives, and then place a check mark next to any item in the list on the right that you want to include. Click **Next** to continue.

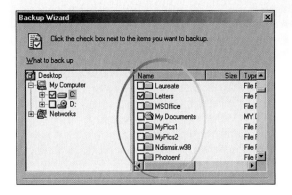

3 Name a Destination

If you've performed a previous backup with the same items, the next window gives you the option to back up all files or only those that are new or changed. Select an option and click **Next**. Then indicate where the backup should be saved. (In this example, the backup becomes a file on a floppy disk.) Select from any additional options that the wizard offers, type a name for the backup file, and click **Start**.

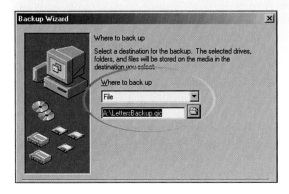

4 Start the Restore Wizard

At some point in the future, you might have to use your backup file to restore damaged or missing files. Start the **Backup** utility and choose the third option in the **Welcome** window, as shown in Step 1. Click **OK**. In the first **Restore Wizard** window, begin by identifying the source of the backup and click **Next**.

Click

5 Select a Backup

Select the backup you want to restore and click **OK**. (In the example shown here, only one backup file is available on the source media selected in Step 4. If you back up your files to a tape drive, for example, several backup files might be on the same tape. In that case, you will have to choose the backup file from which you want to restore.)

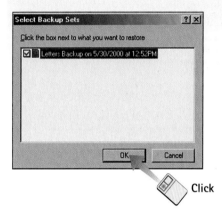

Click

6 Complete the Restore Operation

In the next window, select the files, folders, or drives you want to restore from the selected backup and click **Next**. Subsequent wizard windows give you the opportunity to specify where you want the objects to be restored and whether they should replace existing files. Finally, click **Start** to start the restore process.

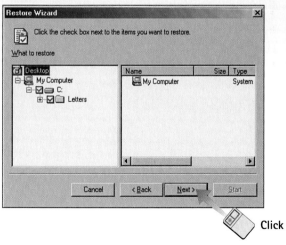

Click

End

How-To Hints

Using the Backup Application Window

The main window for the **Microsoft Backup** application remains on the desktop while the **Backup Wizard** and **Restore Wizard** guide you through the process of preparing or using a backup. The application contains toolbars and menus that give you direct access to the various options. Click the **Backup** tab to define a new backup job; click the **Restore** tab to restore information from a backup.

Finding and Installing Backup

If you do not initially find **Backup** in Your **System Tools** menu, use the **Search** program to see whether it's available on your hard disk. If it is not on your hard disk, you can install it from a file named **MSBEXP.EXE** on your Windows Me distribution disk.

How to Use Desktop Themes

Would you like to transform your desktop into an art gallery, a jungle tableau, a mystery movie set, or a wild display of Sixties psychedelics? If so, the **Desktop Themes** utility is just what you're looking for. Open this program from the **Control Panel** and choose from its diverse list of motifs that will thoroughly change the ambiance of your desktop. Each theme includes a complete set of visual elements—wallpaper, icons, pointers, fonts, colors, and even a screen saver—along with matching sounds.

Begin

1 Open Desktop Themes

Click the **Start** button and choose **Settings** and then **Control Panel**. In the **Control Panel**, click the **Desktop Themes** icon. The **Desktop Themes** window appears.

Click

2 Select a Theme

The window initially displays samples of your current desktop settings. Pull down the **Theme** list and choose the name of a theme you'd like to examine.

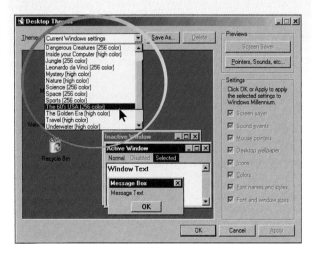

3 View the Theme

The visual elements of the selected theme appear in the window. You'll be able to examine the wallpaper, the icons, the fonts, and the colors associated with the theme. To learn more about the theme, click the **Pointers, Sounds, etc.** button at the upper-right corner of the **Desktop Themes** window. A **Preview** box appears.

Click

4 Explore Individual Elements

The **Preview** box has three tabs: **Pointers**, **Sounds**, and **Visuals**. Select each tab in turn and click items in the corresponding lists. The small **Preview** area shows the element you've selected. Click **Close** when you're finished with the **Preview** box.

Click

5 Deactivate Selected Elements

If you like some elements of the theme but not others, you can deselect items from the **Settings** list on the right side of the **Desktop Themes** window. Click any item to remove the check from the corresponding box.

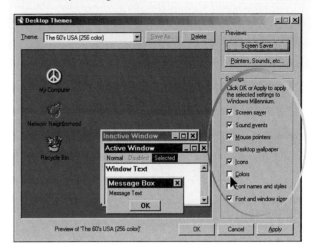

6 Try the Screen Saver

Click the **Screen Saver** button to view the screen saver associated with the selected theme. In this case, the screen saver is a spiral motion that floats around the desktop and distorts portions of the screen. If you decide to apply the selected elements of the current theme to your desktop, click **OK**.

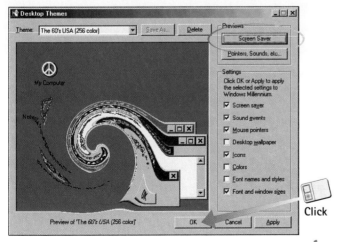

Click

End

How-To Hints

Restoring Previous Settings

If you want to return to the less frenetic settings you were used to before you installed a theme, open **Desktop Themes** again from the **Control Panel** and choose **Previous Windows Settings** or **Windows Default** from the **Theme** list. Then click **OK**. Your desktop returns to normal.

Creating a New Desktop Theme

You can save your current desktop settings as a theme. Use the various tools described in Part 4, "Changing the Windows Me Settings," to change the appearance of your desktop. Then open **Desktop Themes** and choose **Current Windows Settings** from the **Theme** list. Click the **Save As** button, type a name for your theme, and click **Save**.

Task

PART 20

Using the System Tools

In the tasks ahead, you'll explore four of the programs offered in the **System Tools** menu. All these programs provide important benefits that are worth considering for your computer system:

- ✓ **Defragmenter** and **ScanDisk** are designed to improve the efficiency and integrity of disks and the files they store. **Defragmenter** rearranges disk storage so that files are saved contiguously. **ScanDisk** searches for disk errors and fixes them.

- ✓ The **Disk Cleanup** application is a tool for freeing up space on your hard disk by deleting extraneous or unneeded files. Specifically, **Disk Cleanup** lists categories of files—including temporary files, Internet files, and Recycle Bin contents—and gives you the opportunity to delete some or all of these categories from your disk.

- ✓ The **Maintenance Wizard** schedules tune-ups to keep your hard disk in the best possible working order. The scheduled tasks are those performed by the three tools just described: Defragmenter, ScanDisk, and Disk Cleanup.

A list of these utilities appears when you click the **Start** button and choose **System Tools** in the **Accessories** list. If you don't see this folder—or if some items are missing from the list—you'll have to install these programs from your original Windows Me disk. Refer to Task 2, "How to Add Windows Components," in Part 16 for more information. ●

How to Use ScanDisk and Defragmenter

The **ScanDisk** and **Defragmenter** programs are designed to maintain the efficiency and integrity of your hard disk or floppy disks over time. **ScanDisk** searches for errors in the files and folders stored on a selected disk, and optionally checks the disk's surface. **Defragmenter** rearranges storage so that each file on a disk is saved in contiguous blocks of space. This results in faster access to the information on your disk.

Begin

1 Start ScanDisk

Click **Start** and choose **Programs, Accessories, System Tools,** and then **ScanDisk.**

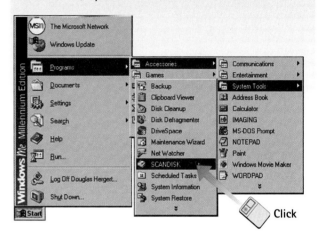

Click

2 Select a Drive

Select the drive you want ScanDisk to check, and then choose the type of test you want to perform. Check **Automatically fix errors** if you want ScanDisk to correct problems without prompting you for instructions, and then click **Start** to begin the test.

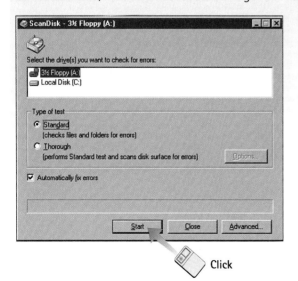

Click

3 View the Results

When the procedure is complete, the results appear in a new window. In addition to statistics about the drive itself, this report tells you about any errors that were located and fixed. Click the **Close** button to close ScanDisk.

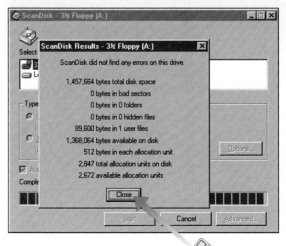

Click

4 Start Disk Defragmenter

To run the **Disk Defragmenter**, choose the program from the **System Tools** list. In the **Select Drive** window, specify the drive you want to defragment and click **OK**.

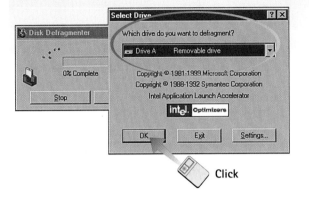

Click

5 View the Progress

The next window charts the Defragmenter's progress. Click **Show Details** to view a full-screen representation of the procedure. Note that defragmenting can take an hour or more on a large hard disk. You can pause or stop the process before completion by clicking the appropriate buttons.

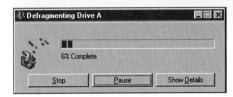

End

How-To Hints

Understanding Fragmentation

Fragmentation occurs over time as you save files to disk. Because of changes in the space available on the disk, files must sometimes be stored in noncontiguous units. Although fragmented files can always be opened and used, defragmentation generally improves the efficiency of disk access.

Choosing Defragmentation Settings

To choose the settings for the defragmentation process, click the **Settings** button in the **Select Drive** window. The program can optionally check the drive for errors in addition to rearranging the files stored on disk; this is a recommended option, but results in a longer defragmentation process.

How to Use Disk Cleanup

The **Disk Cleanup** program collects data about unneeded files on your hard disk and presents you with a list of files that could be deleted to regain disk space. Some of the categories of unneeded files are temporary Internet files, downloaded Web pages, uninstall information for your current version of Windows, and, of course, any files you've moved to the Recycle Bin. If your hard drive is short of space, you may be eager to remove such files. Disk Cleanup allows you to select the categories of files that you want to delete, and then carries out the cleanup for you. In addition, Disk Cleanup makes suggestions for deleting installed applications that you no longer use.

Begin

1 Start Disk Cleanup

Click **Start** and then choose **Programs, Accessories, System Tools,** and **Disk Cleanup.** A small dialog box appears on the screen, asking you to select a drive for the cleanup procedure. Keep the default drive selection, or pull down the **Drives** list and select the drive you want to work on. Click **OK** to begin the process.

Click

2 Wait for an Analysis of Your Drive

The **Disk Cleanup** program examines the specified drive and calculates how much space you can save in several categories if you go forward with the cleanup.

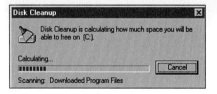

3 Select Categories of Files for Deletion

The first tab of the **Disk Cleanup** window lists the categories of files you can delete from your drive and tells you how much space can be saved in each category. Go through the list and check any category of files you want to delete. Remove the check from any category you want to save.

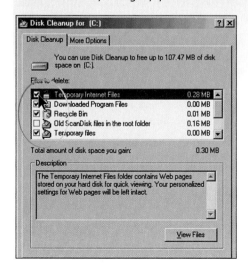

4 View Other Space-Saving Options

Click the **More Options** tab to learn about other ways you can save space on your drive. The first two options suggest deleting Windows components and applications you don't use. If you click either of the **Clean up** buttons, Disk Cleanup opens the **Add/Remove Programs Properties** box so that you can delete software from your system. The third option suggests changing the amount of disk space used by the **System Restore** program, discussed in Part 19, "Restoring, Backing Up, and Customizing."

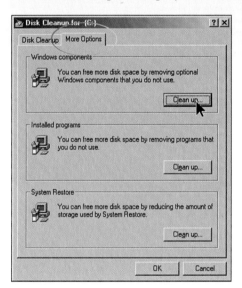

5 Complete the Cleanup

Return to the **Disk Cleanup** tab and click **OK** to carry out the cleanup instructions. A warning box appears on the desktop, informing you that the selected files will be deleted permanently. Click **Yes** if you're sure that you want to delete the files.

Click

End

How-To Hints

Viewing Files in a Category

If you're uncertain whether to select a particular category of files for deletion—and you want to know more about the files in the category—make a selection in the **Files to delete** list (in Step 3) and click the **View Files** button. In response, Disk Cleanup opens a folder in which you can see exactly which files are involved.

Using the Add/Remove Programs Window

To delete certain applications (as outlined in Step 4), you may have to insert the program's original CD-ROM installation disc. See Tasks 2 and 3 in Part 16, "Installing New Hardware and Software," for more information about the **Add/Remove Programs** utility.

How to Schedule a Maintenance Session

The Windows **Maintenance Wizard** helps you schedule specific disk-utility procedures so that they can be performed on a regular basis. The procedures include the **Disk Defragmenter,** the **ScanDisk** utility, and the **Disk Cleanup** program, all described in the previous tasks. When you complete the steps of the **Maintenance Wizard,** the procedures you've chosen are added to your **Scheduled Tasks** folder.

Begin

1 Start the Maintenance Wizard

Click the **Start** button, choose **Programs, Accessories, System Tools,** and then **Maintenance Wizard.**

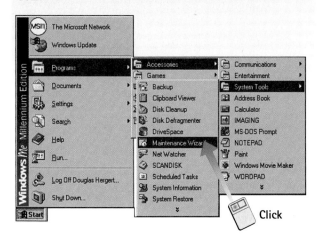

Click

2 Choose a Maintenance Option

If you've used the **Maintenance Wizard** before, a window appears asking whether you want to start a maintenance procedure right away or change your maintenance schedule. (If you've never used this program before, you won't see this window.) To reschedule, select the second option and click **OK.** The first **Maintenance Wizard** window appears.

Click

3 Select a Category of Settings

Select the **Express** option to accept the default settings and click **Next.** (The **Custom** option requires you to make detailed individual decisions about the maintenance settings that follow.)

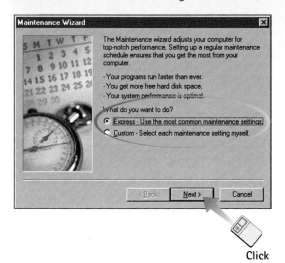

Click

4 Choose a Maintenance Time

Choose a convenient time for the daily maintenance tasks to occur on your system. Click one of the options and read the tip about leaving your computer running. Then click **Next**.

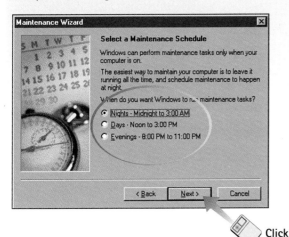

Click

5 Read About Maintenance

The next window lists the tasks included in your tune-up schedule; the corresponding system tools that are scheduled are **Disk Defragmenter**, **ScanDisk**, and **Disk Cleanup**. If you want the first tune-up to be performed right away, select the **When I click Finish** option and then click the **Finish** button.

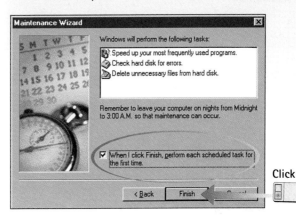

Click

6 Review Your Scheduled Tasks

Any time you want to review the list of tune-up programs scheduled on your computer, choose **Scheduled Tasks** from the **System Tools** list. The **Scheduled Tasks** folder shows icons for each scheduled program.

End

How-To Hints

Customizing Maintenance

If you prefer to choose exactly which procedures to schedule, click the **Custom** option in the first window of the **Maintenance Wizard**. In subsequent steps of the wizard, you can choose to schedule any combination of the available procedures.

Modifying a Task

In the **Scheduled Tasks** folder, right-click a scheduled item and choose **Properties** if you want to modify the task. Click the **Schedule** tab of the properties box to view or revise the timing and repetition of the task.

Adding Tasks

You can add items to your **Scheduled Tasks** folder by clicking the **Add Scheduled Tasks** icon. When you do so, the wizard guides you through the steps of selecting a task and planning a schedule.

Task

PART 21

Working in a DOS Window

*W*indows is the standard operating system for PC applications. Everything you do on your computer occurs on the Windows desktop. But if you've been using personal computers long enough to remember MS-DOS—the command-based operating system that preceded Windows—you might still have a few DOS programs and utilities that you like to use from time to time. The **MS-DOS Prompt** command in the **Programs** menu allows you to open a DOS window. Inside this window, you can run a program or perform a sequence of DOS commands. You can even use the Clipboard to copy information between DOS and Windows applications. ●

How to Run a DOS Program

The **MS-DOS Prompt** command opens a DOS window. In this window, you can run programs, examine the contents of a disk, or perform other DOS-based operations. The **MS-DOS Prompt** window allows you to work with DOS operations and Windows applications side by side on the desktop. You can also switch from the **MS-DOS Prompt** window to a full-screen view of DOS.

Begin

1 Choose MS-DOS Prompt

Click the **Start** button, choose **Programs**, **Accessories**, and then click **MS-DOS Prompt**.

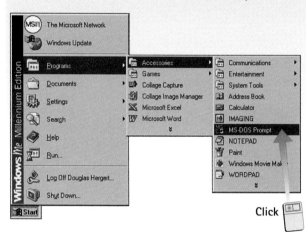

Click

2 Examine the DOS Window

If DOS appears in full-screen mode, press **Alt+Enter** to switch to the **MS-DOS Prompt** window. Inside the window, you see the familiar DOS prompt followed by a flashing cursor, indicating that you can enter commands or run programs.

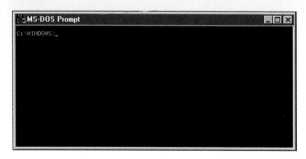

3 Display the DOS Toolbar

A special toolbar is available to simplify your work in the **MS-DOS Prompt** window. If you don't see this toolbar, click the **MS-DOS** icon in the upper-left corner of the window and choose **Toolbar**.

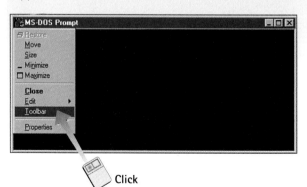

Click

4 Explore the Toolbar

The toolbar contains a row of buttons that allow you to perform specific operations inside the **MS-DOS Prompt** window. Position the mouse pointer over a button, and a small tip box tells you what the button does.

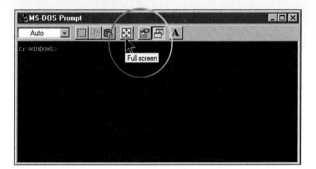

5 Select Property Settings

Click the **Font** button (identified by the label A) to open the **MS-DOS Prompt Properties** box. In the **Font** tab, you can select a new font and point size for the text that appears inside the **MS-DOS Prompt** window. Click **OK** to confirm your selection.

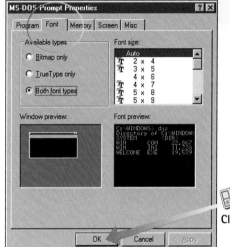

Click

6 Switch to Full-Screen Mode

If you want to switch to a full-screen view of DOS, click the **Full Screen** button on the toolbar or press **Alt+Enter**. Your screen now takes on the appearance of a DOS-based computer.

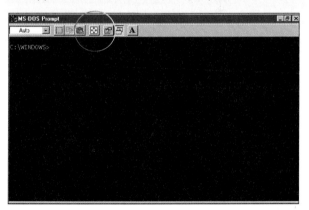

End

How-To Hints

Using Toolbar Buttons

The first three buttons on the DOS toolbar—**Mark**, **Copy**, and **Paste**—are for copying text from the DOS window to a Windows application, or from Windows to DOS. Turn to the next task for more information about these operations.

Minimizing the DOS Window

You can minimize the DOS window by clicking the **Minimize** button in the upper-right corner of the title bar. The window is then represented by a button on the task bar, just like any other minimized Windows application.

Closing the DOS Prompt Window

To close the DOS window, type **Exit** at the DOS prompt and press **Enter** or simply click the **Close** button in the upper-right corner of the title bar.

How to Copy Text Between DOS and Windows

The toolbar at the top of the **MS-DOS Prompt** window gives you simple ways to copy text from DOS to Windows, or vice versa. Like other copy-and-paste tasks in Windows Me, these operations use the **Clipboard** as an intermediate storage place for the data that's copied.

Begin

1 Display Some DOS Text

At the DOS prompt, use commands or programs to generate the text you want to copy from DOS to Windows. (In this example, the **dir** command produces a list of files from a particular disk location.) If the toolbar isn't displayed at the top of the **MS-DOS Prompt** window, click the **MS-DOS** icon at the upper-left corner of the window and choose **Toolbar** from the menu. Then click the **Mark** button on the toolbar.

2 Highlight the Text

Drag the mouse to highlight the DOS text you want to copy, and then click the **Copy** button on the toolbar. This action copies the selected text to the Windows Clipboard.

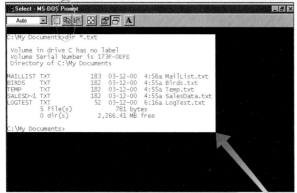

Drag

3 Copy to a Windows Program

Start the Windows application to which you want to copy the text (in this example, the application is Notepad). When the application opens, press **Ctrl+V** to paste the DOS text from the Clipboard into the window.

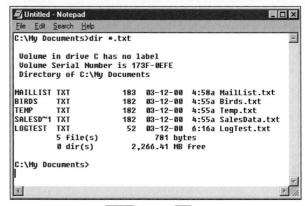

[Ctrl] + [V]

4 Copy Text from Windows

To copy information from Windows to DOS, begin by opening a Windows application and selecting the text you want to copy. Press **Ctrl+C** to copy the text to the Clipboard. In this example, the text is part of a small Basic program that's been developed in the Windows Notepad application.

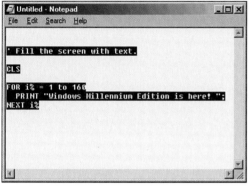

5 Paste into DOS

Activate the **MS-DOS Prompt** window and start the DOS program to which you want to copy the text. Then click **Paste** on the toolbar. This action pastes the text from the Clipboard to the DOS program. In this example, the text has been copied to QBASIC, a DOS-based programming environment, where the program can be tested.

End

How-To Hints

Using the Edit Menu

You can also select **Copy** and **Paste** commands from the menu that appears when you click the icon at the upper-left corner of the **MS-DOS Prompt** window. First, select the **Edit** command from the menu. The **Mark, Copy,** and **Paste** commands in the **Edit** menu perform the same tasks as the equivalent toolbar buttons.

Opening Multiple DOS Windows

You can open more than one **MS-DOS Prompt** window at a time. When you do so, you can use the Clipboard to copy text from one running DOS program to another, just as you can between any open Windows applications.

Glossary

A

Active Desktop The desktop mode that can include regularly updated Web content.

active window The window that displays your current activity on the desktop. Windows uses title bar colors to distinguish visually between the active window and any inactive windows.

address bar In a browser application such as Internet Explorer, the bar in which you type the address (or URL) of the Web site you want to visit. If you follow a series of links to a page, the address bar shows you the address of the page you are currently viewing.

Address Book The built-in application that supplies email addresses for Outlook Express. Address Book is a simple yet versatile tool for storing and retrieving essential information about friends, relatives, and business contacts.

application A software program designed for a particular purpose. For example, Windows comes with text-oriented applications (WordPad and Notepad), a graphics program (Paint), a calculator, and a variety of game programs.

attachment A file attached to an email message. You can sometimes open an attachment directly in the browser window; or you might have to launch the application that created the file.

automatic application A program that starts at the beginning of every Windows session. Automatic applications on your computer are listed in the Startup folder, which you can view by clicking the button and choosing Programs, Startup.

B

Backup A system tool that gives you a simple and reliable way to keep backup copies of your most important files.

bitmap A graphic format in which the Paint program saves files.

BMP A file format in which a single image is stored as a bitmap image, which can easily be read by simple graphics programs such as Paint.

boot To restart the computer.

browser An application designed to help you find, view, and use the information you need on the Web. A browser helps you organize your work online and find whatever information you need. Windows Millennium Edition comes with the latest version of Microsoft's well-known browser, Internet Explorer 5.5.

C

Calculator A built-in program that gives you the equivalent of a multifunction handheld calculator, right on your Windows desktop. You can perform quick calculations and copy the results to other applications using the Clipboard.

capture   In Windows Movie Maker, to acquire video and audio content for a digital movie file. You can capture content from an installed recording device or from existing media files on disk. *See also* transfer.

click   To position the mouse pointer directly over an object and press the left mouse button once. (Note that left-handed users can switch the roles of the mouse buttons. Click the Mouse icon in the Control Panel and choose the Buttons tab to access the appropriate option.)

Clipboard   An area of memory that Windows sets aside to store text, data, or graphics temporarily during cut-and-paste or copy-and-paste operations.

clips   In Windows Movie Maker, convenient lengths of video content that can serve as the building blocks of a movie.

collate   When printing multiple copies of a document, to print all the pages of one copy before beginning the next copy.

collection   In Windows Movie Maker, a container for video or audio clips. When you capture material from a video camera or other device—or when you import material from an existing media file—the Movie Maker lists the content as a new collection.

color scheme   The group of colors used to represent icons, captions, windows, and other objects on the desktop. To change the color scheme, right-click the desktop and choose Properties. The available color schemes are listed in the Appearance tab.

Content Advisor   An Internet Explorer tool that allows you to select acceptable rating levels for content in categories such as language, sex, and violence. A rated site is blocked from use if it goes beyond the levels you've chosen. (An unrated site can also be blocked, depending on options you select.) To maintain your selections in the Content Advisor, you create a private password. Only a person who knows the password can change or override your rating selections.

Control menu   The menu that appears when you click the Control menu icon at the left side of the title bar.

Control Menu icon   An icon at the left side of the title bar in most application windows. Each application has a distinct Control Menu icon. Click this icon to view a menu of options relevant to the application and its window.

copy-and-paste operation   To copy data from one location and insert it in a new location; the original data remains in place.

cross-fade transition   In Windows Movie Maker, a technique for controlling the visual flow from one clip to another. The transition is represented by an overlap between two clips in the timeline view of the Movie Maker workspace. During the transition time, the frames of one clip fade out while the frames of the other fade in.

crossover cable   In a network with only two computers, a cable that successfully handles the signals between the two network cards.

cut-and-paste operation   To delete data from one location and insert it in a new location. Cut-and-paste operations can take place within the content of a single document, between different documents in an application, or even between applications. The "cut" data is temporarily held in the Windows Clipboard.

Defragmenter   A system tool that improves the efficiency of file access by placing all the data from each file in a contiguous area on the hard disk.

desktop   The quintessential visual environment that represents the features and components of Windows. The desktop includes icons, the Start button, and the taskbar; it is the workspace where you run programs, open documents, view Web sites, manage your home network, and organize your work.

digital camera   A camera that captures an image in a digital file format, rather than on traditional negatives. If you have a digital photograph file, you can load it into Imaging for Windows, where you can manipulate and modify the file as you like.

Disk Cleanup   An application tool for freeing up space on your hard disk by deleting extraneous or unneeded files.

disk compression   A process by which the data on a disk is compressed so that you can store up to twice as much information on the disk. The compression process does not result in any degradation of data integrity.

document   A file created in a particular application—for example, a letter written in WordPad or a graphic created in the Paint program. The type of content stored in a document file depends on features of the source application and is often identified by the three-letter extension following the file's name.

double-click   To position the mouse pointer directly over an object and press the left mouse button twice in rapid succession. (Note that left-handed users can switch the roles of the mouse buttons. Click the Mouse icon in the Control Panel and choose the Buttons tab to access the appropriate option.)

drag   A mouse action that moves an object from one place to another in the Windows desktop. To drag an object, point to it with the mouse, hold down the left mouse button, and move the object to its destination. This action can result in a simple move from one place to another on the desktop, or a more significant move from one window, application, or folder to another.

drawing area   In the Paint application window, the area where you create your artwork.

driver   An essential piece of software that controls the use of an attached hardware device such as a printer, a modem, a scanner, or a network card. When you attach a new hardware device to your computer, you must generally install the appropriate driver before you can use the device.

DriveSpace   A system tool that increases the capacity of any disk by compressing the information the disk contains.

E

email   Electronic mail that is sent and received across the Internet. In your email program, you compose a message and click Send, and the message is sent to the named recipient. Programs such as Outlook Express allow you to send and receive file attachments as well as textual email messages.

embedded document   Part or all of a document created in one application that you place in another document in the same or a different application. The embedded document conveniently provides all the features and capabilities of the source application, but is independent of any existing file on disk.

extension   The characters following the period in a full filename. Each application typically appends its own three-character extension to the name of a file, in the form `name.ext`. For example, the WordPad program identifies word-processed documents with the extension `.doc`.

F

Favorites list   A list of links to your favorite Web sites. Most browsers offer this feature, which makes it easy for you to revisit sites. You can add or delete links so that your list always remains useful. In Internet Explorer, you can go directly to a particular site in the list by pulling down the Favorites menu and choosing a link. If you want to see the list of sites in the left pane of the browser window, click the Favorites toolbar button.

file   The basic unit for storing information on disk. A file might contain a *document* you've created in a particular application—for example, a word-processed report, a spreadsheet, a database, or a drawing—or a file might store part of a program that you run on the desktop.

filename   The unique identifier for a file. Windows Millennium Edition allows you to write free-form multiword filenames that are long enough to describe the contents and purpose of each file.

FilterKeys A keyboard option that instructs Windows to ignore certain types of repeated or extraneous keystrokes. FilterKeys is one of the important Accessibility options available in Windows Millennium Edition.

folder A practical way to organize files related to a specific purpose. Given the large amounts of space available on hard disks, folders provide an important multilayered structure for organizing your files. You can create folders on a disk or directly on the desktop. You can also create folders inside other folders. The many programs and documents on a hard disk are typically stored in a hierarchy of folders within folders.

fragmentation A disk condition that results over time as you save files to disk. Because of changes in the space available on the disk, files must sometimes be stored in noncontiguous units. Although fragmented files can always be opened and used, running the Defragmenter program generally improves the efficiency of disk access.

G-H

game controller A hardware device that contains all the controls you need to play an action game. Game controllers include joy sticks, game pads, and so on.

highlight To display in reverse video. For example, if something is normally black on a white background, when it is highlighted, it will appear white on a black background. *See also* select.

home network A network consisting of two or more computers, connected in a way that allows them to share resources. For example, each connected computer might be able to send documents to a single network printer, access Web sites using a shared Internet connection, or read document files located on other computers in the network.

home page The page that appears in your browser window at the beginning of each new online session. Internet Explorer allows you to designate any site as your own home page. Note that *home page* can also refer to the top-level page in the hierarchy of pages belonging to a single online site.

hub In a network with more than two computers, a central device to which you connect the cables from each computer in the network. The hub routes network operations appropriately among the connected computers.

I-K

icon A small pictorial element representing an application, a folder, a file, or a tool available in Windows. Click an icon to start the application or to open the file or folder that the icon represents. Icons appear in special folders such as My Computer and My Documents, in other folders that you create to organize your work, and on the desktop itself. The collection of icons on the desktop represents the most important or commonly used Windows tools; you can add to this collection at any time by creating *shortcut icons* from existing icons in other folders.

ICS host In a network where Internet Connection Sharing is available, the computer that controls the Internet connection.

Imaging for Windows A Windows application that enables you to view, edit, and manipulate digital photographs and other graphic files.

indent settings The paragraph offsets within the current margins of a text document. For example, a text document might have a 1-inch left margin where nothing is printed; the text begins at that point, but the first line of a paragraph might have a half-inch indent—in addition to the space occupied by the margin.

insert mode A word processing feature you can toggle on and off by pressing the Insert key on your keyboard. When you are in insert mode, you can insert text into an existing block of text without overwriting existing text. *See also* overwrite mode.

Internet Connection Sharing A network option that enables multiple computers to sign on to the Web using a single line. This "home network" feature is one of the big advantages of Windows Millennium Edition.

Internet Explorer The Web browser that comes with Microsoft Windows Millennium Edition. The current version is Internet Explorer 5.5.

Internet Service Provider (ISP)   A service that provides you with access to the Internet. You typically pay a monthly fee for an ISP account—somewhat more or less than $20 per month, charged to your credit card. Using your account, you can access the Internet, send and receive email, and participate in any other features that your particular ISP makes available.

L

LAN PC card   *See* network adapter card.

link   A shortcut to information online. When you click a link, the browser takes you directly to the page that the link represents. On a Web page, a link typically appears as an underlined or uniquely colored reference to a specific topic. The Link list in the Internet Explorer address bar contains links to some of your favorite sites; most Web pages also contain links to related information located elsewhere online.

linked document   Part or all of a document created in one application that you insert into your current document. The linked document retains its connections with an original file on disk. If you make changes in the linked information, Windows transfers those changes to the source file.

local area network (LAN)   A group of computers connected together in a limited local environment, such as an office or a campus. If you work in an office where everyone's computer is connected to a LAN, you might not have to use an ISP to go online. You might just connect to the LAN, which in turn provides access to the Web. *See also* proxy server.

M

Magnifier   A Windows tool designed to provide visual magnifications (up to 9 times larger) of portions of the desktop. Using this tool can significantly improve the visibility of desktop details. The Magnifier is one of the important Accessibility options available in Windows Millennium Edition.

Maintenance Wizard   A program that schedules tune-ups to keep your hard disk in the best possible working order.

margin   The blank areas along the top, bottom, left, or right sides of the printed page. Text or graphics are generally not printed within the margins of a page.

menu bar   In most programs, the menu bar is a horizontal arrangement of menu names, located just below the title bar in the application window. This bar contains the main menu commands, such as File, Edit, View, Tools, Help, and so on. Click a name on the menu bar to display a drop-down list of related commands.

modem   The hardware device that allows you to connect your computer directly to a phone line. Most new computers on the market today come with modems that have already been successfully installed.

monitor   In Windows Movie Maker, the area of the application window in which you can preview a movie project in progress.

mouse pointer   The icon that moves around on the screen to represent the movement of the physical mouse on your table top. The mouse pointer initially appears as a solid arrow on the Windows desktop, but it changes to other shapes in different software environments and when positioned over particular objects on the desktop.

MouseKeys   An option that enables you to substitute keyboard techniques for mouse actions. MouseKeys can prove useful for people who find the mouse impractical to use as a pointing device. MouseKeys is one of the important Accessibility options available in Windows Millennium Edition.

MS-DOS   The command-based operating system that preceded Windows. You can open an MS-DOS window on the Windows desktop to perform DOS operations or run DOS-based programs.

multimedia applications   Programs combining video, sounds, photographs, and color images.

N

Net Watcher   A system tool that allows you to monitor activity on your home network. With this tool, you can find out who is connected to the network, what resources are shared, and which files from your own computer are in use on other network computers.

network adapter card   A special-purpose card that you install in an available slot inside your computer or in a PCMCIA slot on your laptop. The card provides the essential resources for attaching your computer by cable to a local area network or a home network.

newsgroup   An Internet location where participants can exchange ideas with one another. Newsgroups are organized by topics; you present your views by posting messages to the group. (You can also send messages to individual members of the group.) Newsgroups can be monitored to maintain a particular focus or might be *un*monitored, in which case the content can often stray from the designated topic.

Notepad   A built-in text editor, designed for creating and editing data files, program listings, or system files.

O

optical character recognition (OCR)   A scanning feature that produces editable text from a scanned text image. You can open the resulting document in your word processor for revision, just as though you had originally typed the text at the keyboard.

overwrite mode   A word processing feature you can toggle on and off by pressing the Insert key on your keyboard. When you are in overwrite mode, the new text you type erases, character by character, any existing text. *See also* insert mode.

P

Paint   A built-in program that helps you create artwork that's engaging, educational, or just fun. Everything you need is close at hand: a palette of colors, an array of tools, and an empty canvas.

PCMCIA   One or more slots available at the side of a laptop computer for installing special-purpose hardware devices such as modems or network adapter cards.

peer-to-peer network   A simple network consisting of two or more connected computers, none of which is necessarily designated as a server or client. A home network that you set up using the Windows Millennium Home Networking Wizard can also be thought of as a peer-to-peer network.

Plug-and-Play device   A hardware device that Windows can detect and install as soon as you attach it to your computer. Windows copies and activates the necessary driver software.

point   To position the mouse pointer directly over an object on the desktop or elsewhere. If your desktop is set up for single-click icons, the pointing action selects the icon for a subsequent action.

pointer trails   An optional visual effect that can help you keep track of the mouse pointer on some display devices. When the Show Pointer Trails option is selected in the Mouse Properties dialog box, subsequent mouse movement produces a trail of pointers.

preview   To see onscreen what a document will look like when it is printed. By previewing a document before you print, you can often catch and correct formatting problems so that you don't waste paper.

print queue   A list of multiple documents in line for printing. If you print documents from several applications to one printer, all the documents are listed in the same queue. You can view and control the queue by clicking the printer's icon.

proxy server   A local network that provides Internet access to individual computers in the network. In Windows Millennium Edition, the Internet Connection Wizard can help you connect to the Internet through a LAN proxy server. *See also* local area network (LAN).

Q

Quick Launch toolbar A special toolbar on the taskbar that contains icons for frequently used applications. The Quick Launch toolbar initially appears just to the right of the Start button. To start an application represented in the Quick Launch toolbar, click its icon. Note that you can add a new item to the Quick Launch toolbar by dragging an icon from the desktop to that location in the taskbar.

quick links Internet Explorer's list of favorite site addresses. Find the list by clicking the double-angle brackets >> to the right of the Links button in the address bar. You can add or delete addresses to this list to customize it for your personal use.

R

Radio bar In the Internet Explorer window, the Radio bar provides links to streamed audio content from local, national, or international radio sites. If the Radio bar does not appear in your browser window, pull down the View menu, choose Toolbars, and then click Radio.

restore point In the System Restore tool, a date-and-time marker to which you can eventually "roll back" your system in the event that something goes wrong with your computer.

right-click To position the mouse pointer directly over an object and press the right mouse button once. (Note that left-handed users can switch the roles of the mouse buttons. Click the Mouse icon in the Control Panel and choose the Buttons tab to access the appropriate option.)

S

ScanDisk A system tool that improves the integrity of your hard disks by scanning for physical problems on the surface of the disk.

scanner A device that produces a digital image of a paper document. The document can contain any kind of content, including color graphics, photographs, text, or any combination of these. The scanner quickly transmits an image to your computer, where you can work with the content in any appropriate application. If the scanned document consists of text, your scanner software might be able to convert the text image into editable text, in a process known as *optical character recognition.*

screen saver A program that displays an animated graphic or design on your screen after your computer has been idle for a specified period of time. Ostensibly, a screen saver is designed to prevent any damage to your screen resulting from long-term display of a single image, although modern display devices are often immune to such damage. A screen saver can also provide a level of security for your system if you establish a password that must be provided to return from the screen saver to the normal desktop.

search service An online tool that helps you locate topics on the Web. Because the Internet is so huge, it is almost impossible for a single search service (sometimes called a *search engine*) to do a good job indexing all possible topics. You might find, for example, that one search service is better for locating scientific topics and another is better for locating current events. Some of the most popular search services include Yahoo!, Infoseek, and AltaVista.

security level The level of safety features assigned to a particular *security zone.* You can accept the default security level for each predefined zone, or you can customize security levels to meet your own safety requirements.

security zone Internet Explorer divides sites into four security zones, each with its own specific safety ratings. In the Internet Properties window, you can assign frequently visited sites to specific zones. For the sites in a given zone, Internet Explorer issues relevant warnings and activates appropriate safeguards.

select To highlight for a subsequent action. For example, selected text in a word processing program is highlighted and ready for formatting. *See also* highlight.

server-client network   A network in which a central server computer provides network resources and controls essential network operations. Any number of client computers can be attached to the server to take advantage of network resources.

shared folder   On a network, a folder that can be accessed by other computers on the network.

shortcut icon   An object on the desktop that gives you one-click access to a program, document, folder, printer, disk drive, Web site, or any other object you use regularly in Windows. To add a new shortcut icon to the desktop, use the right mouse button to drag the icon from its source window to the desktop and then select Create Shortcut(s) Here from the resulting menu. After you've placed a shortcut icon on the desktop, you can click it to open the application it represents.

shortcut menu   The menu that appears when you right-click an object or area on the desktop. The items in the menu control some specific operations related to the object you clicked.

signature   A designated block of text that appears at the end of an email message. For example, in Outlook Express, you can create a signature that includes your name and address, a small graphic, and a link to a Web site.

Start button   The button you click to view a multi-level menu of applications and other resources available on your computer. The Start button is part of the taskbar, and initially appears at the lower-left corner of the desktop. If you move the taskbar to a new location, the Start button is also relocated.

Start menu   The multi-level menu that appears when you click the Start button. The first level contains folder entries representing the major categories of applications, files, and tools that you use on the Windows desktop, including Programs, Documents, and Settings. Select any one of these categories to view an additional level of the menu.

start page   *See* home page.

startup disk   A floppy disk that contains the necessary system software to boot your computer and diagnose problems in the event of a system failure.

storyboard   In Windows Movie Maker, the workspace view that shows the sequence of clips in the content of a movie project.

StickyKeys   A keyboard option that enables you to press multiple keys in succession rather than simultaneously. For example, if an operation requires you to press Alt+F (the Alt key and the F key simultaneously), you can turn on StickyKeys and perform the command by pressing Alt and then pressing F. StickyKeys is one of the important Accessibility options available in Windows Millennium Edition.

streaming media   A technology that allows you to view one part of a video or audio file on the Internet while other parts of the file are still being transmitted or downloaded.

subscription   A Web site whose contents are updated regularly on your computer, according to specific options you select in Internet Explorer. Windows Millennium Edition refers to this arrangement as *synchronizing a Web site* rather than *subscribing*.

synchronize   To download the most recent content from a favorite Web site so that you can later view the information offline.

system tool   A Windows application designed to improve the performance or security of the computer system.

T

taskbar   The bar that includes the Start button and displays additional buttons for each application you open on the desktop. The taskbar traditionally appears horizontally at the bottom of the desktop, but you can move it elsewhere if you prefer. Optionally, you can display special-purpose toolbars along the taskbar, and you can hide the taskbar from view when it is not needed.

theme   In the Desktop Themes feature, a set of sight-and-sound motifs including wallpaper, icons, window colors, fonts, mouse pointers, and distinct sound effects. You can choose a theme to redefine the environment of your Windows desktop.

thumbnail In the My Pictures folder and elsewhere, a small, full-color preview display of a photo, graphic, or other image file. To see thumbnails, pull down the View menu and choose the Thumbnails option.

TIFF A file format that allows you to save multiple scanned pages in a single file. Each page can be an individual scan, an individual photograph from a digital camera, or an image file from disk.

timeline In Windows Movie Maker, the workspace view that shows the duration, timing, and transitions of clips in the content of a movie project.

ToggleKeys A keyboard option that produces an alert tone when you press the CapsLock, NumLock, or ScrollLock key. ToggleKeys is one of the important Accessibility options available in Windows Millennium Edition.

toolbar A horizontal arrangement of icons that represent common operations available in a given software environment. To streamline your work, most Windows applications provide one or more toolbars with useful collections of shortcut icons. You can often choose to display or hide toolbars by selecting options in an application's View menu. Note that you can also display special toolbars along the width of the Windows taskbar. To do so, right-click a blank area in the taskbar and choose Toolbars from the resulting shortcut menu.

transfer In Windows Movie Maker, to acquire video and audio content for a digital movie file. You can capture content from an installed recording device or from existing media files on disk. *See also* capture.

U-Z

URL (uniform resource locator) The address of a Web page. Web addresses typically begin with the letters **www**, and end in "dot" extensions such as **COM** (for a commercial site), **ORG** (for the site of a nonprofit organization), **EDU** (for an educational site), or **GOV** (for the site of a government agency).

wallpaper A repeating visual pattern that can optionally be displayed as the background design of your desktop. To select a wallpaper, right-click a blank position on your desktop and choose Properties from the resulting shortcut menu. Available wallpaper designs are listed in the Background tab.

window A framed area that displays your activity in a particular program. You can open any number of windows on the desktop at a time.

Windows Explorer A Windows application that gives you convenient access to all the contents of your computer. The pane on the left side of the Windows Explorer window lists the major folders, disks, and other resources on your computer. The pane on the right shows the specific files and folders contained in a selected folder or disk. If you set up a home network, Windows Explorer is one available tool for accessing the resources of the network.

WinPopUp A network tool that sends messages from one computer to another across the home network. Each computer on the network can send and receive messages, as long as WinPopUp is running on every desktop.

WordPad The simple word processing application that comes with Windows.

word wrap A feature of most word processing applications. When you reach the end of a line, the insertion point automatically moves to the beginning of the next line; you don't have to press Enter to start a new line within a paragraph.

workgroup name The name of the network you create with the Home Networking Wizard.

workspace In Windows Movie Maker, the horizontal area at the bottom of the application window that shows the clips you've selected for a movie project in progress.

Index

C